Our Unsettled Constitution

LOUIS MICHAEL SEIDMAN

Our Unsettled Constitution

A NEW DEFENSE OF CONSTITUTIONALISM AND JUDICIAL REVIEW

Yale University Press
New Haven &
London

Published with assistance from the Kingsley Trust Association Publication Fund
established by the Scroll and Key Society of Yale College.

Set in Sabon type by Keystone Typesetting, Inc., Orwigsburg, Pennsylvania.

Printed in the United States of America by Vail-Ballou Press,
Binghamton, New York.

Library of Congress Cataloging-in-Publication Data
Seidman, Louis Michael.
Our unsettled constitution : a new defense of constitutionalism and
judicial review / Louis Michael Seidman.
p. cm.
Includes bibliographical references and index.
ISBN 0-300-08531-1 (alk. paper)
1. Constitutional law — United States. I. Title.
KF4550 .S38 2001
342.73'02 — dc21   2001002489

A catalogue record for this book is available from the British Library.

The paper in this book meets the guidelines for permanence and durability of the
Committee on Production Guidelines for Book Longevity of the Council on
Library Resources.

10 9 8 7 6 5 4 3 2 1

For Renee and Dick

Contents

Acknowledgments

Writing this book has been an inexcusable act of self-indulgence. For reasons best known to her, Judith Areen, the dean of Georgetown University Law Center, saw fit to relieve me of all the duties that justify my salary for a solid year so that I could spend that time thinking about constitutional theory. This book is the consequence of that decision. Regardless of whether it was a wise one, I will forever be grateful to her for making it.

Many people helped me in this effort, but two good friends merit special mention. Mark Tushnet has been teaching me about constitutional theory for almost thirty years. Unfortunately, I am not the best of students — he disagrees with much of what I say here. With his usual intellectual generosity, he has managed to suppress this disagreement for long enough to help me sharpen my arguments and avoid embarrassing errors.

Several years ago, Michael Klarman asked me join him in team-teaching a course on constitutional theory at the University of Virginia Law School. Teaching the course turned out to be a humbling experience. I had thought that I had a worked-out position about constitutional law, but I was wrong. Facing Klarman's powerful arguments twice a week forced me to rethink my views from the bottom up. This project grew out of that effort. Both Klarman and Tushnet took the time to read every word of my manuscript. I have

gratefully incorporated many of their suggested revisions and will no doubt
regret not having incorporated more of them.

I imposed on many other friends for help in thinking through the problems I
discuss in this book. I owe a special debt to Steven Goldberg, Jack Getman,
Carlos Vazquez, Alexander Aleinikoff, David Strauss, Girardeau Spann, Gary
Peller, Heidi Li Feldman, Michael Diamond, Julie Cohen, Brian Bix, Carrie
Menkel-Meadow, Florence Roisman, and Vicki Jackson for comments on the
manuscript. Faculty too numerous to mention participated in workshops at
Georgetown University Law Center, the University of Pennsylvania Law
School, the University of Virginia Law School, Washington and Lee Law
School, George Washington Law School, Brooklyn Law School, and the University of Chicago Law School, and provided valuable comments and criticisms.

Being a good editor requires intelligent and sympathetic self-effacement. An
editor must get inside someone else's argument and make sense of it when, on
occasion, the author himself does not know what it means. All this must be
accomplished while strategically administering large doses of flattery to keep
an oversized ego in check. Susan Laity, my editor at Yale University Press, is
spectacularly good at her job. With patience, good humor, and extraordinary
skill, she set about the task of asking probing questions, straightening out
confused grammar, and making sense of half-baked ideas. Her hard work
made this a much better book.

I was blessed with two wonderful research assistants. Daniel Gilman helped
me find my way through the relevant literature and provided insightful comments on many sections of the manuscript. How can I begin to thank Avril
Haines? For a year she regularly worked late into the night tracking down
obscure sources, cleaning up my muddy prose, and providing moral and intellectual support. I am also grateful to Anna Selden, John Showalter, Cathy
Strain, and Roshini Thayaparan for their assistance, and to Fred Kameny for
preparing the index.

For a quarter-century, I have spent virtually every Monday evening talking
with my good friends Frederick Weisberg and Jeffrey Freund about (among
other things) constitutional law. Weisberg is a highly regarded judge on the
Superior Court for the District of Columbia; Freund is an exceedingly successful Washington lawyer. Although both of them have otherwise excellent judgment, they have long thought that my views about the Constitution were, not
to put too fine a point upon it, completely nuts. Many authors need to imagine
an intended audience; Fred Weisberg and Jeff Freund have been mine. I'm not
certain how they will feel about it, but it is simply a fact that this entire project

is no more than an extended (no doubt futile) effort to convince them of the merit of my views.

Ten years ago, Judge Weisberg conducted the ceremony at which Judith Mazo and I were married. Together with the days on which my children, Jessica and Andrew, were born, my wedding day was the most important day of my life. Judy, Jessica, and Andy have provided the love, support, comfort, and caring — the peace at the core — without which nothing is possible.

The two people who have contributed the most to this book have not read a word of it. They are my parents, Irene Seidman and Benedict Seidman. When I was a little boy, they began a life-long project of helping me to think clearly and critically about things that really matter. Many parents give to their children the devotion and unqualified love that provides a solid foundation for what lies ahead. My parents gave me these things in abundance, but they also gave me something else: a habit of questioning and caring, doubting and empathizing, out of which I have fashioned a career and a life. This book is for them.

Introduction
A New Theory of Constitutional Law

I might as well admit it: I am terrified by the title that I myself have given to this introductory chapter.

Is it conceivable that there is something both new and sensible to say about constitutional theory? People have been writing about this subject for several millennia. Surely we are at the point where anything one might say that is original is bound to be silly and anything that is not silly is bound to be unoriginal.

We live in an age of growing doubt as to the utility of any normative theory of constitutional law, much less a new one. Thinkers spanning a political spectrum anchored by Richard Posner on the right and Richard Rorty on the left agree that constitutional theory leads to a dead end. Rebecca L. Brown began a 1998 article by asking her readers to "honk if you are tired of constitutional theory."[1] If the resulting sound was less than deafening, that was only because many legal academics were so tired of constitutional theory they didn't bother to read her fine article.

As inhospitable as the intellectual terrain is to constitutional theory in general, it is even more hostile to any theory that defends judicial review. There have been doubts about the legitimacy of judicial review from the beginning — doubts that Alexander Bickel crystallized more than forty years ago when he tackled the "countermajoritarian difficulty." Around the same time that Bickel wrote his famous book on this subject, Judge Learned Hand proposed a kind of mutual disarmament treaty. Chastened by the still recent struggle over the constitutional validity of the New Deal, he suggested that liberals and conservatives should agree to foreswear judicial power and fight out their differences in the political sphere.[2]

Judge Hand's proposal could not have come at a less opportune time.[3] The Warren Court had just begun its epic struggle against racial discrimination, and judicial intervention seemed to hold out the possibility of authentic social transformation. To be sure, within a decade, Warren Court reform had more or less burned itself out, but for years afterward, progressive scholars continued to resist the bargain Hand suggested because of the lingering, nostalgic hope that constitutional law might yet be harnessed as an effective engine for social reform.

Today, more than thirty years removed from the retirement of Chief Justice Earl Warren, that hope seems remarkably naive. Contemporary constitutional scholarship is dominated by articles and books arguing that judges are ill equipped to solve the social problems that trouble us, that their past efforts to do so have been inept, ineffectual, or worse, and that when their decisions do not merely reenforce current majority sentiment, they unjustifiably impose the views of a cultural and economic elite on the rest of us.[4] The Supreme Court's decision in Bush v. Gore has added fuel to the fire.[5] For many Americans, the decision demonstrated that the Court cannot be trusted to render impartial justice when important political issues are at stake.

Thus, the time may have finally arrived to implement Hand's grand compromise. Robert Bork and Mark Tushnet agree about very little, but they do agree that judicial review is profoundly problematic. Girardeau Spann and Lino Graglia have different views on racial justice, but both of them think that the Supreme Court has made a mess of things. Cass Sunstein, perhaps the most influential constitutional scholar of his generation, captured the emerging consensus when he urged judges to "leave things undecided" and the rest of us to accept "judicial minimalism."[6] For some, the only real question is whether even Sunstein's tentative, limited, and ambivalent defense of occasional judicial intervention goes too far.

The short of the matter, then, is that this hardly seems like the moment to propose a new, comprehensive constitutional theory that defends an expansive version of judicial review. Yet paradoxically, the current pessimism about constitutional theory in general and the hostility to judicial review in particular can also be seen as laying the necessary foundations for a new approach. Three interrelated points provide the reasons why a new theory may be useful after all.

First, whatever the doubts of the critics, the fact remains that the Supreme Court continues to begin a new term on the first Monday of every October. Not only has the Court stubbornly refused to go out of business; it is more activist than ever. "Conservative" and "liberal" justices alike regularly vote to invalidate laws on a wide range of subjects. Although politicians occasionally grumble about judges who "make" rather than "enforce" the law, the country is far from being in open revolt against this practice. Judges and lawyers frequently accuse constitutional theorists of being out of touch with the "real world."[7] This charge may be aimed at the wrong target. It is the anti-theorists who seem to hold themselves arrogantly aloof from a practice that people in the real world take for granted.

Perhaps judicial review is simply illegitimate. Yet it is a striking fact that even after Bush v. Gore, many Americans who thought that the decision was politically biased and wrong nonetheless continued to support the Court as an institution.[8] Isn't it at least worth asking whether there is some intellectually respectable way to justify a practice that is so widely accepted? In the spirit that Robert Nozick gracefully expressed in his book *Philosophical Explanations,* we might ask how belief in the practice is *possible* even as we avoid the temptation to try "to get someone to believe something whether he wants to believe it or not."[9] I think that there is a coherent explanation for judicial review, an explanation that the anti-theorists should engage with, even if they are not ultimately persuaded by it.

The second point is that however unfashionable, constitutional theory is in some sense inevitable.* After all, judicial restraint is itself a theory of constitutional law, and a controversial one at that. Why should elected officials, who may be short-sighted, poorly informed, or venal, have the final say on constitutional disputes? There may be good reasons for judicial restraint, but they should be put on the table just like the justifications for any other constitutional theory.

Consider, in this light, Judge Posner's recent attack on constitutional theory.[10] Posner complains that it "has no power to command agreement from people not already predisposed to accept the theorist's policy prescriptions." Yet in the same article that asserts the worthlessness of constitutional theory, Posner advances a theory of his own, which he labels "pragmatism." Posner is too intelligent to miss this irony, so he takes pains to argue that pragmatism is

---

*This statement should not be confused with an assertion that any particular version of constitutional law is inevitable. In particular, I do not want to insist that there is anything inevitable about the American system of judicial review. A defense of the system is necessary precisely because it is not inevitable.

really an anti-theory. Apparently, pragmatism amounts to no more than careful attention to empirical facts and the ways in which judicial decisions interact with those facts.[11] How could anyone be against this?

Yet to precisely the extent that pragmatism is an anti-theory, it begs questions that only theory can answer. The instrumental rationality that Posner favors yields determinate outcomes only if we first agree on what it is we are trying to accomplish. But even the most careful and comprehensive empirical study cannot settle disputes about ends.*

Posner also candidly directs attention to a second question that his pragmatism begs. As he admits at the end of his essay, often the facts are unknown or even unknowable.[12] When this is true, judges must nonetheless resolve disputes. Which resolution they choose will depend upon who bears the burden of proof, and surely this decision requires some theoretical justification.

Although Posner is less than crystal clear on this point, apparently he would place the burden on those who wish to reverse political outcomes on constitutional grounds. He expresses "considerable sympathy" with the view that judges should "take a back seat to the other branches of government," and should intervene only if their "sense of justice is sufficiently outraged." Moreover, the very structure of Posner's argument reflects this stance. It is telling that Posner chooses constitutional adjudication as the target for his complaint about the failure to attend to facts on the ground. There is no a priori reason to suppose that judges are more guilty of this sin than legislators or executive branch officials.[13] Posner's choice of target strongly suggests that his default position is respect for decisions made by the political branches.

This position has the virtue of answering one of the questions pragmatism begs, but it does so only by advancing the kind of theory that Posner wants to avoid. As I have already noted, "judicial restraint" is also a theory of constitutional adjudication, which should enjoy no more presumptive correctness than the theories that Posner attacks. If his general thesis is right, then it must be that this theory, like any other constitutional theory, "has no power to

---

*For example, Posner faults the Supreme Court for its inattention to scientific evidence that might demonstrate that homosexuality is spread "from flaunting or public endorsement of the homosexual way of life." Richard A. Posner, *Against Constitutional Theory*, 73 N.Y.U. L. Rev. 1, 20 (1998). But this evidence (which, by the way, Posner himself considers nonexistent) would be relevant only if homosexuality were a moral or social evil. This question, in turn, cannot be answered by empirical data. As Posner himself acknowledges, "There is no way to assess the validity of [the belief that homosexuality is morally blameworthy] and what weight if any such a belief should be given in a constitutional case [is] an equally indeterminate question." Id.

command agreement from people not already predisposed to accept the theorist's policy prescriptions."

One can hardly fault Judge Posner for falling into this trap. Being a thoroughgoing and consistent theoretical skeptic is hard work. Sometimes anti-theorists try to make the job easier by relying on some of the negative connotations contingently associated with the word *theory*. The theoretical enterprise is treated as if it were necessarily abstruse, metaphysical, and impractical. To be sure, some theorists are guilty of these sins, but there is nothing about theory itself that requires their commission. Stripped of these negative connotations, all that *theory* amounts to is the offering of justifications for the decisions one makes that are comprehensible to the audience to whom they are offered.

Anti-theorists are surely correct when they maintain that this enterprise can never be wholly successful. There will always be some people excluded from the intended audience. I am reasonably confident that Thomas Aquinas, Josef Stalin, Friedrich Nietzsche, and Antonin Scalia would be unmoved if exposed to the theory that I offer in this book. It does not follow that theory as such is worthless or unnecessary, however. To give up on the theoretical enterprise merely because it will never be wholly successful is to give up on the possibility of communicating with others about the reasons for one's actions.* And that is something that most people are simply unwilling or unable to do. We need to consider the implications of the fact that Steven Smith's intelligent and original attack on the role of reason in constitutional theory is itself carefully reasoned, or that Judge Posner not only advances a theory of his own but also ends up articulating a theoretical argument against constitutional theory.[14]

All of which leads to the third point: although I cannot demonstrate that it is true, my guess is that the real target of the anti-theorists is not constitutional theory per se but rather a particular kind of tendentious and unconvincing constitutional theory. The sort of theory that rubs skeptics the wrong way is one that dresses up controversial policy prescriptions in the garb of timeless and acontextual principle — a theory that tries to "command agreement," in Posner's words. Posner and his fellow critics are right to object to this sort of

---

*I do not mean to suggest that this communication must be in the form of reasoned argument in the philosophically rigorous sense of the term. We often successfully communicate by methods that are not "reasonable" in this sense — for example, by moral demonstration or empathic connection. In any event, the boundaries of "reasoned argument" are themselves unclear and contested. I use the term "reasons" more loosely to include any account of one's actions that is comprehensible to its audience.

theory, and there is plenty of it around to object to. Consider, for example, John Rawls's notorious assertion that "any comprehensive doctrine that leads to a balance of political values excluding [a] duly qualified right [to an abortion] in the first trimester is to that extent unreasonable." Are we really to expect that abortion opponents will give up on their deepest moral and political commitments because of this claim?* And Rawls is hardly alone. Constitutional theories offered by scholars as diverse and talented as Frank Michelman, Ronald Dworkin, Michael Perry, John Hart Ely, Michael Sandel, and Richard Epstein all claim that the theoretical enterprise can resolve some of our deepest political and moral disagreements.[15]

There is a sense in which these efforts are quite noble. They reflect a faith in the power of reason and persuasion that is admirable. At their best, theorists can help us to understand positions we might otherwise reject out of hand and build empathetic and intellectual bridges to political opponents. Unfortunately, though, constitutional theorists, like the rest of us, are not always at their best. Sometimes theorists claim that their work shows not just that their views are possible or plausible but that opposing views are irrational or illegitimate. When theorists try to command agreement rather than begin discussions, they are bound to be unsuccessful — and to enlarge rather than shrink the political and moral gulf that separates us.

Through a kind of guilt by association, the failures of these theories have brought into question not only the theoretical enterprise more generally but also the practice of judicial review. Instead of legitimating exercises of judicial power, tendentious theories have tended to discredit them. Anti-theorists argue that if judicial decisions on controversial subjects like abortion, religion, gender, or sex really rest on the weak normative foundations supplied by academic theorists, then there is no good reason why these decisions should be entitled to our respect or obedience. Because these theories cannot justly command dissenters to give up their positions on these topics, decisions based on the theories amount to no more than an exercise of raw power masquerading as disinterested reason. Modern skepticism about theory and modern hostility to judicial review are therefore linked by a common worry about elitism and authoritarianism in constitutional analysis.

*John Rawls, Political Liberalism 243 n. 32 (1993). To his great credit, Rawls himself has retracted this assertion. See John Rawls, The Idea of Public Reason Reconsidered, 64 U. Chi. L. Rev. 808, n. 80 (1997). As Rawls himself has written, "[I]t is often thought that the task of philosophy is to uncover a form of argument that will always prove convincing against all other arguments. There is, however, no such argument. People may often have final ends that require them to oppose one another without compromise." John Rawls, The Law of Peoples 123 (1999).

These concerns are legitimate and healthy. There is, indeed, a problem with most *theories* of constitutional law. It does not follow, however, that there is a problem with constitutional *theory*. The criticisms of the anti-theorists should provide a goad to do better, not an excuse for giving up. The challenge for a modern theorist is to formulate a general approach to constitutional law that takes into account the intractable nature of our political disagreements instead of attempting to suppress them. Our efforts should be directed toward building a new theory of constitutional law that starts by acknowledging the weakness that has so often bedeviled the theoretical enterprise.

The thesis of this book is that we can accomplish this task by reversing the two central assumptions upon which most prior theory has been based: that principles of constitutional law should be independent of our political commitments and that the role of constitutional law is to settle political disagreement. It is just these assumptions that have discredited so much prior theory. To critics it is obvious that theories offered by academic constitutionalists are not apolitical. Rather, they serve as rationalizations for a set of political commitments that precede the theory. It is obvious as well that these commitments are appropriately contestable and that disagreements with regard to them cannot be settled by any theoretical construct.

It does not follow, however, that all theories are subject to these criticisms. Suppose that we start by acknowledging that the critics are right. Just as they claim, the content of constitutional law does and must reflect contestable political views. And just as they claim, no constitutional theory will settle our disagreement about these views. Can we build a successful theory of constitutional law that rests on these concessions?

We can start by relaxing the first assumption. Judges regularly insist on the political neutrality of their role, but most ordinary citizens are not fooled. According to polling data, a large number of Americans think that the decision in Bush v. Gore was influenced by politics,[16] and they are surely right. Are we really supposed to believe that it "just so happened" that the Court's most conservative Justices read the equal-protection clause in a way that favored George W. Bush while their more liberal colleagues read the same words so as to favor Al Gore? Of course, Bush v. Gore was an extraordinary case, but the point can be made more generally. It requires more faith than most people can muster to suppose that it is mere coincidence when Justice Antonin Scalia, a conservative Republican, regularly finds conservative principles embedded in the Constitution, while Justice Ruth Bader Ginsburg, a liberal Democrat, regularly discovers liberal principles lurking in the same document.

Does this obvious fact discredit constitutional law? Viewed from one perspective, perhaps it does. It means that opinions about the content of constitutional law cannot be separated from political opinions. People will therefore favor or oppose particular interpretations of constitutional law based upon their political positions.

Suppose, though, that we try to view constitutional law from the outside. Instead of thinking of ourselves as participants in political disputes, we could imagine that we are anthropologists investigating the function served by a particular practice in an alien culture. Viewed from this perspective, the political contestability of Supreme Court decisions is hardly fatal. To be sure, it would be if one thought that the function of constitutional law was to settle ordinary political disagreements, for we can hardly expect constitutional law to resolve these disagreements if it simply reflects them. But it is precisely because most judges and constitutional theorists are committed to a settlement theory that they insist on an Alice-in-Wonderland world where judicial interpretation of the Constitution is uninfluenced by politics.

On the other hand, if we relax the second assumption — if we assume that the function of constitutional law is not to settle disputes but to unsettle any resolution reached by the political branches — then the political contestability of constitutional doctrine is much less troubling. To see why this is so, we need to consider what we should expect from constitutional law in the first place.

Like its rivals, unsettlement theory begins with the premise that in a free and diverse society, there is bound to be political conflict. Like its rivals, unsettlement theory takes the purpose of constitutional law to be the maintenance of a just community in the face of this conflict. Our ultimate objective should be to provide a just reason why individuals who lose political battles should nonetheless maintain their allegiance to the community. Unsettlement theory differs from its rivals by making the paradoxical claim that constitutional law can help build such a community by creating, rather than settling, political conflict.

Any constitutional settlement is bound to produce losers who will continue to nurse deep-seated grievances, and we would be hard put to offer reasons, convincing within their own normative frameworks, why these losers should abide by settlements they deeply oppose. But a constitution that unsettles creates no permanent losers. By destabilizing whatever outcomes are produced by the political process, it provides citizens with a forum and a vocabulary that they can use to continue the argument. Even when they suffer serious losses in the political sphere, citizens will have reason to maintain their allegiance to the community — not because constitutional law settles disputes but because it provides arguments, grounded in society's foundational commitments, for why the political settlement they oppose is unjust. In short, an

unsettled constitution helps build a community founded on consent by entic-
ing losers into a continuing conversation.

It is important to understand that unsettlement theory does not preordain
any particular outcome to this conversation. In particular, it provides no guarantee that the conversation will result in the reversal of the initial decision. A
preordained outcome entails a settlement; it is the very indeterminacy of the
outcome that makes the constitution unsettled. Thus an unsettled constitution
is different from a system with a settled mechanism for power sharing. Unsettlement does not promise losers that they will eventually get their way. It
promises them only that they will have a continued opportunity to engage
their opponents in a good-faith, open-ended discussion about what is to be
done.

Of course, standing alone, this argument provides no reason for judges to
play a special role in implementing the unsettled constitution. If the content of
constitutional law is indeed inseparable from contestable, political commitments, one might fairly ask why a tiny number of unelected judges should be
able to exercise political power over the rest of us.

In order to tackle this objection, it is necessary to emphasize, once again, the
distinction between a community member and an anthropologist. If constitutional law is not politically neutral, then it follows that each individual's opinion about constitutional law will turn on the politics of the law in question.
For example, my own views about judicial authority to invalidate laws restricting abortion or providing for affirmative action depend upon my substantive beliefs about the morality and wisdom of these practices and on my
empirical judgment about whether judges are likely to share those beliefs. This
fact is a necessary implication of the claim that constitutional law cannot settle
political disputes.

It does not follow, however, that there is nothing to be gained from attempting to abstract from the disputes. From the perspective of an anthropologist, it
still makes sense to ask whether a particular form of constitutional law allows
a community to live in peace by offering reasons that make sense to its members for why political divisions should not lead to a severing of ties. When we
ask this question, it turns out that there is a strong argument to be made for
vigorous judicial review. Judges have the potential to play a special role, not
because they can settle our disputes but because they stand astride a series of
contradictions that can unsettle any resolution of them. The best way to see
this is to examine some of the criticisms that have been made of judicial review.

Sometimes critics argue that judges are not accountable to the people.[17]
These critics start with the assumption that our disputes should be settled by

democratic means. On other occasions, however, critics complain about the "myth" of judicial independence, pointing out that judges do not effectively protect individual rights because they have neither the inclination nor the ability to depart much from the contemporary popular consensus.[18] At first it would seem that these criticisms cannot both be right. Oddly, though, it is the very fact that both *are* that provides the justification for judicial power. Precisely because judges are both public and private, both independent and accountable, they are able to police a boundary that is never fixed.

The point missed by the critics is that both a democratic, collective mechanism for resolving our disputes and a private, individualist mechanism are contestable settlements. Losers have no more obligation to accept these outcomes than they have an obligation to accept any other settlement. A large part of what divides us is precisely the question of whether particular issues should be resolved publicly and democratically or privately and individually. There is no reason to expect this argument to be settled to everyone's satisfaction by assuming the primacy of one resolution or the other. Because judges straddle the public-private line — because they are both independent from the political branches and in some sense accountable to them — they are well suited to the job of keeping the division between public and private permanently unsettled.

Another set of criticisms of judicial review points to the supposed indeterminacy — some would say incoherence — of the standard tools of liberal constitutionalism.[19] For someone skilled at the relevant moves, open-ended constitutional text and vague judicial precedent can be made to support a wide variety of arguments. Moreover, the core distinctions around which constitutional law is organized — the difference between freedom and coercion, public and private, feasance and nonfeasance — are easily deconstructed. Many skeptics have complained that this manipulability of constitutional doctrine means that judicial judgments are inevitably political. To the extent that one thinks of constitutional law as providing a politically neutral method of resolving our disputes, this criticism is on target.

But the skeptics have failed to notice that this fact about constitutional argument can also be a virtue. An odd feature of constitutional rhetoric is that it is at once analytically empty and uniquely powerful. For example, no matter how persuasive the demonstration that the private can be collapsed into the public or the free into the coerced, few people are able to give up on these fundamental concepts around which most of us organize our experience of the world. If one believes that judicial decisions are legitimate not because they settle disputes but because they utilize an analytic technique well suited to unsettling them, then we should celebrate the fact that constitutional rhetoric provides powerful support for virtually any outcome to any argument.

In order to make these assertions convincing, I shall have to set them out in much greater detail. I do so (I hope persuasively) in the pages that follow. For now, I want to add a few words about the audacity — one might say arrogance — of the project itself. I make large claims for the argument that follows, and I am well aware of the risk that they will turn out to be pretentious, unconvincing, or simply silly. It may indeed be foolish to suppose that there is something both new and sensible to say about constitutional theory or, more to the point, that I am the one to say it. In short, I feel justified in my own terror.

Nonetheless, I take some solace from the modesty of my normative goals. Although I like to think that my formulation of it is new, there is a sense in which this theory of constitutional law is actually no more than a description of what we have been doing all along. In the end, I do not want to insist that what we have been doing is just. Ultimate judgments on that question may well turn on the very political disagreements that drive the theory in the first place. Instead, my claim is that this characterization of constitutionalism shows the practice in its best, most defensible light. If my argument is successful, then readers who want to believe in constitutionalism will find a set of reasons that support their desire. Of course, there will also be readers who follow everything I say but nonetheless reject the practice. My hope is that these readers can take satisfaction from the knowledge that they have rejected it in its strongest form. For it is only this sort of strong rejection that provides the solid base upon which something truly new can be erected.

I

The Impossible Constitution

Modern constitutional theorists and judges rarely ask the most fundamental questions about constitutional law. Preoccupied with figuring out
what the Constitution commands and *how* the Constitution's commands
should be enforced, they almost never think about why the Constitution *ought*
to be obeyed and whether it *can* be.

The "what" question is about the substance of constitutional law. Sometimes it concerns specific constitutional doctrine. Does the Fourteenth Amendment, properly understood, guarantee a right to die? Can Congress delegate to
the president the power to veto portions of legislation? Does a state have the
power to require its employees to live within the state? On other occasions, the
question concerns more general issues about techniques of constitutional interpretation. Should the Constitution's text be interpreted according to the
original intent of the framers? Are there nontextual sources of constitutional
law, such as tradition, moral theory, or commonly held presuppositions about
the nature of government? Should the Constitution be interpreted broadly or
narrowly?[1]

The "how" question is about the means by which constitutional ideals
should be realized. Here most of the debate has centered around the efficacy
and legitimacy of judicial review. Do judges have the ability to enforce their in-

terpretation of constitutional norms when confronted with significant opposition? If they have that ability, are they likely to have the inclination? And even if they have the ability and the inclination, is it legitimate for them to do so?[2]

Although scholars have devoted endless pages to the "how" question, the "what" question is in the foreground of most Supreme Court cases. Consider, for example, the Court's decision in United States v. Morrison.[3] Morrison claimed that a statute creating a federal remedy for gender-motivated crimes of violence exceeded Congress' constitutional powers. After analyzing the Constitution's text and history, as well as its own prior decisions interpreting that text and history, the Court concluded that, as a substantive matter, Congress had indeed exceeded its powers.

But although substance was in the foreground, means of enforcement were necessarily in the background. By answering the substantive question in the way it did, the Court also tacitly held that contested questions about constitutional limitations on national government should be resolved by courts, rather than, say, by members of Congress, who may have interpreted the Constitution differently.

Only occasionally does the enforcement question move to the foreground. When the Court deals with matters like the political question doctrine, standing, and other justiciability issues, the "how" question is at the surface of its opinions.[4] Even when the issue is not justiciability, the Court sometimes discusses enforcement issues. For example, the extraordinary plurality opinion in Planned Parenthood of Southeastern Pennsylvania v. Casey, in which the Court reaffirmed the essential holding of Roe v. Wade, includes a lengthy meditation on the importance and fragility of judicial review.[5] On some occasions, the Court has held that the Constitution is best enforced by mechanisms other than judicial review. In Garcia v. San Antonio Metropolitan Transit Authority, the majority held that the extent of Tenth Amendment limitations on the federal government should be determined by the political branches, rather than by the Court.[6] The Court's many decisions utilizing "rational basis" review in equal-protection cases, affording deference to political actors in free-speech or due-process cases, or broadly construing congressional power as against federalism and separation of powers objections can be understood as decisions about constitutional substance, but they are also at least influenced — and perhaps determined — by ideas about appropriate mechanisms for enforcement.[7]

I know of no theory that successfully predicts or explains when the Court will put the "what" question in the foreground, when it will concentrate instead on the "how" question, and when it will conflate the two. There are, however, two additional, logically antecedent, questions that are almost never in the foreground. First, the Court hardly ever asks why policy questions *ought to be* determined by constitutional principle.

Suppose that the Constitution, properly understood, does not permit Congress to enact legislation prohibiting gender-motivated crimes of violence. So what? Either it is a good idea for Congress to enact the prohibition or it is not. In either event, it is not obvious why we need constitutional principle to decide what to do. If the idea is a bad one, isn't its badness reason enough to object to the legislation? If the idea is a good one, why should we allow constitutional principles to prevent us from doing something that would, by hypothesis, make the world a better place?

Careful separation of the "what" and "how" questions puts this "ought" question into sharper focus. Often our reaction to the "ought" question is colored by our commitment to democracy and concerns about an elite and unaccountable judiciary. Judges should be sharply constrained, on this view, because otherwise the people will be deprived of the right to rule themselves. Judges ought to obey the Constitution because without this obligation, they will be unconstrained, thereby threatening democratic values.[8]

There are two difficulties with this argument, however. First, it assumes an answer to the "what" question that may not be correct. Perhaps the Constitution, properly understood, does not embody democracy.[9] Perhaps its broad and indeterminate phrasing is meant to give extensive power to unelected judges and deprive the people of the right to rule themselves.[10] If this is a proper interpretation of the Constitution, but if we believe in democracy, then we are confronted in dramatic fashion with the "ought" problem: Why should we feel bound by such an arrangement in the face of our commitment to democracy?

Second, the argument assumes an answer to the "how" question that may also be incorrect. Perhaps an unelected judiciary should be sharply constrained, but constraining judges does not resolve the conflict between constitutionalism and democracy. Even if, as a "how" matter, judges never enforced constitutional commands, other political actors — members of the legislative and executive branches — would still have to answer the "ought" question. On occasion, this question will force them to choose between doing what the Constitution mandates and doing what, all things considered, they or their constituents think best. A commitment to constitutionalism requires an explanation of why they should choose the former.[11]

This "ought" question is logically anterior to the questions that have preoccupied courts and theorists. Only if we determine that the Constitution ought to be obeyed need we trouble ourselves with what it requires or how to secure obedience to it.* Moreover, there is another question anterior even to the "ought" question. Since "ought" generally implies "can," we need to ask whether it is *possible* to decide contested issues by reference to the Constitution. If it turns out to be impossible — if we cannot be bound by the Constitution even if we want to be — then we need not concern ourselves with whether we want to be.

At first blush, there seems to be little mystery about why the Court rarely addresses these anterior questions: the answers seem easy. Almost two hundred years ago, Chief Justice John Marshall thought that he had satisfactorily disposed of the questions in his celebrated opinion in Marbury v. Madison. "That the people have an original right to establish, for their future government, such principles as, in their opinion, shall most conduce to their own happiness is the basis on which the whole American fabric has been erected," he wrote. And because the people have the right to establish such principles, it logically follows that there is an obligation of obedience to them once established:

> The constitution is either a superior paramount law, unchangeable by ordinary means, or it is on a level with ordinary legislative acts, and like other acts, is alterable when the legislature shall please to alter it.
>
> If the former part of the alternative be true, then a legislative act contrary to the constitution is not law: if the latter part be true, then written constitutions are absurd attempts, on the part of the people, to limit a power, in its own nature illimitable.
>
> Certainly all those who have framed written constitutions contemplate them as forming the fundamental and paramount law of the nation, and, consequently, the theory of every such government must be, that an act of the legislature, repugnant to the constitution, is void.[12]

For two centuries, this answer has seemed good enough. Yet the answer, if indeed it can be called that, is remarkably unpersuasive. Much of the remainder of this chapter is devoted to a detailed demonstration of its inadequacies, but even a superficial examination of Marshall's logic reveals significant flaws.

Marshall begins with the hypothesis that the people have the right to establish constitutional principles. If so, it does indeed follow that the principles

*There is, to be sure, a sense in which the "what" question is anterior. Most people are uninterested in buying a pig in a poke. They might sensibly take the position that they would like to know what kind of constitution we are talking about before making a commitment to obey it. Put differently, our quest might be to choose a "what" for constitutional law that creates an obligation to obey. But we still need to start by investigating the potential circumstances that would create a duty to obey.

they establish should be obeyed. As Marshall explains, the idea of an obligation to obey seems built into the concept of constitutional principles. But where does this right come from? A "right" of people alive in 1789 to establish constitutional principles interferes with the "right" of people alive in the twenty-first century to govern themselves.* Marshall's formulation therefore begs the question of why people today lack the right of self-determination.† Marshall contended that framers of the Constitution intended it to be binding. Of course they did. But that historical fact tells us nothing about why we should feel bound.‡

---

*The problem is made even more serious by the fact that the initial rules were not established by all the people living in the United States in 1789. Indeed, the majority of people — including women, slaves, and nonproperty holders — had no role in the decision.

†Of course, constitutions can be amended. People alive today can govern themselves if they manage to overcome the special hurdles established by the amendment process. But it is much more difficult to amend the Constitution than to enact ordinary legislation, and these special hurdles to amendment seem built into the idea of constitutional law. As Marshall argued, if there were no special hurdles, constitutions would be no different from ordinary legislation and, hence, have no point. It follows that precisely to the extent that they have a point, constitutions raise issues of self-governance.

At first blush, there may seem to be a symmetry between the special difficulty in amending constitutions and the special difficulty in entrenching them in the first place. On this view, their extraordinary binding effect is justified by the extraordinary efforts required to ratify them. There is some force to this argument, which has been developed with great sophistication by Bruce Ackerman, among others, but it does not respond to the intergenerational difficulty. First, the current generation may not agree that the ratification process was sufficiently onerous to bind. Certainly few people today would agree that a process limited to property-holding white men — the one adopted in 1789 — is sufficient. Second, no matter how onerous the original ratification process, the fact remains that constitutions prevent a current generation from deciding what is best for itself. No one would maintain that the Dutch parliament can legitimately make laws for the United States as long as it enacts them by a special supermajority designed to ensure that participants in the lawmaking process are publicly engaged. Why then can an earlier generation of Americans make law for the current generation?

‡Sometimes people respond to this line of argument by claiming that the problem of constitutional legitimacy is no different from the problem of political obligation more generally. After all, statutes also purport to bind. To be sure, statutes may not be as deeply entrenched as constitutions, but neither can they be discarded at will. Many statutes are also old and were also written by people who are now long dead. Why, one might ask, should we be so hung up about constitutional law when all of law poses the same difficulty?

There is a problem with explaining political obligation more generally, but beginning

Nor does it help to assert, as Marshall does a few paragraphs later, that failure to enforce the Constitution "would subvert the very foundation of all written constitutions" and therefore "[reduce] to nothing what we have deemed the greatest improvement on political institutions — a written constitution."[13] All the work in this sentence is done by the word *we*. If "we" in fact currently believe that our Constitution is "the greatest improvement on political institutions," then we will follow it because we think that it is a good idea to do so, rather than because we are bound to do so. The binding force of the Constitution affects only the people outside the "we" that Marshall invokes — that is, people who would not otherwise obey its commands but do so out of obligation. For these people, Marshall's argument amounts to an assertion that they ought to be bound by the Constitution because, if they were not, there would be no binding constitution.*

This final argument does, perhaps, suggest a solution to the "ought" question but only at the cost of raising the "can" question in acute form. Marshall writes that if a legislative act could trump a constitutional provision, "written constitutions [would be] absurd attempts, on the part of the people, to limit a power, in its own nature illimitable."[14] Apparently this proposition itself is so absurd as to require no refutation. Yet there is a puzzle here. The framers of

---

our inquiry with this problem puts the relation between the puzzles of constitutional and political legitimacy in the wrong order. Instead of helping to solve our difficulties with constitutional law, the statutory obligation puzzle only makes the search for a solution more urgent. For if we had a satisfactory explanation to why constitutions bind, then the answer to our statutory problem would be easy. Law made pursuant to a scheme that is binding is itself binding precisely because it is made pursuant to a binding scheme. For example, if a constitution permits statutes to be entrenched, and if the constitution itself is legitimate, it would follow that the entrenchment the constitution permits is also legitimate. There is thus an asymmetry between the problems of constitutional and statutory legitimacy. If we could come up with a satisfactory theory of constitutional legitimacy, the more general problem of political obligation is likely to solve itself. But if, as also seems likely, statutes are legitimate only because they are enacted pursuant to a legitimate constitution, asking questions about statutory legitimacy first will not get our inquiry off the ground.

*Perhaps Marshall's claim is that there is universal agreement as to the value of constitutions in general but not universal agreement as to the value of each of command of the U.S. Constitution. People who agree that constitutions are worth having are obliged to obey portions of the constitution they disagree with. Even as reformulated, however, the argument does not speak to anyone who thinks that constitutions in general are not worth preserving. Perhaps more important, it provides no answer to those who value constitutions in general but think that the U.S. Constitution could be improved upon by changing some of its specific commands.

the Constitution, now long dead, have no coercive power over us. Perhaps the "ought" question can be answered with the observation that it is, after all, we, the living, who choose to follow constitutional principles.[15] If following these principles is our choice, then there is no longer an "ought" question that need concern us; this is simply what we have chosen to do because, all things considered, it seems best to us.

The difficulty with this resolution of the problem is that if constitutional principles control only to the extent that we now wish them to, then it can no longer be said that we are (or can be) bound by them. The principles themselves are doing no work. They "bind" us only to the extent that they correspond to some other normative framework that (contingently) makes it seem like a good idea to follow them. Apparently our power not to follow them is indeed illimitable.

Most people who think about constitutional law today have followed Chief Justice Marshall in treating the "what" and "how" questions as difficult and contested, while the "ought" and "can" questions, if they are asked at all, are regarded as easy and uncontroversial. Much of this book is devoted to the claim that this hierarchy should be reversed. Not only are the "ought" and "can" questions difficult; but once they are answered, the "what" and "how" questions more or less answer themselves.

The argument in support of these propositions is complex and will require considerable explication. Before we can embark upon it, however, we need a more precise specification of the function of constitutional law.* Once we establish such a function (at least provisionally), we can then explore in more detail the difficulties posed by the "ought" and "can" questions.

What Does Constitutional Law Do?

What, then, does constitutional law consist of? Unfortunately, when we try to formulate an appropriate definition, we confront an immediate problem: as the previous discussion indicates, both the "what" and "how" of con-

---

*I do not mean to claim that authoritativeness and function are necessarily linked. At least conceptually, it is possible to imagine a constitution that people are obliged to obey even though doing so makes things worse rather than better. Indeed, I shall argue below that the only way constitutional law can create a just community for people of divergent views is by giving them a motive for identifying themselves with the community even when that community's constitution yields results with which they profoundly disagree. Still, we need to give these people some sort of reason to obey, and this task will be easier if we can imagine a function for constitutional law that makes sense within their own normative frameworks.

stitutional law are contested. It would therefore be a mistake to build a resolution of these issues into our initial definition.

It will not do, for example, to define constitutional law as consisting of judicial enforcement and interpretation of the constitutional text.[16] We may ultimately decide that this is the form of constitutional law that best satisfies the "ought" and "can" questions, but we cannot establish it at the outset by definitional fiat. Instead, our initial definition should be general enough not to prejudge the very questions we wish to investigate.

A more promising approach is to ask what we can reasonably expect from constitutional law. What is constitutional law good for? Even if we cannot agree (at least initially) about its form, we might agree (again, at least initially) about its function. Perhaps we can begin by provisionally defining constitutional law as a system designed to prevent the polity from *de*constituting.* It accomplishes this task by establishing terms of agreement to which all members of the polity can subscribe (or at least can be *expected* to subscribe) and which prevent the polity from disintegrating when confronted with political disagreement.[17]

I want to emphasize at the outset that this definition is provisional. Indeed, I shall ultimately argue that the definition must be modified because it leads to the unsatisfactory conclusion that constitutional law is both impossible and inevitable. The modifications necessary to avoid this paradox constitute the bulk of this book. Nonetheless, I start with this provisional definition because I must, after all, start somewhere, because the definition seems at least initially plausible, and because an exploration of its problems turns out to be a useful expository strategy.

The definition insists on a sharp distinction between ordinary political disagreement, which is inevitable and desirable in any political community, and constituting principles. Members of any political community will regularly favor different policies, make different trade-offs between goods, and believe in different moral and religious values. Perhaps citizens disagree about the appropriate funding method for social security, or about the propriety of capital punishment, or about whether to send troops to a foreign conflict, or about the truth of Christianity. At some point, these disagreements might be

---

*I do not mean to take a position here as to whether constitutional law *constitutes* the polity. Perhaps on some occasions the act of constitutional creation provides the mechanism by which communities come into existence. In many other instances, though, constitutional law reflects an organic, preexisting community rather than creating a new one. Even in the latter situations, however, constitutional law might serve as a mechanism for maintaining community cohesion in the face of inevitable disagreement.

severe enough—or numerous enough—to justify a severing of ties. Much more frequently, however, it will be better for all concerned to find a way to resolve the disagreement. If people are not to come to blows or go their separate ways, there must be an agreed-upon method by which the community can settle the dispute and move on.

What constitutional law amounts to, then, is a series of metarules or principles that allow people to abstract from ordinary disagreements. For convenience, I shall call these the rules of constitutional settlement.[18] Constitutional settlement can take three forms. Sometimes, constitutional law itself specifies an answer. For example, the U.S. Constitution, by its terms, answers the question of whether there should be taxes on exports (it prohibits them).[19] Sometimes constitutional law specifies a public, political process by which an answer can be determined; most of the Constitution consists of an elaborate blueprint for public resolution of disputed questions, allocating lawmaking power among branches of the federal government and between the federal government and the states. Finally, sometimes constitutional law requires that the answer be remitted to the private, individual sphere. For example, the U.S. Constitution specifies that the truth claims made by various religions should be determined individually, rather than collectively.*

Whichever form it takes, constitutional settlement can achieve its objective in two ways. First, there can be a substantive settlement. Perhaps I start out believing that there are sound policy reasons for imposing a tax on exports. I then discover that the Constitution prohibits such a tax. I therefore change my mind and decide that taxes on exports are bad policy. Although substantive settlement is theoretically possible, it seems implausible. Why would the bare fact that such taxes are constitutionally banned cause me to change my mind about them? It seems far more likely that I would conclude that the Constitution is bad insofar as it bars such taxes.[20]

At least superficially, the possibility for procedural settlement seems more plausible. As a substantive matter, I might continue to believe that taxes on exports are a good idea, but I am also committed to constitutionalism as a procedure for resolving disagreements of this sort. The issue is therefore settled by agreement on procedural norms despite my continuing substantive disagreement.†

*Interestingly, the U.S. Constitution never requires a public resolution.

†Note that procedural settlements can take any of the three forms of constitutional settlement. One could be committed to a particular resolution dictated by the constitutional text, to a particular voting mechanism specified in the text, or to an allocation to the private sphere specified in the text. In each case, the settlement is procedural in the sense that people agree to the procedure for resolution without settling their substantive disagreement.

Whether procedural or substantive, the settlement produced by constitutional law comes about because once citizens recognize "higher" areas of agreement, they are able to reason from them back down to the political level so as to resolve political disputes in a fashion that is generally accepted as justified.

What sort of metaprinciples might serve this function? Once again, it is important not to prejudge the issues that divide us. At least hypothetically, we can imagine a variety of different sources for the metarules. A potential source would be a canonical text, but it is not the only one. The rules might be derived from what rational people would agree to in the "original position" or in a hypothetical "social contract." They might be derived from teleological views about the appropriate context for human flourishing; utilitarian views about the greatest good for the greatest number; pragmatic, functional, or instrumental views about institutions likely to make the wisest decisions; or even religious views about revealed truth demonstrating the will of God.[21]

The Definitional Dilemma

For the most part, attacks on constitutionalism have focused on the gap between the rules of constitutional settlement on the one hand and the resolution of political disputes said to follow from those rules on the other. The standard argument is that the rules are indeterminate and do not or cannot dictate unique resolutions.[22] This is a powerful criticism, but it is not, in my judgment, the most powerful one. The indeterminacy critique runs up against the experiential reality that most judges feel constrained by constitutional doctrine.[23] Once a background culture has been specified, it is simply not true that actors feel completely unconstrained when they follow rules.[24]

A more fundamental problem is built into the very effort to define the practice of constitutional law. Our strategy of beginning with a definition seems sensible—how else can we start a discussion about whether constitutional law is justified and possible? Yet the strategy introduces an immediate problem. Recall the insistence on a definition so general it will not prejudge the issues in dispute. This effort is essential if we are to avoid an "ought" problem. If we define constitutional law more narrowly, consisting of the application of a particular, contested metarule, then we will provide no reason why adherents to rival rules ought to affiliate themselves with constitutional law. But the effort to avoid "ought" problems reintroduces the "can" question. If we formulate a definition that is broad enough not to prejudge the conflict between metarules, how can these rules resolve our political disputes? Even if the indeterminacy critique is wrong, and a particular constitutional settlement yields a unique resolution to every political dispute, such a resolution remains illusive if there is more than one possible constitutional settlement. What we are likely to end up with, in other words, is contesting constitutional settlements yielding contesting political outcomes.[25] Instead of metarules permitting escape from political conflict, the conflict is simply transferred to the metalevel, where it is even more dangerous and destabilizing because loss at this level implies not just political defeat but exclusion from the political community.

This problem is not solely the product of the fact that participants in contemporary political debate adhere to a variety of inconsistent metarules. Even in the teeth of this disagreement, we could satisfactorily answer the "ought" question if we could provide reasons why people "ought" to adhere to one set of metarules rather than another. But what could these reasons be?

All too frequently, constitutional theorists attempt to justify the rules of settlement in terms of the rules themselves. It is said, for example, that Supreme Court Justices are obligated to obey the text of the Constitution because obedience to text is what constitutional law demands.[26] It should be obvious that this is not a reason at all—or at least not a reason that will convince anyone who does not already believe in the set of rules. It is just another attempt to end the argument through arbitrary definition.

If the rules cannot be justified by reference to themselves, then we must look either below them or above them for justification. We look below if we justify the rules by reference to their consequences. One might argue, for example, that we should all adhere to our Constitution's text because this is the best way to ensure that the government avoids taxes on exports.[27] But now we are reasoning from contested political positions to rules for constitutional settlement, rather than the other way around. If the rules are going to settle political contests, then their content cannot be determined by the contests they are intended to settle.

We might look above by justifying the rules in terms of some still more fundamental principle—a set of meta-meta-rules. Unfortunately, however, our definitional difficulty reemerges on this higher level. How are these rules to be justified when people disagree?

Constitutional Evil

These problems are compounded by what J. M. Balkin has called the problem of "constitutional evil."[28] For constitutional law to work, it must require individuals to accept outcomes they would not accept in its absence. If constitutional law did not produce this result—if it did not at least occasionally provide the motivation for people to do things they would not otherwise do — then it could be reduced to whatever does provide the motivation. But it is unclear how rules of constitutional settlement — in either their substantive or procedural manifestations — can accomplish this objective.

Consider first the problem of substantive settlement. An analogy to religious debate serves to illuminate the difficulty. Some liberal adherents to Roman Catholicism purport to disagree with certain of the church's teachings — for example, its stand against the ordination of women.* Conservative Catholics have attacked the liberal view as amounting to what they derisively call "cafeteria Catholicism."[29] Although their point is not usually made this way, the conservatives are arguing in essence for a substantive settlement. On this view, if Catholicism is to provide a reason for action, Catholics cannot be allowed to pick and choose which aspects of the religion they adhere to; a Catholic whose Catholicism is contingent upon coincidence between Catholicism and some other foundational premise (for example, a commitment to a particular version of gender equality) is not really a Catholic at all. For Catholicism to do work, it must require adherents to believe and do things they would not otherwise believe and do. Hence, the fact that liberal Catholics disagree with the church's teaching (at least as an initial matter) should not be dispositive. Their Catholicism, on this view, should provide sufficient reason for them to change their mind.

This argument seems correct as far as it goes, but it leaves mysterious how, as a psychological matter, and why, as a logical matter, such a change would occur. Liberal Catholics are likely to respond in one of two ways. If they are indeed convinced that Catholicism requires them to give up their commitment to gender equality, they may say so much the worse for Catholicism and leave the church. Alternatively, they may remain within the church but contest the meaning of Catholicism. They can claim that they are the real Catholics and that their conservative critics have misunderstood or misrepresented Catholic teaching.

These two responses are thus different forms of the "ought" and "can" questions. If a proposed substantive settlement really does require outcomes that are evil, then why *ought* one accept it? If only those settlements that avoid substantive evil ought to be accepted, then how *can* the settlement bind people to do things they otherwise would not do?

At first, it might seem that this problem could be resolved by dividing the

---

*By using the example of "liberal" Catholics, I do not mean to suggest that the problem I discuss has an ideological valence. The same points could be made by discussing the opposition of various conservative Catholics to the church's teachings regarding capital punishment or to some of the reforms resulting from Vatican II.

group into smaller communities. Imagine, for example, that dissident Catholics break off from the church and form a new community. Its constituting beliefs consist of traditional Catholic doctrine modified by the principles of gender equality. Surely now this new group has formulated a settlement that is binding on it. But the old problem reemerges: the principles of gender equality, like traditional Catholic doctrine, do work only to the extent that they compel people to believe things they would not otherwise believe. When individuals come up against a conflict between gender-equality principles and what they otherwise believe to be right, they will once again confront the question of whether to abandon gender equality or reformulate it so as to avoid substantive evil.[30]

If this argument is correct, it leaves us with a mystery. We know that individuals do affiliate themselves with groups, formulate principles of constitutional settlement, and perceive these principles as providing motives for action. How does any of this come about? One answer is that these groups rely upon a procedural, rather than a substantive settlement. A highly simplified example illustrates both the possibilities and limitations of procedural settlement.

Suppose a small group of friends decides to form an investment club. At their initial meeting, the friends agree that it will require a two-thirds vote of members to invest in a security.* At a subsequent meeting, they take a two-thirds vote to purchase a particular security, but one member believes that the purchase is a bad idea. Even if the other members are unsuccessful in persuading the dissenter to agree as a substantive matter, he might nonetheless agree to accept the vote because of his commitment to the procedural settlement.

Two types of reasons might support this decision. First, a procedural settlement can operate as a rule of thumb. Perhaps the dissenter believes that the security is a bad investment, but he also feels some humility about his own beliefs. The two-thirds rule is a procedural mechanism designed to produce wise decisions. With more time to do more research, the dissenter might feel comfortable substituting his own judgment for that of the group. But given the limited time for the decision, it may be a sensible strategy to adopt the general practice of deferring to group decisions.†

Perhaps even after the dissenter has taken into account the views of others,

---

*Note that this is not the only form a procedural settlement can take. The agreement might provide that only securities of a certain type could be purchased or that individual dissenters could opt out of certain purchases. These examples correspond to the types of constitutional settlement discussed above.

†To the extent that the dissenter actually changes his mind about the correctness of the decision, his motivations shade into the substantive settlement category.

he remains convinced that his initial assessment is correct. A second reason for nonetheless adhering to the procedural settlement is that such adherence may be necessary to preserve the group. The dissenter might believe that even though this decision is bad, over the range of cases the group will make enough good decisions to compensate for the bad ones. And even if most group decisions lose money, the camaraderie and connection that the group provides might be worth the cost. To be sure, the dissenter might attempt to renegotiate the rules that hold the group together, but there is no guarantee that his effort will succeed. Even if the rules are in some sense suboptimal, they may be the only rules that the group as a whole can agree upon. Moreover, even if the renegotiation is successful, the cost in time and the disruption caused by continual efforts to restructure the deal may be greater than the benefits likely to be achieved.

Motivations of this sort go a long way toward explaining the willingness of individuals to comply with rules of procedural settlement. Consider, for example, the decision by the U.S. Senate to confirm the nomination of Clarence Thomas as Associate Justice of the Supreme Court. The fight over Thomas' nomination was extraordinarily rancorous and the vote close. Many Americans were angered by the outcome, and it is hard to believe that most of them changed their minds about his qualifications simply because a narrow majority of the Senate approved the nomination. Still, once the vote had been tabulated, principles of procedural settlement caused almost everyone to accept the legitimacy of the outcome. No one suggested that Thomas was not, in fact, a member of the Court[31] because, say, the Senate is not apportioned according to population.[32] People were prepared to accept the outcome — perhaps because they believed that, whatever happened in this case, over the range of cases the Senate was likely to reach wise conclusions, more likely because, as angry as they were, this one bad decision was insufficient cause to unravel a set of rules that had held the country together for two hundred years.

But although people unquestionably adhere to rules of procedural settlement, it does not follow that they adhere to these rules *because of* the settlement. Indeed, it is hard to see why anyone would. Consider, again, the members of our hypothetical investment club. As outlined above, a dissenting member may agree to go along with the procedural settlement either because he is convinced that the two-thirds rule is more likely to produce wise decisions than his own judgment in the absence of the rule or because the value of preserving the group is greater than the disutility produced by obeying the rule.

It is important to understand that neither of these motivations is the same as a motivation rooted in obligation to obey the terms of the settlement. A dissenter who believes that the two-thirds rule is likely to produce wise outcomes abides by the rule not because of a felt obligation to respect the procedural settlement but because of his present, all-things-considered judgment as to the wisest course of action. Put differently, the rule motivating his actions is not the rule of procedural settlement (two-thirds can bind the group) but rather a rule providing that he should always invest an optimal level of effort in making wise decisions. As a contingent fact, in this case, it turns out that this rule leads him to respect the two-thirds requirement, but there is no guarantee that the same outcome will result in a future case. A person who adopts this approach does not *bind* himself to follow the procedural settlement *because* it is the procedural settlement.[33]

Similarly, a dissenter who wishes to maintain group cohesion is motivated by this desire rather than by an obligation to obey the settlement. Indeed, sometimes a devotion to group cohesion will require disregard of the procedural settlement. Imagine, for example, that some members of the group unilaterally announce that they are no longer willing to comply with the rules and that from now on a three-fourths vote will be necessary before an investment is made. Suppose further that these members threaten to break up the group if their threat is not acceded to. Of course, these demands are in blatant violation of the procedural settlement. Yet a person who valued the group might well accede to them.

There are good reasons why the rules of procedural settlement qua procedural settlement cannot bind. In our initial hypothetical, we simply specified that the parties had agreed to the two-thirds requirement. But this specification begs the crucial question: What procedures were used to establish the two-thirds procedure? Procedural settlements cannot work because in order for them to take effect, there must already have been a procedural settlement in place.[34] Suppose, for example, that at the club's first meeting the two-thirds voting rule was established by majority vote. Why should this vote bind the minority? For club members to be bound by this settlement, there would have to be some binding, antecedent settlement establishing a majority voting rule. But then there would have to be some settlement that supports this settlement, and so on.

We might think that these problems could be avoided if the initial vote were unanimous or if individuals joined the club with the understanding that there was to be a two-thirds voting rule. Of course, neither of these conditions was satisfied when our own constitutional settlement was put into place. Moreover, even if they were, we would still have to confront the issue posed by people who change their minds. The dissenting member of our hypothetical investment club might say that although he agreed to a two-thirds rule at the time, he no longer does. Why should his past, abandoned views control his current actions? A procedural settlement can never successfully entrench a particular procedure against an argument of this sort. Perhaps the settlement itself specifies that members agree not to change their minds or agree to a particular amendment procedure if they do. But even this settlement cannot bind people who change their minds about whether they should be allowed to change their minds.

Many will no doubt be unsympathetic to this argument in the highly simplified context of an investment club. When we are talking about individual commitments, we regularly allow our past selves to bind our future selves. Indeed, our ability to bind ourselves — to plan and control our own future lives — is crucial to the concept of personal identity over time.[35]

Even on the individual level, however, the problem is more complicated than one might at first suppose. It is not always clear that individual autonomy requires preference for past decisions over present ones. And the problem is much more complex when procedural settlements purport to bind other individuals. Perhaps I, as an individual, should be bound by my own prior commitments even if I change my mind, but it certainly does not follow that I should be allowed to bind others.[36] I as an individual never agreed to give every state two votes in the Senate. Indeed, none of my ancestors agreed to it.* Had I been asked, I like to think that I would have strongly objected to this procedural settlement, and I am quite certain that I would not have agreed to the procedures by which this procedural settlement was entrenched.† Why, then, should I be bound by it?

This embarrassment regularly leads to slippage whenever political theorists engage in social-contract talk. Instead of insisting on actual, personal agreement, they substitute a kind of hypothetical agreement.[37] On this view, the constitutional settlement is binding because it is what all rational people *would have* agreed to in a state of nature, or behind a veil of ignorance, or whatever. A great deal of ink has been spilled over precisely how this hypothetical, impersonal agreement generates an actual, personal obligation to

---

*To be sure, my ancestors at some point probably took an oath to support and defend the Constitution of the United States as a condition of their obtaining citizenship. It is not obvious that the oath was freely given in light of the context in which it was administered and the alternative courses of action available. Nor is it obvious what version of constitutionalism my ancestors committed themselves to. In any event, an institutional settlement could hardly work if only those who had personally agreed to support it were thereby bound.

†It must be acknowledged that there is some difficulty in articulating who, precisely, the "I" is in this counterfactual.

obey, over whether it really exists, and, indeed, over whether one can even speak of people making choices or commitments when they are stripped of their surrounding culture or their individuating characteristics.[38]

Without rehearsing these matters here, it is sufficient for our purposes to note that, at best, the argument from hypothetical agreement is convincing when defending the broad outlines of a political theory. It is barely plausible that all rational individuals would agree to the maximin principle[39] or to a Lockean conception of property rights. It is simply not plausible that all rational individuals would agree to equal state representation in the Senate or to a ban on the taxation of exports. Arguments for this particular constitutional settlement are certain to persuade some but not others. Those who are persuaded will not need an argument from obligation to motivate their actions while those who are not cannot be provided with one.

Getting by without Constitutional Law

The previous two sections outlined two groups of interlocking reasons why constitutional settlements are bound to fail. The settlements are supposed to allow us to resolve contested political disputes by reference to a "higher" set of rules on which there is agreement. But there is in fact no agreement on the higher set of rules, and to the extent that the competing sets of rules are foundational, there is no prospect of formulating arguments that would (or should) create agreement. Moreover, even if there were agreement, there is no reason why people should feel bound to follow the rules in circumstances where those rules produce results that are perceived as undesirable.

These two problems interact in the following way: When a political actor discovers that a particular settlement produces results she considers undesirable, she is likely to find another settlement, which cannot be definitionally excluded from constitutional practice and which will achieve her objectives. There is no reason why she should feel bound to the first settlement and no argument exterior to the first settlement for why the second settlement is worse than the first. The result is certain to be a proliferation of constitutional settlements, with a settlement to match every political position. It follows that the settlements cannot lead to resolution of political disputes and that constitutional law cannot serve the function we have identified for it.

In this section, I consider some possible implications of this analysis. Each of the proposals I discuss below involves, in different ways and to a greater or lesser extent, giving up on constitutional law as a means of maintaining community cohesion. I conclude that each of the proposals is unsatisfactory and that the only way out of the dilemma is to rethink what we expect from constitutional law.

One approach involves assuming a perspective external to the practice of constitutional law. A social scientist can examine an alien culture and by careful study determine the *grundnorm* in place for that society. For the external observer, this discovery carries no normative import. It is simply an observable fact that those within the society attach normative significance to a particular settlement.[40] Some of our most perceptive constitutional scholars have attempted to think about constitutional law in this fashion. They are ready to concede that there are no arguments for a particular constitutional settlement that will persuade those outside the settlement. Constitutional law is binding for those within a particular practice but provides no mechanism for mediating between practices.[41]

One might express some skepticism about the ability of contemporary observers, writing about our own constitutional practices, truly to get outside of those practices. But even if we put this problem to one side, the views of such an external observer are of no help to those of us (all of us) acting within a society. An external observer has the luxury of studying from the outside, but an internal participant must decide what to do.[42] A participant needs to know whether she is obliged to follow a particular constitutional settlement and if so, why. The empirical observation that many others act as if they feel bound to it cannot answer these questions for her.

An external observer might assist us in understanding a slightly different, more subtle point. Such an observer could help us see that we are bound in the existential rather than the moral sense of the word. Perhaps constitutional law is literally constitutive, on the individual as well as the societal level. I have argued above that because "ought" implies "can" we need not worry about whether we ought to adhere to a constitutional settlement if we cannot adhere to it. But of course the same argument also holds if we cannot *avoid* adhering to it. And perhaps we cannot. It does no good to pretend that our country has not had the history that it has in fact had and that we are not located within the culture that in fact surrounds us. Perhaps this history and this culture bind us to a way of looking at the world and a set of constitutional settlements whether we like it or not.

Frederick Schauer has made a related point: constitutional law must, at bottom, be grounded in the social fact of acceptance rather than in normative judgment.[43] Our investment club hypothetical again illustrates the point. Suppose we insist that the club's settlement be normative all the way to the bottom. On one view, this would mean that the settlement should be obeyed only if the norms it contains are substantively right. As we have already seen, however, this view attaches no weight to the settlement itself. We would then obey the settlement only to the extent that it corresponds to the norms.

Obedience to the settlement, as opposed to a set of norms that it might or might not contain, requires the conclusion that the settlement was itself put in place by a normatively attractive method. But at this stage of the argument, the difficulty repeats itself. If we are to make an independent judgment about the norms by which the settlement was put in place, then our obligation to obey the settlement is once again only contingent. So the method by which the settlement was put in place must itself be justified according to some prior settlement, and so on.[44] It seems to follow that at the bottom of the chain must be the raw social fact of acceptance unsupported by a preceding norm.

There is force to this argument, but the force is limited. One problem is that the social facts themselves are ambiguous. We have more than a single history and a single culture. Various versions of our history and culture wage a continuous struggle for primacy. Thus, the choice between different sets of social facts must be normatively driven. The choice might not be unlimited, but we surely have some leeway about which bits of our history and culture to emphasize and which to repress. Indeed, the struggle between contending constitutional settlements can be conceptualized in precisely this way.

Moreover, there is a special irony in the role an external observer plays with regard to this struggle. A social scientist can help us see that our constitutional settlement is rooted, at bottom, in social fact. But the very act of identifying the bonds of our prior history causes them to dissolve. As long as the bonds remain unconscious, they limit freedom. As soon as they are introduced into consciousness, we acquire the illusion of choice. It will then seem that we can abandon them if we wish to.* If prior settlements are really supported by no more than social fact, then we are motivated by this realization to reject them and replace them with a settlement that can be normatively defended.

---

*Consider, for example, the well-known argument against determinism involving a hypothetical "book of life." If determinism is true, then in principle it would be possible to have a "book of life," which accurately predicted one's next action. So long as the agent has not read the book, there is no difficulty. But as soon as the agent has read the book, it would seem that he is presented with the choice of frustrating its author by choosing to do something other than what the book predicts. One response to this argument is that the "choice" may reflect no more than the failure to consult the right book. The "true" book would include the agent's consultation of the false book in its calculations concerning the agent's next action. The result is an infinite regress, which, perhaps, demonstrates why the illusion of free will, even if no more than an illusion, is impossible to extirpate. For a discussion, *see* Alvin I. Goldman, A Theory of Human Action 186–96 (1970); *and* Alf Ross, On Guilt, Responsibility and Punishment 145–52 (1975).

To be sure, the possibility of accomplishing this goal may be no more than an illusion, but it is an inescapable one, and, for as long as we are under its spell, we will wonder about what choice to make.* A social scientist who is external to our struggle cannot answer that question for us.

Other theorists have attempted to assimilate skeptical arguments while remaining within the practice of constitutional law by insisting on its thinness. These theorists in effect invert the hierarchy I have described. On my model people start out by disagreeing about ordinary political disputes and use a constitutional settlement to resolve their disagreement. Perhaps instead people start by *agreeing* about most ordinary questions. What they disagree about is the fundamentals.

One version of this thesis suggests that people might be able to use their agreement on the lower level to reach agreement on the higher level — the reverse of the process I have described. On this version, constitutional law does not constitute the community. Instead, people who already value political community may come to discern and protect an "overlapping consensus" that preserves the community.[45]

A slightly different version suggests that political community can be preserved with only minimal agreement — or perhaps no agreement at all — on the higher level.[46] This position finds support in the historic ability of Americans to put to one side the abstract theoretical and foundational disputes that have racked Europe. Americans, it is claimed, are not united by a creed or philosophy but by their pragmatic insistence on making the pie as big as possible for everyone.[47] Our constitutional settlements should therefore remain "incompletely theorized"[48] because the very effort to secure agreement is likely to produce, rather than resolve, conflict.[49]

There is surely some truth to both these versions. As a theoretical matter, constitutional law is necessary only where there is political disagreement, and trying to reach a constitutional settlement may produce disagreement where none previously existed. But I think that these theories overstate the extent to which we can do without constitutional law. There are several difficulties.

First, to the extent that these views rest on a consensus theory of American history, they are not likely to be persuasive to those who see more conflict beneath the surface. Moreover, to the extent that there is consensus on the political level, we must entertain the possibility that the consensus is produced

---

*I should make clear that my point relates solely to a choice as to the "what" of constitutional law. I do not mean to argue that there is a choice as to whether to have constitutional law. Indeed, the point of this section is that some form of constitutional law is inevitable.

by the unjust, legitimating power of our constitutional settlement. If the arguments I have made are correct, there is no good reason why people *ought to be* motivated by the settlement. But this proposition is not inconsistent with the possibility that people might be tricked into believing that they have an obligation which, in justice, they do not have. Perhaps, then, constitutional law amounts to no more than a mystification that helps entrench an unjust social order.[50]

The most sophisticated expositors of consensus theory avoid these traps. They argue that it is precisely because of the inevitability and desirability of political conflict that we need to forge an overlapping consensus. Moreover, this consensus should not be a mere modus vivendi or cynical device for manipulating others. Rather, it should consist of views, honestly held, that we can reasonably expect others within our political community to share.[51]

This ideal is an attractive one, but standing alone, it does not tell us what to do when consensus runs out. Even if Americans agree about many things, they don't agree about everything. Consider, for example, the controversy over gay marriage. People on both sides of this issue are motivated by sincere, foundational beliefs that do not overlap, and the set of sincere beliefs that do overlap may be too small and incomplete to resolve the question.[52] To be sure, a peace maker might reproachfully ask people on both sides whether they really wish to dissolve the political community over this question, but there is no reason in principle why one side should have to sacrifice its position in order to preserve the union. Both sides might reasonably stand their ground, waiting for the other to back down.

A frequent reaction to impasses of this sort is to argue that when no constitutional settlement is possible, the matter should be remitted to democratic decision making. But this is a grave mistake. Remitting the question to democratic politics is *itself* a constitutional decision that reflects a contested constitutional settlement. For example, Justice Antonin Scalia has argued that in the face of disagreement, we should remit issues like homosexual marriage and euthanasia to collective, majoritarian politics.[53] In contrast, advocates of gay rights and a "right to die" argue that in the face of disagreement, we should remit the question to individual decision making. Instead of a choice between constitutional law and something else, this dispute requires a choice between competing versions of constitutional law. Both positions rely upon a contested constitutional settlement, and neither presents a reason why advocates of the competing settlement should abandon their position.

Perhaps Justice Scalia has not assimilated the full implications of the skeptical position. Instead of arguing for democracy, a thoroughgoing skeptic might take the view that there is nothing worth saying about one resolution as opposed to another. There will be a struggle of some sort, and things will come out the way they come out. What this position amounts to, though, is an effort to regain the perspective of an external observer, an effort that is bound to fail. Letting things come out the way they come out is also a constitutional settlement — and a particularly unattractive one, at that. For a disengaged external observer it may be possible to let the chips fall where they may. For anyone within a society, committed to a position on the issues that divide it, this sort of passivity has little to recommend it. Only a believer in divine providence will suppose that things must come out the right way. (And on this belief, divine providence will work its will no matter what arguments we make about constitutional settlements.) Unless we are ready to give up not just on constitutional law but on all of our political commitments, there is no escape from the effort to structure the settlement in a way that will vindicate those commitments.

The upshot is that constitutional law (at least as we have defined it so far) is not only impossible, it is also unavoidable. When there is real disagreement, the disagreement must somehow be resolved, and any resolution will reflect a settlement. We simply do not have the option of abandoning constitutional law. The only choice that remains is to try to reformulate it in a fashion that is at once coherent and attractive. In the next chapter I begin that task.

2

Strategies for a Just Peace

If the argument of the previous chapter is correct, we need to think harder about what we should expect from constitutional law. At least as we have defined it so far, constitutional theory provides no reason for citizens to accept constitutional principles that lead to political outcomes with which they disagree. This chapter explores how constitutional theory could be reformulated to provide a reason. I shall argue that the best hope for such a theory is to give up on some of the claims that have been made for the theories that failed. Specifically, we must relax two interrelated assumptions that have been central to our inquiry so far: the assumption that constitutional law serves as a mechanism for settling ordinary political disputes and the assumption that we can formulate constitutional principles of settlement that are independent of those disputes.

At first it may seem that giving up on these assumptions is an unlikely strategy for providing answers to our "ought" and "can" questions. After all, why ought people to obey constitutional principles if those principles reflect, rather than resolve, political disagreement? How can constitutional law settle disputes if contesting principles of settlement simply reproduce those disputes?

These are fair objections, but they are grounded in a controversial conception of political community. In order to answer the objections, we must first see how traditional principles of constitutional settlement are tied to a particular view of political community and then examine how an alternative view might lead us out of our dilemma.

At least since Thomas Hobbes, political theorists have been preoccupied by the supposed fragility of political community. The specter haunting theorists is the threat posed by irreconcilable conflict. They have obsessively worried that unless conflict is somehow controlled, political communities will collapse and ordered society will degenerate into a nightmare of violence and chaos.

One need look no further than Bosnia or Rwanda to see that there is some basis for this fear. The question, though, is what to do. For many thinkers, the solution has involved finding a method for avoiding conflict. At the risk of much oversimplification, we can sketch three strategies for accomplishing this end.

First, there is the strategy embraced by Hobbes himself — the creation of an all-powerful state with the ability, through brute force, to suppress destabilizing disagreement.[1] There is more to be said for this solution than is sometimes realized. We may yet come to regret the break-up of the old Soviet empire if, as still seems possible, a power vacuum leads to a war of all against all. But although Hobbes's solution might ultimately prove the only one possible, its disadvantages are obvious. It trades the risk of tyranny in a private sphere, where the strong prey on the weak, for that of tyranny in the public sphere, where the governing prey on the governed. Perhaps the trade is worth it, but the history of twentieth-century totalitarianism must give us pause. In any event, it is easy to see why one might be motivated to search for alternatives that avoid this hard choice.

The second strategy, with roots in republican thought, is to form relatively homogeneous political communities where conflict is unlikely to arise.[2] This task might be accomplished through the creation of numerous subcommunities, each with its own ethnic, cultural, or political identity.[3] Some modern arguments for localism, for certain forms of multiculturalism, and for ethnic self-determination are grounded in this approach.[4] Alternatively, the state might play a strong role in inculcating uniform public values that subsume private disagreement or in limiting activities that produce such disagreement.[5] For example, some republican theorists have been attracted to public education as a means of inculcating public values,[6] and to redistribution as a means of reducing the disparities of wealth thought to give rise to social conflict.[7] Similarly, prohibitions on hate speech, norms discouraging public displays of solidarity by ethnic or cultural subgroups, and fostering national symbols and civil religion can be understood as efforts to create unity and suppress conflict.[8]

Republican solutions avoid the overtly totalitarian implications of Hobbes's approach, but they have disadvantages of their own. Revolutionary developments in mass communication, cheap and fast transportation, and the accompanying growth of transnational markets make the disentanglement of divergent communities extremely difficult.[9] As the Bosnian example illustrates, efforts at disentanglement can cause, as well as circumvent, conflict. Moreover, even if disentanglement is successfully accomplished, the resulting fragmentation loses the advantages of coordination and economies of scale, and often substitutes inter- for intra-community conflict.

The alternative republican strategy — government efforts to suppress conflict and build unity in a larger state — has problems as well. History teaches that these efforts are often unsuccessful. Instead of fostering a common civic culture, the cultivation of public values sometimes amounts to (or at least is perceived to amount to) the forced imposition of the majority culture on the minority. This problem might be mitigated by state inculcation of a bland, universally acceptable civic culture, but at best, this effort buys civic peace at the cost of conformism and the discouragement of creative thought. At worst, it shades over into Hobbesian totalitarianism.

The third possibility is liberal constitutionalism — the approach outlined in the previous chapter. The great claim for liberal constitutionalism is that it can avoid totalitarianism on the one hand while maintaining diversity on the other. As already explained, it does so through a constitutional settlement that allows contending groups to maintain their identity while resolving disputes between them.

In spite of the theoretical difficulties discussed above, defenders of liberal constitutionalism can claim that this solution has been successful — at least as implemented in the United States. Today, the United States is one of the most socially diverse countries in the world, yet it is also one of the most politically stable. True, our record has been far from perfect when it comes to the peaceful and just reconciliation of the claims of competing groups. Our history is punctuated by violent spasms that have regularly filled the vacuum when conversation has broken down. Yet the fact remains that today most people routinely accept results they oppose so long as those results comport with our constitutional settlement. How, one might ask, can anyone claim that constitutionalism is impossible when it has worked so well?

There are two responses to this challenge. The first, which I have already mentioned, is that liberal constitutionalism works only by systematically fooling people into believing that they have obligations they do not in fact have. Perhaps sophisticated students of political theory, who have read and absorbed the argument of the first chapter of this book, can pierce the veil of legitimation created by constitutional rhetoric, but most ordinary citizens are more easily manipulated. For them, the powerful, if empty, symbols of constitutionalism will make it seem as though they have no choice but to give up on their own political commitments when they are defeated according to the rules of a particular constitutional settlement. On this version, liberal constitutionalism is not a device for self-government but rather a potent tool that eliminates political autonomy by a species of mind control.[10]

One could insist that manipulation of this sort is the lesser of two evils. A Straussian might argue that a fully informed citizen would, indeed, trade the possibility of victory with regard to particular issues for the stability that comes with the maintenance of political community. Most citizens are not, and cannot be, fully informed, so we must use dishonest rhetoric to persuade them to do what they themselves would choose if they were more sophisticated.[11]

Notice that this version of the liberal argument is really a disguised form of Hobbes's position. It effectively concedes the impossibility of meaningful consent to a constitutional order for the sake of avoiding a war of all against all. The only difference is that citizens are controlled more subtly — through trickery, rather than violence. At bottom, it reflects an unwillingness to treat fellow citizens as fully autonomous actors with the ability and obligation to choose what is best for themselves.

Perhaps the liberatory hopes of constitutional liberals are simply unrealistic, and we should be grateful to substitute thought control for torture and death — no small advance, after all. There is even a sense in which citizens are not fooled. If a belief in constitutionalism is necessary to maintain community, and if maintaining political community is a good of overriding importance, then citizens do indeed have the obligation they think they have to obey a constitutional settlement that preserves the peace.

It is here, though, that the second response to the argument for liberal constitutionalism takes hold. The premise for liberal constitutionalism is that some sort of relatively permanent settlement is necessary to preserve political community. In this respect, liberal constitutionalism shares a bias with Hobbesian and republican theories for a static view of community. All three of the theories we have discussed assume that community is preserved through some sort of final "working out" of conflict, whether by the imposition of totalitarian rule, the creation of a unified society, or agreement to a constitutional settlement. But why should anyone think that this strategy will be successful?

Liberal Neutrality

On the face of it, the claim is strikingly implausible. In the real world, most settlements produce winners and losers. Because we are talking about a *constitutional* settlement, these are not the sort of temporary or partial victories and defeats that are the stuff of quotidian politics. A constitutional settlement is a deeply entrenched, fundamental charter that defines the political community for the indefinite future. Defeat on this level can amount to virtual expulsion from the community. The losers in this high-stakes struggle are unlikely to accept their losses; they will almost certainly continue the battle in ways that are bound to destabilize the political community.

It is for this reason that constitutional liberals often insist that a just settlement must produce no losers. It must be an agreement that all members of the community — or at least all rational members — can accept.* What sort of settlement satisfies this requirement? Liberals often insist that the settlement must be neutral between contending forces within a society.[12]

This ideal of a level playing field, fairness, and neutrality is so deeply ingrained in our ways of thinking about political institutions that it may be difficult at first to recognize how misguided it is. Still, if we can manage to penetrate the vague cloud of rhetoric that usually accompanies such talk, it quickly becomes apparent that liberal neutrality is simply not a sensible goal.

One difficulty is that reasonable people within our culture disagree not only about substantive matters but also about the meaning of the neutrality requirement itself. Consider, for example, the problem of religious observance in public schools. Both opponents and proponents of prayer in school invoke the ideal of neutrality. Opponents argue that no meaningful prayer could possibly be neutral between religious sects or between believers and non-believers.[13] Proponents argue that the state is hardly being neutral when public schools inculcate secular values but bar competing religious perspectives.[14]

In order to resolve this dispute, we need a neutral mechanism for defining neutrality. Unfortunately, however, the idea of neutrality is contested on the meta level as well. Some argue that democracy is a neutral mechanism for settling disputes. On this view, giving each individual an equal "say" in decision making provides a level playing field. Perhaps individual school districts should decide, by majority vote, whether to recite prayers in school and, if so, what prayers to recite. But even if we put to one side the inconvenient fact that we do not agree on which version of democracy satisfies the neutrality require-

---

*To be sure, some constitutional liberals advance more sophisticated versions of the neutrality argument. For example, Ronald Dworkin is prepared to concede that constitutional interpretation is inevitably influenced by the contestable political theories of the interpreter. Yet even Dworkin eventually insists that such interpretation is disciplined by the politically neutral requirement of "fit." *See* Ronald Dworkin, Taking Rights Seriously 131–49 (1977); *and* Ronald Dworkin, Freedom's Law: The Moral Reading of the American Constitution 10 (1996). This concession is no accident, for if he, and other constitutional liberals, were to concede that constitutional law merely reflected political disagreement, they could not also insist that it legitimately settled disagreement.

ment nor on what, if any, background preconditions are necessary for democracy to function, the invocation of majority rule hardly settles the dispute. Democracy is a public process under which winners coerce losers. Opponents of public resolutions argue that neutrality requires the government to provide a neutral framework which maximizes the freedom of individuals to resolve disputed questions as they choose. Proponents of this view will insist that state imposition of a particular religious view is nonneutral, even if the view is determined by a process in which every person has equal access to the ballot. True neutrality requires the state to be equally beneficent to all privately held religious beliefs.

As bad as these difficulties are, the problems with liberal neutrality become even worse when we focus on the level of constitutional detail. Virtually every provision in every constitution is nonneutral in the sense that it affects political outcomes in one way or another. How could it be otherwise? In the U.S. Constitution, for example, the First Amendment makes it more difficult to regulate campaign finance,[15] the Fourth Amendment makes law enforcement more costly,[16] and the war and treaty voting rules affect the likelihood of armed conflict and peace.[17] These provisions clearly create winners and losers. Someone who favors campaign finance reform would rather not have a First Amendment, at least in its current form; those who think that we are not doing enough to control crime might prefer a very different sort of Fourth Amendment; and pacifists are bound to favor a supermajority requirement for declarations of war.*

In the face of this obvious fact, liberals sometimes retreat to the ex ante perspective. Of course, constitutional structures determine outcomes, they say, but we need to judge the neutrality of these structures without respect to the outcomes they produce. From behind a veil of ignorance, reasonable people, unbiased by their particular political commitments, will agree on structures that are fair to all.[18]

Unfortunately, this claim is only slightly more plausible. In the first place, it seems to assume that there is a "correct" answer to every question of constitutional structure and that if we disagree about what that answer is, this is only

---

*It must be acknowledged that the interpretation of at least some of these provisions is contested. Not everyone agrees that the First Amendment, properly understood, bars or makes more difficult campaign finance regulation. But if the First Amendment does permit such regulation, then the people who oppose regulation will be the losers. Of course, if the implications of the First Amendment were perfectly indeterminate, it would not produce winners or losers. But then it would not be a settlement. Conversely, if the First Amendment is a settlement that has determinate consequences, then someone is bound to be unhappy with them.

because we have failed to take an ex ante perspective. Once again, attention to detail makes plain how silly this claim is. Does anyone really suppose that there is a correct answer to whether the president's term of office should be four, rather than five years? To whether searches should be permitted on probable cause or reasonable suspicion?[19]

Even if one believed that there were correct answers to these and countless other questions, it seems extremely doubtful that any real constitution could hit on all of them.[20] The drafters of real constitutions do not sit behind a veil of ignorance. They have political commitments and an idea about how constitutional structures will affect those commitments. A constitutional settlement inevitably entrenches structures that facilitate the achievement of a particular set of political goals and that will be seen by the losers as doing so.* And even if this were not so — even if somehow we came up with an ideal constitution that all unbiased, reasonable people accepted — we are left with the fact that the real communities that constitutions govern are not made up of unbiased, reasonable people. Real human beings, who perceive that a settlement impedes their efforts to vindicate their political commitments, are bound to object to it and make trouble for the community, even if those hypothetical reasonable and unbiased people would not do so.

Bargaining Equilibrium

It simply will not do, then, to insist that constitutional settlements produce no losers. Still, one might counter this objection by advancing a theory of settlement based on a bargaining equilibrium. This theory starts by conceding the obvious. Of course, some people will oppose individual components of any given settlement. It does not follow, however, that these objections imply opposition to the settlement as a whole. Settlements are compromises made

---

*It is true that the passage of time puts constitution makers behind a partial veil, at least with regard to narrow, political consequences. When Republicans, frustrated by Franklin Roosevelt's third and fourth terms, pushed for enactment of the Twenty-Second Amendment, they had no idea that it would prevent Dwight Eisenhower and Ronald Reagan from running for reelection. With regard to more general political aims, however, the effect of constitutional text is more predictable. For example, the original framers were plainly concerned about redistributive legislation and two hundred years later, their language continues as a check on such legislation. Moreover, for reasons explained in more detail below, the very factors which blind constitution makers to the long-term consequences of their decisions also tend to undercut their claim to the legitimacy of their work. This is so because as circumstances change in unpredictable ways, the initial bargaining equilibrium that supported the constitution is likely to dissolve.

necessary by the fact that no one will be entirely satisfied with an agreement that everyone can accept, and made possible by the fact that everyone can accept an agreement that leaves no one entirely satisfied.[21] On a bargaining theory, the settlement provides the basis for a just stability so long as every member of the community believes that no better settlement can be negotiated at acceptable cost and that the chaos that would follow a breakdown of negotiations is worse than the settlement itself.

Unfortunately, this theory provides only a slightly more plausible basis for the claim that settlements build political community. The most obvious difficulty is that there will be powerful incentives to cheat on the deal. It is important to understand that a constitutional settlement is not the same as an outcome produced by the distribution of social power at a given moment. A constitutional settlement differs from the Hobbesian conception of civic peace precisely because it reflects a bargain to which all citizens agree, rather than a ukase to which they all submit. But if this is so, it follows that the settlement will often be in conflict with outcomes that individuals could achieve through the exercise of social power. As a matter of constitutional morality, perhaps these individuals should refrain from exercising the power available to them. Unfortunately, however, history provides little support for the thesis that the powerful will be self-restrained.

Moreover, even on the level of constitutional morality, any bargaining equilibrium is bound to be unstable. Perhaps at the moment of entrenchment, a given settlement will embody the optimal resolution of conflicting preferences. As the settlement ages, however, it is unlikely to remain optimal. New generations will have different preferences and, even if they do not, new material, technological, and cultural facts will disrupt the old nexus between preferences and entrenched institutional arrangements.[22] In the face of these changes, the rigidity of any constitutional settlement is bound to produce dissatisfaction.

Numerous examples from our own history demonstrate how the inflexibility of constitutional settlements obstructs, rather than promotes, political community when the situation changes. Consider, for example, the dilemma faced by Rhode Island in 1789 after the other twelve states had ratified the new constitution. The ratification was in blatant violation of the previous constitutional settlement represented by the Articles of Confederation. Yet it was Rhode Island's reluctant acceptance of this violation, rather than its stubborn insistence on the terms of the original settlement, that ended up creating community.*

---

*Originally, Rhode Island refused to send a delegate to the Philadelphia convention on the entirely plausible ground that amending the Articles of Confederation in this fashion

A second set of examples comes from the Civil War period. Although the point is disputed, some believe that Chief Justice Roger Taney faithfully interpreted our constitutional settlement when he invalidated the Missouri Compromise.[23] This dogged insistence on enforcement of the original settlement did nothing to maintain political community. On the contrary, it contributed to the tensions producing a civil war. When the war ended, President Andrew Johnson argued, as Abraham Lincoln had before him, that secession was unconstitutional. It logically followed that the Confederate states had not legally seceded and that their exclusion from Congress, as well as all military reconstruction, was therefore unconstitutional.[24] This position was at least arguably faithful to the constitutional settlement. It was also disastrously wrong.

A final example comes from the New Deal period. In a series of famous cases invalidating New Deal programs, conservative justices insisted that changes in the structure of our economy in the 150 years since the founding were irrelevant to their legal obligation to enforce the original bargain.[25] It followed that much of the modern regulatory state, which the New Deal inaugurated, was unconstitutional. Of course, the Justices holding this view were eventually displaced, and constitutional law was radically revised so as to accommodate the twentieth century. Is it plausible that political community would have been promoted if the Old Court had had its way? The Court's insistence on respect for the constitutional settlement produced a constitutional crisis.* Surely, it was the willingness to depart from the settlement, rather than the faithful adherence to it, that led to a return to civic peace.

---

violated the Thirteenth Article. When the convention nonetheless adopted a new constitution, the Rhode Island legislature declined to convene a ratifying convention. Instead, it organized a referendum on ratification, which led to the overwhelming defeat of the Philadelphia draft. Despite this vote, the legislature eventually reconsidered, and authorized a ratifying convention, with Governor Collins casting the tie-breaking vote after citing "the extreme Distress we were reduced to by being disconnected with the other States." Although a majority of delegates to the convention had been instructed by their constituents to reject the new constitution, two delegates violated the instructions, and the constitution was ratified by a vote of 34–32. For a good account of these events, see Bruce Ackerman and Neil Katyal, *Our Unconventional Founding,* 62 U. Chi. L. Rev. 475, 528–37 (1995).

*Of course, people still disagree as to whether the Old Court was, in fact, faithful to the constitutional settlement. Nothing I have said turns on how this controversy is resolved. My point is that even if the Justices were faithful to the settlement, their decisions were disastrous from the perspective of maintaining community cohesion.

Internal Constitutional Change

Constitutional settlements need not permanently entrench the original bargain. Virtually all constitutions provide mechanisms for change. The open texture of many clauses of our own Constitution seems to invite changed readings in new circumstances.[26] Moreover, to the extent that the text is resistant to change, Article V provides a detailed blueprint for amendment.

These internal mechanisms for revision do not save the settlement strategy, however. There are two difficulties. First, the processes for revision cannot eliminate the evils of entrenchment because the processes themselves are entrenched. The framers chose to make some provisions of the Constitution vague and flexible (for example, the requirement that searches and seizures be "reasonable") and some clear and fixed (the requirement that the president serve for four years). Modern generations cannot easily shift clauses from one category to the other based upon current views as to which should be entrenched. Moreover, one of the clear and fixed provisions concerns the amendment process itself.[27] I have argued above that the bargaining equilibriums that produce settlements are unstable over time. Surely, this instability infects bargains concerning the extent of entrenchment as well. There is no more reason for a modern citizen to be bound by the framers' wishes regarding Article V than by any other provision in the Constitution.

Second, precisely to the extent that textual vagueness and the amendment procedures relax the rigidity of constitutions, they dissipate the supposed advantages of settlement. Imagine first a polar case. Suppose that the language of a constitution was completely indeterminate or that it made no distinction between its amendment procedures and the ordinary mechanisms by which political decisions are made. A constitution of this sort could not settle political controversy. Controversy that would otherwise exist on the political level would simply be transferred to the constitutional level because, by hypothesis, the political level would be indistinguishable from the constitutional. A putative settlement of this type would not really be a settlement at all. Some sort of entrenchment against ordinary change is built into the very idea of a settlement.

Of course, we do not want to fall victim to the fallacy of focusing only on polar cases. Perhaps a regime of *partial* entrenchment would capture some of the advantages of constitutional settlement while avoiding some of the disadvantages. But this seemingly sensible compromise will not work either. The advantages of constitutional settlement *are* the disadvantages. Recall that we were motivated to search for a constitutional settlement by the desire to avoid civic strife. But we have also seen that to the extent that a settlement is entrenched, it raises questions of legitimacy that we have so far been unable to answer. The settlement's rigidity prevents us from answering the "ought" question for people who never agreed to the settlement and see no reason why they should be bound by it. If the argument in the preceding paragraphs is correct, settlements cause the very unrest they are designed to avoid by creating losers who are effectively excluded from the political community. To be sure, making the settlement less rigid lessens this difficulty, but only because it makes the arrangement less settled. If settlements are causing the problem they are designed to solve, why entrench them at all?

Two Theories of External Change

One might read Bruce Ackerman's sophisticated and subtle theory of dualist democracy as an effort to respond to these difficulties.[28] Ackerman is prepared to concede that a constitution cannot entrench itself. Indeed, the U.S. Constitution, he claims, has been amended without bothering with the internal Article V requirements. During periods of ordinary politics, citizens focus on their private lives and, without much reflection, adhere to the constitutional settlement. But during "constitutional moments," a different sort of politics takes hold. An aroused and politically engaged citizenry rethinks fundamental questions and revises the initial settlement.[29] On Ackerman's account, there have been three such episodes in our history: the founding period, Reconstruction, and the New Deal. Each of these periods resulted in a revision of constitutional understandings that was legitimate even though it violated the internal, textual basis for amendment.[30] Ackerman would doubtless be quick to point out that each of my examples above, where constitutional flexibility rather than rigidity helped build community, came at one of the constitutional moments he has identified.

There is much to be said for this approach. Ackerman's theory builds in a mechanism by which settlements can be changed so as to respond to new situations. Moreover, it provides a normative basis for the entrenchment of the change. Law produced at constitutional moments is entrenched against ordinary law because it is the product of true public engagement. The people speak in their public capacity only occasionally, but when they do, popular sovereignty requires obedience.[31]

Yet for all its power, Ackerman's theory fails to rescue constitutional obligation. Ackerman's theory is intended to rebut an alternative approach which he calls "rights foundationalism."[32] For a rights foundationalist, constitutional obligation is tied to the substantive content of the constitution in question:

constitutions are binding only to the extent that they conform to some preconceived idea of fundamental rights.

It is easy to see why Ackerman is dissatisfied with this approach. As outlined in Chapter 1, a rights foundationalist has no answer to our "ought" question because she makes constitutional obligation dependent on the contingent overlap between a particular constitution and a nonconstitutional conception of fundamental rights. But what is the alternative to this approach? The alternative Ackerman propounds is a theory of popular sovereignty. The constitution is binding, whether or not it embodies principles that are morally "true," because it is the authentic voice of "we, the people.[33] Unfortunately, this answer begs yet again a very old question. Since Ackerman rejects rights foundationalism, he must believe that there is a gap between the authentic voice of the people on the one hand and the demands of justice on the other. What, then, binds us to choose the former rather than the latter?

Even if we put aside this nagging dilemma, there are other serious problems. Critics like Michael Klarman[34] and Frank Michelman[35] have uncovered one: How do we know when we are in a constitutional moment? Ackerman's account provides a detailed set of criteria for identifying such moments, involving carefully specified interaction between the courts, the political branches, and the electorate.[36] It is unclear, however, why Ackerman's antiformalism extends only to the constitutional text. If an aroused citizenry can indeed override the textual limits on amendments, why are they confined by a theory of constitutional moments choreographed with all the rigidity of a minuet?

Mark Tushnet has suggested that the problems we have identified so far can be explained if we take Ackerman as engaging in an interpretive, rather than a normative, project.[37] On this view, Ackerman's claim is not that decisions at constitutional moments are normatively superior but that the American people understand their own tradition as giving weight to such decisions.[38] The formal requirements for constitutional momenthood serve simply to identify our own self-understanding of when this higher lawmaking has taken place. It is this self-understanding, rather than anything about the decisions themselves, that gives them normative force. As Tushnet puts it,

> Such a history overcomes the normative difficulty associated with explaining why we today should be bound by decisions made by people long ago, its proponents claim, by demonstrating how we today are in some important — though constructed — sense the very People who made those decisions. . . . And, because national identity — or at least some supra-individual identity — is normatively valuable, interpretive narratives that create communities (beyond face-to-face exchanges) have normative weight.[39]

I shall have more to say about the relation between national identity and obligation below. For now, though, we need to see that this reading of Ackerman's theory substitutes one problem for another. Even if we are successful in identifying a constitutional moment, how do we know that it is "our" constitutional moment? Suppose that the aroused and engaged citizens of South Africa enunciate constitutional standards during a constitutional moment. Do these standards have any impact on the U.S. Constitution? For Ackerman these standards would be irrelevant to the United States: Ackerman does not think that the authentic voice of South Africans binds American citizens. Yet in important respects, late twentieth-century South Africans have more in common with us than late eighteenth-century Americans. Even if we ignore differences produced by the passage of time, we must focus yet again on the fact that not even the majority of late eighteenth-century Americans were among the aroused citizenry. No women, no African Americans, no Indians, no people without property participated. My own ancestors, who were someplace in Russia or central Europe at the time, hardly followed the proceedings in Philadelphia with rapt attention. What do these people have to do with us? In short, if we want to use a dualist approach to explain constitutional obligation, Ackerman must develop a theory of political continuity that takes these embarrassments into account.

One obstacle to such a theory is the constitutional dualism Ackerman favors. A dualist approach insists that the "authentic" voice of the people can be heard only at constitutional moments. But viewed from the perspective of community preservation, Ackerman's approach seems positively perverse. Can constitutional law really maintain community stability if it is made only occasionally and convulsively? Can it maintain community solidarity if it is made only on the occasions when the community nearly comes unstuck? Consider the constitutional moments that Ackerman has identified: more than half a million Americans died during our Civil War.[40] By 1787 the existence of a United States of America was in doubt. And in 1933 many sensible people thought that democratic government was doomed. Each of these occasions might have ended differently. We were at the brink of rupture and nearly went over the brink. Moreover, even ending as they did, each occasion produced losers who were not prepared to accept defeat and took years to be reconciled to their loss. If occasions such as these provide the only opportunity for constitutional creation, our political community is in serious trouble indeed. It is hard to see how constitutional law can foster cohesiveness if it can be legitimately promulgated only when we are at one another's throats.

Ackerman offers dualist democracy as a theory for constitutional change, yet his theory is really a consequence of rigid entrenchment. Geologists understand that sudden, violent earthquakes occur when pressure gradually builds with no prospect of release. Similarly, one consequence of relatively rigid entrenchment is that when change does occur, it will be wrenching and dangerous. Communities built on faultlines of this sort must live in continual dread of upheaval.

In fact, it is simply wrong to suppose that American society is erected on such a faultline. Throughout our history, constitutional law has been made and remade without a dramatic change of regime. Our constitutional history is not one of a few tumultuous shifts followed by long periods of stasis. Rather, it is characterized by continuous struggle and unceasing pressure on constitutional order. Constitutional arrangements are continually being reformed and renegotiated as new challenges arise and political balances shift.

Often, these changes are so undramatic they go virtually unnoticed. Consider, for example, the regular application of stare decisis to constitutional cases. At first it may seem that respect for stare decisis serves the interests of entrenchment rather than change. When a court applies the doctrine, it is insisting on a maintenance of the legal status quo. There is a sense, of course, in which the doctrine does entrench. On closer examination, though, stare decisis also illustrates how gradual constitutional change is linked to stability. Stare decisis works solely in cases where, but for its application, the court would have ruled differently. It follows that whenever the doctrine makes a difference in the outcome of a constitutional case, the court's decision is contrary to constitutional requirements as the court then best understands them. As originalists like Gary Lawson recognize,[41] invocation of stare decisis is hardly an act of conservativism. On the contrary, the doctrine provides a method for legitimating constitutional change outside the requirements of Article V. The court is saying, in effect, that even though the Constitution previously required one result, we are now prepared to treat it as requiring a different result.

Significantly, courts are least likely to rely upon stare decisis at constitutional moments, and when they do invoke the doctrine, they often speak of the twin goals of stability and predictability.[42] Their regular reliance on this doctrine in times of ordinary politics thus amounts to a recognition that stability and predictability are best served by gradual shifts in constitutional obligation rather than by either rigid entrenchment or its inevitable partner, convulsive regime change.

The same pattern is apparent when we focus on particular substantive areas of constitutional law. To take but a single example,[43] consider the history of federalist limits on the powers of Congress. One looks in vain for any consistent, doctrinal strand running from the Marshall Court's first encounters with this problem to the present. The history is characterized neither by a few sudden revolutions (although, to be sure, there have been some of these) nor by a gradual, evolutionary march toward a particular resolution. There has been no settlement, no long-term trend, no final working out—but rather, a long, inconclusive struggle marked by continuous cycling between inconsistent views.

There are several reasons for this cycling phenomenon, but surely one of them is the fact that the contending settlements have been linked to contested political positions. The Marshall Court's nationalizing decisions were grounded in a particular political ideology, as were the pre–New Deal Court's restrictions on federal power, the Warren Court's expansive reading of the commerce clause, and the Rehnquist Court's revival of the Tenth Amendment. In short, instead of settling political disputes, commerce clause jurisprudence has mirrored the ebb and flow of an ongoing political struggle.

Ronald Dworkin's seminal work on "law as integrity" provides a theory for constitutional change that helps account for the incrementalism that Ackerman's theory seems to ignore.[44] Like Ackerman, Dworkin sees his project as "constructivist," by which he means that it is grounded in, and intended to reflect, the most attractive possible interpretation of our existing constitutional history.[45] Unlike Ackerman, Dworkin ties his theory to a view of political community that purports to provide a normative basis for constitutional obligation even as constitutional law changes incrementally in ways that are linked to contested political positions.

Dworkin's constructivism extends not just to our legal institutions as a whole but also to the act of constitutional interpretation. On his view, when deciding a "hard case," a constitutional actor should start with the constitution's text as well as our constitutional history. The actor should use this material to reach the most morally attractive result the material can yield.[46] It follows that an important component of constitutional interpretation is "fit." Dworkin distinguishes his approach from that of a "legal pragmatist," who simply reaches the best possible result by her lights in every case. Principled judges

> may not read their own convictions into the Constitution. They may not read the abstract moral clauses as expressing any particular moral judgment, no matter how much that judgment appeals to them, unless they find it consistent in principle with the structural design of the Constitution as a whole, and also with the dominant lines of past constitutional interpretation by other judges. They must regard themselves as partners with other officials, past and future, who together elaborate a coherent constitutional morality, and they must take care to see that what they contribute fits with the rest.[47]

But although judges should not start afresh, neither should they feel themselves completely constrained. It is their duty to produce the best possible results from the material they are given. The great open textured clauses of the Constitution, Dworkin claims, are subject to a "moral reading" which will, inevitably, be contested by those who approach the clauses with different moral theories.[48] Judges committed to law as integrity will "find the best conception of constitutional moral principles — the best understanding of what equal moral status for men and women really requires, for example — that fits the broad story of America's historical record."[49]

Dworkin's theory helps explain how constitutional law can bind even as it changes through political struggle. Because the constitutional text itself invites contested moral theorizing, no interpretation that is true to the text will be completely independent of political views. Because judges are obligated to build on what has gone before, the Constitution's meaning will gradually change over time as new generations of interpreters put their stamp on our constitutional heritage.

But if Ackerman's theory of dualist democracy focuses too much on rupture, Dworkin's theory of legal integrity is too concerned with continuity. It is important to Dworkin that "force not be used or withheld, no matter how useful that would be to ends in view, no matter how beneficial or noble these ends, except as licensed or required by individual rights and responsibilities *flowing from past political decisions about when collective force is justified.*"[50] But why should we be bound by these past political decisions? Dworkin candidly acknowledges that the requirement of fit imposes costs paid for in the coin of justice.[51] If fit constrains at all, it must prevent some outcomes we would reach if we were simply applying the best moral theory. Dworkin's approach thus reopens the problem of constitutional evil: Why should past evil political decisions bind us to future evil decisions? Why not cut our losses?

Significantly, Dworkin's response to this riddle is rooted in ideas about the best way to achieve political community. If we think of ourselves as simply a random collection of people who contingently inhabit the same territory at the same time, there is in fact no reason why we should not view politics as a struggle "in which each person tries to plant the flag of his convictions over as large a domain of power or rules as possible."[52] True political obligation, Dworkin insists, arises from membership in a community of principle which is bound together by a common history and extends over time. As Dworkin puts it,

> Members of a society of principle accept that their political rights and duties are not exhausted by the particular decisions their political institutions have reached, but depend, more generally, on the scheme of principles those deci-

sions presuppose and endorse. So each member accepts that others have rights and that he has duties flowing from that scheme, even though these have never been formally identified or declared. Nor does he suppose that these further rights and duties are conditional on his wholehearted approval of that scheme; these obligations arise from the historical fact that his community has adopted that scheme, which is then special to it, not the assumption that he would have chosen it were the choice entirely his. In short, each accepts political integrity as a distinct political ideal and treats the general acceptance of that ideal, even among people who otherwise disagree about political morality, as constitutive of political community.[53]

Dworkin is on the right track when he insists that constitutional obligation must rest on some sense of community membership. Because the ideal of individual consent is unrealizable, there must be some moral basis rooted in the nature of the community that makes "its act . . . in some pertinent sense my act, even when I argued and voted against it, just as the victory or defeat of a team of which I am a member is my victory or defeat even if my own individual contribution made no difference either way."[54]

The difficult question, however, is how to establish such a community? Dworkin goes astray when he argues that a "fit" requirement builds community membership. Instead of providing a reason for constitutional obligation, "law as integrity" establishes the sort of exclusionary community that, for those excluded, offers a strong argument for disobedience. In effect, the "fit" requirement creates a vertical community between past and present at the expense of a horizontal community between citizens in the here and now.

To see why, we need to disaggregate the "fit" requirement into its two separate components. For a new legal rule to fit within a prior legal regime, we must first specify what that regime consists of. Then we must operationalize the concept of consistency by testing a new legal principle against this prior regime. It turns out that each of these operations excludes some people from the community of principle that is supposed to bind them.

Consider, first, the specification of the prior legal regime. Dworkin insists that this regime has been formed not just by our written constitution but also by important political acts throughout our history. But who is the "our" whose history we are to examine? Unfortunately, Dworkin's constructivism applies only to the second of the two operations that compose the "fitting" exercise. His theory depends upon the construction of law from the intersection of past historical events and decisions on the one hand and contested political ideals on the other. But for this constructivism to work, he must treat the history itself as fixed and simply "there." It is the material around which future law is constructed.[55]

This is surely a mistake. "Our" history is also constructed. There is no natural boundary around the community whose past events and decisions provide the fixed mold to which legal developments must conform. Histories are formed not only by shared experiences but also by how human beings choose to react to those experiences. Feelings of solidarity and antipathy, of connection and separation, do not simply exist. They are created as individuals decide how to interact with events in the external world. Since the boundaries of the resulting communities are constructed through political struggle, the contours of the history of "our" community are the subject of struggle as well.

A skirmish in this struggle occurring in 1997 provides a useful example. A school district in Louisiana touched off a national controversy by removing George Washington's name from a predominantly African American high school.[56] In the broader culture, this decision was met with widespread derision and dismay.[57] Yet surely the school officials had a point. Why should African Americans treat a person who owned their ancestors as the starting point of their history?

Patricia Williams has movingly described how her very genetic identity is bound up in the outrage that was slavery.* Yet even if it is true that biology is destiny, history is not. Although Williams cannot choose her genes, she can choose which of her ancestors to identify with. "Our" history need not begin with the brutal exploits of Columbus or the political musings of wealthy slaveholders in Philadelphia. It need not include events that occurred long before "our" ancestors arrived here or omit formative experiences occurring in countries outside the British Empire. Our history might begin in Africa or in Eastern Europe or in China or in Central America. Our shot heard round the world might have been fired against Pinkerton operatives in the far west, at U.S. soldiers at Wounded Knee, or, for that matter, at FBI agents at Ruby Ridge.

None of this is to deny that there is value in creating a myth of a common history even if there is no genetic basis for it. For the same reason that history is constructed, it is surely sensible to construct a history that binds us together, rather than one that drives us apart. The question, though, is what strategy best achieves this end. I shall return to this problem at the end of this chapter. For now, it is sufficient to note that specifying a particular version of our

---

*According to Williams, her great-grandmother was raped and impregnated by her great-grandfather, a slaveholder. Williams' mother told her that she had lawyering "in her blood" because her great-grandfather had been an attorney. Patricia J. Williams, The Alchemy of Race and Rights 154–56 (1991).

history by fiat is unlikely to achieve unity. This history is bound to be perceived as exclusionary from its inception, and the groups who are excluded — whose history commands no requirement of fit — will feel no obligation to the community of principle it establishes.

Matters are made worse when we move to the second step and attempt to operationalize the consistency requirement. Even if we assume that our prior history is fixed and uncontested, "fit" itself seems infinitely malleable. As Mark Tushnet brilliantly demonstrated, in principle any new legal rule can be reconciled with any set of past legal decisions by anyone inventive and original enough to tell a story that encompasses past and present.[58] Oddly, though, the ideal of integrity would actually be less troubling if, as Tushnet insisted, it did not constrain. To be sure, the "fit" requirement would then be meaningless, but at least it would leave us all free to invent our own connections between the past and whatever future we preferred. Indeed, if fit did not constrain, there would be no problem with the arbitrary specification of some prior community history, since any result could be made consistent with the prior history of any community.

The real problem with the "fit" requirement is the opposite of the one that troubled Tushnet: even if it does not constrain in some abstract logical sense, it does so as a social fact. Part of the difficulty is that some people will be better at imagining connections than other people. Law as integrity means that people who are especially skilled at a certain kind of logical game have more social power than those who are less skilled. Akhil Amar, for example, has made a successful academic career out of finding clever, if eccentric, "fits." Amar has managed to find connections between the Thirteenth Amendment and a constitutional prohibition against private child abuse; the public trial requirement and the unconstitutionality of the exclusionary rule; and the Fifteenth Amendment and bans on racial challenges to jury members.[59]

Of course, if differential ability at this sort of thing were the only problem, the "fit" requirement might result in nothing more serious than the enrichment of lawyers who could be hired by excluded communities to play the "fit" game. Unfortunately, the problem is not so easily solved. Dworkin's formulation fails to account for the phenomenon of "crazy constitutionalism." Consider, for example, the constitutional jurisprudence of the Militia Movement. As David Ray Papke points out, Militia members differ from past legal "heretics" in their profound respect for constitutional law.[60] They fetishize the constitutional text with all the fervor of the most rigid originalist and have a sophisticated, worked-out jurisprudence that, on the face of things, seems no more far-fetched than Amar's arguments. Indeed, as Susan Koniak has shown, some of their views bear an eerie resemblance to mainstream constitutional theorizing.*

And yet Militia constitutionalism is different from what is taught in the academy or argued in the courthouse. As one judge remarked after sitting through a trial dominated by Militia rhetoric, "You can't follow their arguments because they're listening to a different music no one else hears."[61] Crazy constitutionalism is not different because it is somehow logically deficient; it is different because it is, well, *crazy*. It rests on a series of postulates and a worldview that "sensible" people do not share. The "fit" requirement, in turn, in the hands of someone like Dworkin, privileges a way of understanding the world that sensible people do share. Selecting one version of "fit" rather than another is an exercise of social power, rather than abstract logic.

Or at least so it will seem to the person listening to a different sort of music. For even if in some absolute sense, Dworkin is right, and advocates of crazy constitutionalism are actually crazy, the "fit" requirement nonetheless has the effect of *labeling* them as crazy. Virtually everyone reading these words is likely to agree that such people richly deserve this label, but that is not the point. Dworkin's argument is that law conceived of as integrity will build a community of principle that provides people with a motivation to treat earlier community decisions as their own. Labeling people crazy is hardly a strategy calculated to accomplish this objective.

If this problem were confined to a few cranks outside the mainstream, perhaps it would not be fatal. But it cannot be so confined. Consider, for example, Dworkin's claim that a constitutional right to die and to secure abortions satisfies the "fit" requirement while a constitutional right to subsistence does not.[62] What are we to make of the fact that others, whom we do not consider crazy, will find these claims far from self-evident?[63] The difficulty here is not just that Dworkin himself may be listening to music that others do not hear. People have a right to choose their own music. The problem is that Dworkin's theory elevates these disagreements to the level of fundamental principle. Advocates of welfare rights and opponents of euthanasia and abortion are not merely taking a different political position.[64] On Dworkin's theory, either these advocates have made a fundamental *logical* mistake or they have misunderstood the basic thrust of our political history.

---

*For example, Militia constitutionalism insists, with Ackerman, that the New Deal accomplished a fundamental constitutional transformation without comporting with the legal requirements of Article V. *See* Susan P. Koniak *When Law Risks Madness,* 8 Card. Stud. in Law & Lit. 65, 79–80 (1996).

If Dworkin were able to convince his adversaries that these claims were true, their conversion might provide the rock upon which a community of principle could be built. But how likely is it that there will be many such conversions? Most of Dworkin's opponents will view the requirements of logic and history differently. They will surely claim that their logic is not crazy and that their understanding of our national experience is every bit as profound as Dworkin's. To put the matter bluntly, this is not a dispute that will be resolved by calm discussion. If constitutional argument requires us to settle questions such as these, it is certain to devolve into a fist fight. The mystery is why anyone would believe that dealing with the disagreement in this manner would help form a community of principle that motivated all participants to accept results with which they disagree.

Our Unsettled Constitution

Both Ackerman and Dworkin have asked the right question. Both understand that constitutions can gain respect only if we are able to solve the riddle of creating an ongoing community from people with disparate views. Yet both efforts founder on the ancient difficulty with constitutional settlements: if things are settled, why should the losers remain attached to the community? No matter how sophisticated the effort, it seems that theories of settlement always run into this brick wall.

How might the wall be avoided? At this point, it is necessary to challenge the two troublesome assumptions that have driven our analysis thus far. Is a constitutional settlement really necessary (or even helpful) in maintaining political community? And is it really necessary for constitutional law to be independent of ordinary political struggle?

We might start by observing that these assumptions may attach more significance to legal structure than is warranted. Perhaps political community is best understood as a consequence of cultural, social, or economic factors, rather than legal regimes. Surely many political communities rest on a shared worldview that preexists legal norms. For communities such as these, it is wrong to think of constitutional law as a constituting force. Their constitutions will reflect, rather than shape, their social vision.

Our own community may not fall into this category. The diversity produced by waves of immigration into this country may make law more important as a constituting factor. Yet even here, American political quietism rests at least to some degree on the avoidance of deep issues of constitutional structure, rather than on engagement with these problems. As many have argued, the American success in maintaining community may well be a consequence of political indifference created by material abundance and the hope for a better life rather than of a worked-out constitutional theory.[65]

To the extent that cultural solidarity or material abundance maintains community in the absence of a settlement, we have the luxury to look for other functions for constitutional law — functions I set out below. Of course, it remains possible that certain constitutional structures help produce solidarity and abundance. Societies that are riven with ethnic or political strife are not notable for their economic achievements. Perhaps a certain kind of constitutional law minimizes the risk of such strife. Still, even if constitutional law *is* linked to solidarity and prosperity, it remains unclear why a version of constitutional law with apolitical settlement at its core would best achieve this goal. For reasons we have already explored at length, the effort to achieve a settlement seems likely to produce more conflict than it settles.

The claim I wish to defend is that the traditional views about political community discussed so far have things backward. Healthy political communities are not fixed and static, and they do not have things worked out. Their past, as well as their future, is not settled. Instead, they are constantly reinventing their own histories and meaning. Moreover, this reinvention cannot be channeled or confined by the structures that both Ackerman and Dworkin try to impose upon it. The reinvention does not happen only at constitutional moments, and it is not constrained by the requirement of integrity. Indeed, it is not constrained at all. Political community is maintained precisely because there is no permanent settlement and, indeed, no exclusive, agreed-upon method for amending temporary settlements. Instead, the community is built upon an endless battle, with no fixed rules and no hope of final resolution.

An analogy to individual commitment helps make the point. Conventional constitutional theory — Hobbesian, republican, or liberal — is attached to what might be called the romantic-comedy version of community. Everyone knows the basic structure of the Hollywood romantic comedy. In the world according to Tom Hanks and Meg Ryan, life is divided into three parts. First comes prehistory — the unhappy and essentially irrelevant period before the couple meet. Then there is history, which typically constitutes the bulk of the movie. During this period, the couple meet, become involved in a series of conflicts and misunderstandings, and eventually reach what, in this context, we might call a constitutional settlement. Finally, there is the end of history. The couple marry, and nothing else happens. They live happily ever after.

Anyone involved in a real relationship knows that this is not the way things work. Relationships are never finally worked out, and there is no "happily ever after." Moreover, healthy relationships do not change only at points of near rupture, and the changes are not channeled or confined by a fixed conception of their essential nature. Instead, successful relationships gain permanence through contingency. A relationship constantly remakes itself as the individuals in it develop and change. As Woody Allen famously remarked to Diane Keaton in his brilliant, antiromantic comedy *Annie Hall,* "A relationship is like a shark, you know; it has to constantly move forward or it dies, and I think what we got on our hands is a dead shark."[66]

Lest we produce a dead shark, we need a theory of the constitution that keeps us moving. What would such a theory look like? It would begin by putting to rest the obsessive concern about the destabilizing effect of political conflict. Even without an agreed-upon mechanism for resolving such disputes, people have strong incentives to find resolutions. Inertia, indifference, efficiency, and the fear of political unraveling that Hobbes invoked all provide reasons for communities to remain static. Most of the real risks are on the other side. Paradoxically, it is the natural tendency toward stasis, not the threat of political argument, that ultimately poses the greater threat. A static society with a fixed settlement will not adapt to changed material, cultural, or demographic circumstances. Over time, such a society loses the link between its fundamental structures and the values and aspirations of its people.[67] And even if this is not true for most people, such a society is bound to create permanent outsiders — people who have lost their constitutional struggle and have a strong incentive to disrupt the community. In contrast, a society with no fixed settlement makes no distinction between outsiders and insiders. Because everything is always up for grabs, no one is permanently excluded.

Of course, the fact that there is never a *constitutional* settlement does not mean that things are not settled. No society can successfully function in a world where there is all argument and no action. Discussion and deliberation are great, but eventually the long evenings must end. Elections must be won or lost, wars fought or avoided, highways built or foregone. The question, though, is what role constitutional law should play with regard to these subconstitutional decisions. My argument is that constitutionalism does more harm than good when it entrenches them. The kind of constitutionalism that best answers the "ought" and "can" problems is one that provides a permanent platform from which the losers can always criticize and unsettle the winners.

Roberto Unger's ambitious proposal for an "empowered democracy" bears a superficial resemblance to my conception of an unsettled constitution. As part of his plan for comprehensive institutional reform, Unger would create a special branch of government devoted to "a systematic intervention in large areas of social practice and the consequent disruption of major institutions."[68] He would also create explicit "destabilization rights" that would "protect the citizen's interest in breaking open the large-scale organizations or the extended areas of social practice that remain closed to the destabilizing effects of ordinary conflict and thereby sustain insulated hierarchies of power and advantage."[69]

There is no doubt that constitutional provisions of this sort would unsettle. However, I do not share Unger's view that a constitutional revolution is necessary to achieve this goal. I argue below that ordinary legal institutions currently in place have the capacity to serve the unsettlement function. Doubtless, Unger favors much more comprehensive reform because he has bigger fish to fry. In this sense, his aims are actually antithetical to the aims of an unsettled constitution. Unger's radical institutional restructuring is linked to a substantive program of "bold transformative projects."[70] He imagines a comprehensive political and personal renewal that would break down the distinction between routine and revolution and, by "context smashing," free "social life more fully from false necessity."

These substantive goals can be attractive, but they are controversial. It is therefore not surprising that Unger's many critics, who think that his substantive program is utopian, unattractive, or terrifying, also resist institutional reform designed to implement it. In this sense, Unger's constitutional project falls victim to the same difficulty as the constitutional projects he attacks. It embodies yet another settlement, designed to achieve yet another contested set of substantive goals. Like all settlements, it fails to provide a reason comprehensible to people with different substantive views why they should adhere to it.

Unger believes that if disagreements are brought out into the open and translated "into detailed schemes of collective life," the differences between us will no longer seem nonnegotiable and the traditional liberal fear of unrestrained conflict will dissolve.[71] Perhaps he is right, but for those of us who are less confident, an unsettled constitution provides a second-best solution. For this reason an unsettled constitution does not systematically break up or "smash" subconstitutional settlements because of a belief that radical transformation is necessary to achieve human potential. Its aims are much more modest. It unsettles by a vocabulary and an institutional mechanism that losers can always use to criticize political outcomes, but it provides no assurance that the losers will prevail. The hope it creates is that even when they don't, both they and their adversaries will recognize that their arguments, too, are grounded in our society's core commitments and that the winners must somehow take account of them. The promotion of unsettlement is a good not because we all agree that "context smashing" or Unger's conception of human freedom is correct. Rather, it is a good because we differ among ourselves as to the good, and only a constitution that promotes unsettlement of these questions can produce a community to which people with different views on this subject can lend their allegiance.

Still, one might argue, is not the unsettled constitution also just another settlement? There are two kinds of concerns, which look in opposite directions. First, to the extent that losers fail to persuade the winners, doesn't an unsettled constitution help entrench the winner's victory? If an unsettled constitution indeed persuades losers to accept their loss, doesn't it legitimate outcomes that might otherwise be contested? Second, to the extent that the losers do succeed in systematically destabilizing outcomes, doesn't this devalue the views of people who would like to see the outcomes settled? If I am a person who values stability and settlement, why should I affiliate myself with a community that has, as its foundational principle, an unwillingness to achieve what I desire?

These are serious problems, and they deserve a lengthier response than I can provide in a preliminary discussion. Ultimately, the answer will have to come in the form of a response to a third, more specific question: How, precisely, are constitutional actors — for example, Supreme Court Justices — supposed to function if they adhere to an unsettled constitution?

For reasons we have already explored, any stance they take will embody some constitutional settlement. For example, it will not do for destabilizing Justices simply to defer to democratic outcomes. More than half a century ago, John Dewey defended democracy on the ground that it engendered a skeptical attitude about any "truth" — an attitude, he thought, well calculated to allow people with different views to live together in harmony.[72] But Dewey failed to apply this skepticism to democracy itself. Democracy is also a contested constitutional settlement, and a truly unsettled constitution must attack it as well.

Perhaps, then, we should advise a Supreme Court Justice to side with whoever is currently losing the political struggle. But this advice is perverse. When the Court decides a constitutional case, it cannot avoid at least partially entrenching a constitutional settlement with regard to that particular case. Either prayers in school are forbidden or they are permitted, and either way, the result will rest on a view about constitutional law. It would be nonsensical for the Court to choose a particular version just because that version is least acceptable to a majority of the people likely to be affected by the decision. And even if we could somehow defend this outcome on the ground that it avoided calcification, we would still be confronted with the difficulty, discussed above, that such an approach in effect calcifies the avoidance of calcification.

It seems clear, then, that we still have a great deal of work to do if we are to develop a satisfactory answer to our "can" question. My hope is that the chapters that follow, spelling out with some specificity how our unsettled constitution functions, will at least mitigate these doubts. For now, it is enough to foreshadow the argument by noting that we might make some progress by shifting our focus. Perhaps there is no need to inquire into what decisions a conscientious Justice devoted to an unsettled constitution would render.

There are two reasons why this inquiry may be beside the point. First, there may be something about the nature of constitutional law — or at least about a certain kind of constitutional law — that serves to unsettle regardless of what Justices and other constitutional actors do. This is hardly a new idea. The Federalist Papers, written at our founding, embody a version of it. Madisonian democracy is premised on an anti-settlement theory. On Madison's view, the complex system of overlapping powers and constituencies which the Constitution established was designed to generate conflict, thereby preventing control by any dominant faction.[73] Madison did not place much stock in pious advice to political actors.[74] Instead, he thought that the Constitution had established a structure that worked to build community more or less automatically regardless of how individual actors behaved.

To be sure, the Federalist Papers reflect the kind of faith in a structural settlement that I have attacked. Although Madison did not believe in stasis, he did seem to believe that institutions promoting unsettlement on the political level would produce a societal settlement that protected the private sphere. But this means only that he failed to carry his theory far enough. Perhaps the right kind of constitutionalism generates conflict not just on the political level but also between the public and private power.

A second approach might focus on individual constitutional actors but address the spirit in which they approach their task, rather than the outcomes they reach. The right kind of constitutionalism may help foster a tentativeness and uncertainty that will build political community even in the teeth of particular outcomes some members of the community hate. Justices imbued with this version of constitutional law will certainly reach decisions in cases, and these decisions are bound to be controversial. But they will reach them with an understanding that there is nothing inevitable or logically necessary about the outcome. A pervasive sense of epistemic modesty — a realization that even our most strongly held views are uncertain and temporary — might build community by fostering a sense of identification with political opponents.

Of course, a great deal more needs to be done to explain the ways in which constitutional law might achieve these goals. The chapters that follow are designed to accomplish this task. My hope is that in the course of this explanation, we will answer our "what" and "how" questions without really trying.

The "what" and "how" of constitutional law flow more or less automatically from answers to the "ought" and "can" questions. If our "ought" and "can" answers are right, then the "what" of constitutional law is those doctrines, decisions, institutions, and traditions that allow us to enjoy the benefits of a sustained, just, and legitimate political community. Paradoxically, the "how" of constitutional law is the unsettling of any doctrine, decision, institution, or tradition that constitutional law itself manages to establish.

3

Constitutional Boundaries

The preceding chapter set forth an account of how constitutional law might help us to achieve a just and legitimate political community. I have said nothing so far, however, about the specific mechanisms by which it accomplishes this task. For those who adhere to a settlement theory, there is nothing mysterious about these mechanisms: the Constitution embodies a settlement that resolves disputes between community members, thereby ensuring social peace. It is much less clear, though, how anything resembling constitutional law might serve to unsettle current arrangements. After all, isn't constitutionalism necessarily about entrenchment and settlement?

In this chapter, I hope to explain how we might recharacterize the ordinary practice of American constitutional law so as to achieve the unsettled community I advocate. For reasons set out below, it turns out that the very effort to achieve constitutional closure can serve the ends of an unsettled constitution. This is so because contradictions at the core of our ordinary constitutional practice always allow losers to make plausible claims that their constitutional rights have been violated. Two additional characteristics of ordinary constitutional practice make these claims especially powerful. First, these unsettling concepts need not be imported from the outside. They are already and always how we understand what constitutional law is all about. Second, although internal to constitutional practice, the concepts are nonetheless reenforced from the outside. They are not merely legal but reflect the fundamental framework we use to make sense of the world.

Settlements and Boundaries

It would be a mistake to claim that only constitutions built along the American model are capable of producing political justice and legitimacy. Although I do insist that all just regimes must have a mechanism that gives political losers a reason, comprehensible within their own framework, for affiliating with the polity, the nature of that mechanism is culturally and historically contingent. The system of strong judicial review coupled with indeterminate rights claims that I describe below can serve this function in our time and place, but plainly it is not for every time and place. With this understanding, the rest of this chapter investigates how we can best use our own particular constitutional tradition to serve destabilizing goals.

As I have already argued, part of the difficulty for standard constitutional theory is that we are not in agreement about the substantive content of that tradition. Still, there is surprisingly broad agreement about its structural features. Paradoxically, even though the overarching aim of liberal constitutionalism is to bring us together in a just community, most of its structure involves boundaries and separation.[1] This is true on the macro level, where liberal constitutionalism attempts to create community by enforcing boundaries around the individual, but it is also true on the micro level, where the actual practice of constitutional law requires the demarcation of boundaries between a series of paired opposites.

These macro and micro processes are linked. Individual rights are protected by maintaining the boundaries between the paired opposites. The relative impenetrability of these boundaries, in turn, is thought to provide the protection that allows individuals with different aims and values to form a community.

What are the boundaries policed by constitutional law? Most constitutional cases require exposition of the distinction between private and public, free will and coercion, local and national, nonfeasance and feasance, or equality and inequality.[2] Judges typically resolve these cases by slotting the facts into one category or the other. In most situations, this division will resolve the dispute because each paired opposite has a dominant and a subservient component.[3] In its classical form, constitutional law privileges private over public, local over national, freedom over coercion, feasance over nonfeasance, and equality over inequality.*

Each of the paired opposites, in turn, is linked to the others in an intricate, mutually reenforcing web. Consider, for example, how a liberal constitutionalist might defend the "right to die." An advocate might start with the assumption

---

*As we shall see below, modern constitutional law sometimes flips the priorities between these categories.

that individual, private choices about life and death are presumptively free, whereas public intervention is problematic because it creates coercion. People make free decisions in a private sphere when the government remains passive by not interfering with these decisions (nonfeasance). In contrast, there is no constitutional right to government intervention (through public subsidization of either palliative medical intervention or doctor-assisted suicide, for example) that facilitates the making of the decisions. Instead, when the government acts (feasance), there is a risk that it will invade the private sphere. Government action restricting the right to die is problematic because it denigrates old and sick people by not respecting their considered decisions, thereby failing to treat them as equals before the law. If regulation is appropriate, it should be promulgated on the local level, which is least invasive of freedom, in part because of the greater ease with which individual dissenters can "vote with their feet" to escape regulation.

This interlocking web of justification provides powerful support for a constitutional settlement that bounds individual rights. Notice, however, that the settlement does not entirely eliminate the disfavored categories. There will always be residual cases that are appropriately public (decisions involving the mentally incompetent, for example). How do we decide which cases go into which category? Superimposed on all the linked pairs is the master distinction between law and politics. This distinction, in turn, is defined by still another series of subsidiary linked pairs. Law is neutral, nondiscretionary, objective, and rational. Politics is biased, idiosyncratic, subjective, and nonrational. Legislatures engage in politics; courts enforce the law. Law (together with its subsidiary linked categories) is the favored category because it embodies the protections for individual rights that make a just community possible. The rationality of law means that all reasonable people can accept it as the basis for a constitutional settlement. Whereas legislative coercion risks crossing the boundaries that separate individuals through the exercise of raw power, thereby driving the community apart, legal decisions, protecting individual choice, provide the separation that makes unity possible. It follows that law, rather than politics, is the method by which we decide which cases are ordinary and which are residual. Indeed, the most important task for constitutional law is finding ways to wall off the residual cases so that they do not contaminate the ordinary ones.[4]

The famous majority opinion in Lochner v. New York[5] illustrates how this process works. A New York State law established maximum hours for workers in bakeries. In the Court's view, the law was unconstitutional because it treated decisions by workers and their employers about conditions of employment as public rather than private. So long as these decisions were private, they were exercises of freedom of contract. Government inaction left this preexisting freedom intact, but government regulation (feasance) unjustifiably limited the freedom. This limitation, in turn, treated bakers as if they were not full citizens capable of deciding what was best for themselves — in other words, as unequal and inferior.*

It did not follow, however, that the category of permissible public decisions was a null set. As many have pointed out,[6] even during the heyday of substantive due process, the Supreme Court upheld much more regulatory legislation than it invalidated. Indeed, in *Lochner* itself the Court affirmed an earlier decision upholding legislation of hours for miners.[7] Liberal constitutionalism can tolerate a fair amount of government regulation. It insists only on a legal boundary between the realms of public and private. The problem in *Lochner,* then, was not government regulation per se. It was rather that the decision to regulate amounted to an exercise of political power rather than a reasoned judgment. The central purpose of constitutional law is to police this boundary. As the Court put it,[8]

> In every case that comes before this court . . . where legislation of this character is concerned, and where the protection of the Federal Constitution is sought, the question necessarily arises: Is this a fair, reasonable and appropriate exercise of the police power of the State, or is it an unreasonable, unnecessary and arbitrary interference with the right of the individual to his personal liberty . . . ?
>
> This is not a question of substituting the judgment of the court for that of the legislature. If the act be within the power of the state, it is valid, although the judgment of the court might be totally opposed to the enactment of such a law. But the question would still remain: Is it within the police power of the state? and that question must be answered by a court.

The *Lochner* example might suggest that these structural features of constitutional settlement have now been abandoned, along with *Lochner* itself. I hope to show that they have not and, indeed, cannot be. Still, it is true that for most of the twentieth century, this method of thinking about constitutional law has been under attack. The overall critical strategy has been to probe for weaknesses in the master distinction between law and politics. Critics argued that there was no single, uniquely rational way to engage in the sorting process on which constitutional law depended. The result has been the proliferation of conflicting yet plausible constitutional settlements described in Chapter 1,

---

Lochner itself applied to local, rather than national decisions. However, during the first part of the twentieth century, the Court also relied upon the local/national distinction to invalidate important federal programs. *See, e.g.,* Schechter Poultry Corp. v. United States, 295 U.S. 495 (1935); Carter v. Carter Coal Co., 298 U.S. 238 (1936).

where each settlement sorts cases in a different way and supports a different resolution of contested political issues.

The critical assault has taken two forms. First, critics have claimed that the factors that justify slotting the exceptional cases into the disfavored category also justify putting the ordinary cases there.[9] Because there is no principled difference between cases categorized in one way and cases categorized in the other, the Court's categorization must be discretionary rather than mandatory — that is, political rather than legal. For example, in *Lochner* itself, Justice Harlan's dissenting opinion cited scholarly sources purporting to demonstrate that bakers suffered risks to health comparable to the health risks of miners.[10] If mining could be treated as public, Harlan argued, then baking could be as well.

Superficially, arguments of this sort might seem benign. After all, Harlan's opinion demands no more than a slight expansion of a category already conceded to exist. But defenders of traditional constitutionalism rightly saw this maneuver as an effort to get the camel's nose under the tent. As Justice Peckham's majority opinion points out, all professions are unhealthy to some extent.[11] To allow government regulation whenever there is any degree of unhealthiness is to permit the exception to swallow the rule — the ultimate nightmare for traditional constitutionalism. Yet conceding that the permissibility of regulation turned on matters of degree (just how unhealthy *are* various occupations?) was dangerous as well. When cases are aligned along a continuum, rather than on one side or the other of a bright line, categorization is inevitably discretionary and arbitrary.

Faced with this dilemma, the *Lochner* Court opted for insistence on a formal, rigid distinction between the categories. It refused to be drawn into a discussion of which professions were healthy and which were not. Instead, it declared that bakers were different from miners because — well, because everyone knew they were just different.[12] Given the alternatives, one can easily see why the Court opted for this solution. Yet the insistence on formalism also played into the critics' hands. The arbitrariness of the formal line — the failure to provide the kind of reasoned explanation that the Court itself insisted upon — seemed to undercut the central claims made for liberal constitutionalism.

The second critical strategy was even more insidious than the first. The problem was not just that arguments for the exceptional cases could also be made in ordinary cases; it was also that the categorical distinctions between special and ordinary were themselves incoherent. Thus, the private *was* the public, because public decisions structure the markets where private bargains are struck.[13] For example, public influence over economic decision making through budgetary and monetary policy and publicly determined rules of property and contract formation made big differences in the bargaining positions of labor and capital when the bakers and their employers entered into contracts providing for long work hours. The free *was* the coerced because supposedly free decisions were always located within a constellation of forces that put pressure on the choices.[14] It was fanciful to suppose that bakers chose to work long hours because this was how they wanted to spend their time. The shape of the labor market and the need for money to purchase necessities pressured bakers into accepting conditions of employment they hated. Nonfeasance *was* feasance because the failure to control private power was itself a governmental choice that had the effect of delegating coercive, lawmaking authority to one segment of society at the expense of another.[15] Here the government faced a choice about whether to treat bakery owners like mine owners. A decision not to do so is something more than a failure to act. It is a policy determination that has predictable consequences.

Since each of the opposites could be collapsed into its pair, it seemed to follow that when the Court labeled an activity private rather than public, free rather than coerced, or inaction rather than action, it was making an arbitrary and discretionary decision, rather than an objective and neutral one. This labeling was a method of announcing conclusions masquerading as a statement of reasons for them. In short, the labeling exercise was, once again, politics rather than law.

To be sure, traditionalists were not defenseless against this assault. Critical arguments had bite only if one assumed that the legal distinctions were freestanding, not linked to some extralegal standard. Perhaps from a purely legal perspective the various categories could be collapsed into one another. The categories might, nonetheless, be defended if they corresponded to "natural," or prelegal, distinctions. These distinctions might be grounded in a worked-out theory of natural rights—the sort of theory that contemporary scholars like Richard Epstein[16] and Robert Nozick[17] have provided. But the distinctions need not be theoretical. They can also be grounded in custom, intuition, tradition, or conventional morality.

As we shall see, the argument for grounding constitutional law on these extralegal sources has more force than is sometimes recognized, but it does not really solve the problem. We have already identified the reasons why: It is true that virtually no one in our culture is prepared to give up on the various linked opposites upon which constitutional law depends. Whatever the analytic difficulties, almost everyone thinks that there is indeed a distinction between public and private, freedom and coercion. What we are lacking, though, is a single prelegal theory that would give content to these categories. Instead, as the right to die and maximum-hours examples illustrate, we have a variety of prelegal theories, intuitions, customs, and traditions, and the result is contested rather than fixed boundaries between the paired opposites.

It is not surprising, then, that many people who agree with the critical argument when it is applied to *Lochner* reject it when applied to a right to die. Yet there is no inherent, logical reason why the argument suddenly loses force when applied to end-of-life decisions. The categorization process between, say, the terminally ill making "rational" choices to die and the merely depressed making "coerced" decisions is just as contested as the distinction between bakers and miners, and the risk that the disfavored category will engulf the favored one just as real. Similarly, patients who "choose" to die, like employees who work long hours, are sometimes pressured into their choices by social and economic conditions for which the government may bear responsibility. Government nonfeasance, allowing patients to die, can easily be characterized as government action designed to kill them, especially if the nonfeasance takes the form of denial of Medicare or Medicaid reimbursements for life-prolonging procedures.

But although the analytic structure of the argument is identical, the prelegal suppositions that cause one set of facts to be decoded as private and free while the other is seen as public and coerced are contested. This stubborn fact of moral and epistemic pluralism, in turn, serves to undermine the master distinction. Faced with a constitutional case, a court can give content to constitutionalism's analytic tools only by choosing between different potential settlements resting on different prelegal theories. Precisely because the theories are prelegal, the choice cannot be made according to law.

Wrong Turns

What follows from these critical arguments? Mainstream constitutional theory has responded in three ways to the effort to eradicate constitutional boundaries. One response has been to reverse the presumptive status of the various linked categories. Today the Supreme Court often starts with the assumption that activity is in the public sphere unless special reasons can be shown for placing it within the private. The modern court has treated both end-of-life issues and workplace issues as presumptively public.[18] Public resolution of these and other questions is now conceptualized as free, in the sense that the decision is democratically arrived at. Private resolution is coerced, in the sense that the Court's protection of a private sphere limits the freedom of democratic majorities.

Similarly, modern Justices and theorists sometimes reverse the local versus national distinction. Local decisions are treated as coerced because there is a greater risk of capture by faction at the local level[19] and because competition between local governments constrains choice by threatening a race to the bottom.[20] National decisions are free because they reduce the risks of externalities and avoid prisoners' dilemmas.*

These reversals might be thought to follow logically from the attack on the law-politics distinction. If the sorting process is not, in fact, insulated from political choice, then it seems appropriate for the process to be accomplished by overtly political institutions. The reversals were also congenial to the New Deal Justices who populated the Court after the *Lochner* debacle and who shared the Roosevelt administration's ideological preference for subjecting the economy to greater national and public control.

However, the simple transposition of the public and private categories cannot resolve the contradictions uncovered by the critical attack. First, transposition provides us with no better tools for sorting between the dominant and the residual categories. Although the Court has been content to leave regulation of the choice to die mostly in the public, political sphere, for example, virtually no one thinks that nothing should be slotted in the now disfavored private category. A fractured Supreme Court has indicated that there are circumstances, albeit dimly defined, when private choices to terminate treatment or hasten death must prevail.[21] To be sure, the Court's majority has been attacked for these statements,[22] but the attackers themselves are unprepared to eliminate the disfavored category. Is there anyone now sitting on the Supreme Court who would relegate the choice of life, as opposed to the choice of death, to the public sphere? If, as I suspect, all nine Justices would condemn a forced euthanasia statute, we must explain why private choices to live are presumptively free while private choices to die are presumptively coerced.

Second, the transposition does not respond to the claim that the categories collapse into one another. End-of-life issues again provide a useful illustration. Critics of a right to die argue that the choice is unlikely to be free.[23] In an age of managed care there is, indeed, reason to worry that vulnerable, terminally ill patients will be pressured in a variety of economic and social ways to end treatment. But to use coercion of this sort to justify public intervention is to

---

*Although less common, Justices have also occasionally reversed the feasance-nonfeasance distinction. For example, Justice Scalia has written that a patient who declines available treatment for an illness is analytically no different from a patient who actively commits suicide. *See* Cruzan v. Director, Missouri Dept. of Health, 457 U.S. 261, 296 (1990) (Scalia, J., concurring). In his majority opinion in Roe v. Wade, 410 U.S. 113 (1973), Justice Blackmun seems to have assumed that the state's failure to prevent abortion would violate constitutional rights if the fetus were a person within the meaning of the due-process clause. *See* id., at 156.

miss the critical point. Patients — or any one else for that matter — are never in a pristine state where their decisions reflect an unfettered will. *All* decisions are coerced, or at least all can be so characterized. Decisions to abort a fetus, affiliate with a religion, or support a political candidate are also substantially influenced by outside forces that could, if we so chose, be characterized as coercive.* Shifting end-of-life decisions from the private to the public arena does no more than readjust the boundary. It fails to respond to the argument that no such boundary can possibly exist.

Nor is it obvious that public decisions are free in the sense that they amount to the unmediated reflection of popular will. Because our conceptions of democracy are contested, it is always possible to label any political outcome undemocratic. There is now a small academic industry devoted to demonstrating that progressive legislation of the type invalidated in *Lochner* resulted from various imperfections in the democratic process.[24] Similar demonstrations can be made regarding legislation prohibiting suicide and euthanasia. Many of the laws that prohibit assisted suicide, for example, are both old and unenforced.[25] Paradoxically, the existence of these laws, as a practical matter, leaves euthanasia almost entirely unregulated in many parts of the country. Doctors make secret decisions about life and death that are largely shielded from public control.[26]

Perhaps advocates of public, democratic decision making should favor Supreme Court invalidation of these laws. Were the Court to strike them down, its decision might prompt a modern legislative reexamination of the problem, much as its decision a generation ago invalidating capital punishment statutes led to a rewriting of these laws.† The result might be a truly public discussion, culminating in the kind of effective public regulation that opponents of a right to die favor.

A second response to the critical assault has been to shore up the legal,

---

*For example, the absence of adequate child-rearing assistance for working mothers might be said to coerce abortions. Indeed, when the German Constitutional Court upheld a restrictive abortion law, it simultaneously held that the government had a constitutional duty to provide support during pregnancy and after childbirth. For an account, see Vicki C. Jackson and Mark Tushnet, Comparative Constitutional Law 121 (1999). Parental and spousal "coercion" often influences religious and political choices. *See, e.g.,* Wisconsin v. Yoder, 406 U.S. 205, 241 (1972) (Douglas, J., dissenting).

†The Court's decision in Furman v. Georgia, 409 U.S. 902 (1972), had the effect of invalidating every capital sentencing scheme in the country. By the time the Supreme Court revisited the issue in Gregg v. Georgia, 428 U.S. 153 (1976), at least thirty-five states had enacted new capital sentencing statutes. *See* Sanford H. Kadish and Stephen J. Schulhofer, Criminal Law and Its Processes 524 (6th ed., 1995).

nondiscretionary character of the boundaries by linking them more overtly to some external referent. Various flavors of textualism and originalism illustrate this response, as do efforts to locate the boundaries with maps drawn from tradition, the teachings of moral philosophy and political theory, or convention. For example, some have claimed that *Lochner* was wrongly decided not simply because the Court overrode a decision reached by the political branches but because it paid insufficient attention to constitutional text[27] or because its decision amounted to bad economics or bad political or social theory.[28]

I have already discussed the reasons why these efforts are bound to fail, and they need not now long detain us. Although advocates of various external referents criticize the *Lochner* Court, their efforts are really no different from Lochnerean formalism. As such, they run into the twin problems of multiple constitutional settlements and constitutional evil, both discussed in Chapters 1 and 2. As the *Lochner* Court discovered, making the boundaries more rigid will make them appear more legitimate only if there is general acceptance of the basis upon which the lines are drawn. Advocates of originalism, for example, must contend with the fact that not everyone accepts originalist methodology as a uniquely privileged settlement. Insistence on this settlement to the exclusion of others simply delegitimates constitutional law in the eyes of those who believe in other settlements.

Moreover, the very rigidity of the boundaries means that they are certain to produce some results that are evil — results that could be avoided by drawing the boundary in a different place. Consider once again the example of originalism. As explained in Chapters 1 and 2, if originalism is to work, it must lead to judgments that would not be reached under an all-things-considered approach. Originalists must then explain why we should reach a "worse" outcome when a "better" one is available. It will not do simply to assert that this is the result originalism requires, since the very issue in dispute is whether we ought to be chained to originalist methodology. Any explanation originalists offer must therefore be outside the bounds of the originalism they advocate, thereby denying the very claim that they are making.*

A third response looks in the opposite direction from the second. Instead of shoring up the boundaries, this approach attempts to do away with them.

---

*As explained in Chapter 1, an originalist might claim that we should adhere to the original bargain even when it produces evil results because no better bargain can be struck. But this claim rests on an empirical assertion that becomes increasingly dubious as the original bargain ages. In any event, the claim assumes that some bargain is required to preserve political community. The central thesis of this book is that this assumption is wrong.

Advocates of this response attempt to reconceptualize constitutional law as pragmatic policy management.[29] Cases are no longer decided by slotting them into preconceived categories. Instead, good judges are sensitive to the fact that most issues involve matters of degree and judgment, rather than bright lines. On this view, judges should end their pointless obsession with theory. Instead, they should balance interests, weigh costs and benefits, and pay attention to the probable practical effects of their decisions.

It should be apparent why this response, too, is unlikely to solve the problem. Either policy management yields determinate outcomes or it does not. If it does, it is just formalism, drawing a rigid line premised on still another constitutional settlement. Instead of insisting on adherence to text, or original intent, or moral philosophy, advocates of this settlement insist that we reach results dictated by the "science" of policy management. This settlement begs all the same questions as competing settlements. We might, instead, abandon the pretense that policy management is a science. We might treat it as open-textured and indeterminate. But then a court must face the choice of how to interpret the lessons policy managers have to teach us. By hypothesis, the choice is not dictated by policy management itself. It would seem to follow that the choice must be political, rather than legal, no different in principle from the political decisions for which the *Lochner* Court was justly criticized.

The failure of these mainstream responses is not especially surprising. If the critical attack is right, the responses are bound to fail. The critical apparatus is powerful, and it would be remarkable if things could easily be patched up once it is deployed. What is more interesting is the failure of imagination of some of the critics themselves.

One response to critical constitutionalism has been the retreat to nihilism. Perhaps the best exemplar of this position is Arthur Leff, whose mordant, biting essays still rank among the most entertaining and uncompromising works of American legal scholarship.[30] Leff understood better than any of his contemporaries the dark corner to which anyone cursed with critical insights was driven.[31] By the end of his life, he had seemingly retreated completely from normative discourse, devoting his time to an unfinished legal dictionary that was equal parts bizarrely obsessive positivism and delightfully wicked cynicism.[32]

Leff's clear-eyed skepticism and zero tolerance for cant are undeniably bracing, but few would want to follow his path into waspish withdrawal. The problem for most of us is that no merely theoretical argument can eliminate from our consciousness the distinctions upon which constitutional law rests. Whatever the critics say, most of us continue to see distinctions between individuals and the collective or between acts that we undertake freely and those that are coerced. Our sense of ourselves as choosing and purposive agents seems to rest upon distinctions of this sort.

Moreover, even if we could eradicate these frameworks we use to organize the world, it is far from clear why we would want to. After all, waspish withdrawal is itself a choice. As the ancient Greeks understood, this choice also presupposes a free will that nihilists doubt, and any reasons offered in support of it presuppose a normative framework that nihilists dispute.[33]

We might avoid these difficulties by maintaining our normative commitments but giving up on offering reasons in support of them. Consider, for example, the work of Philip Bobbitt.[34] Bobbitt understands the critical insight that there can be no mediating principle between rival constitutional settlements. For Bobbitt settlements are simply practices, which are meaningful and have normative content for those already within them but which cannot be normatively justified to those outside of them. Yet Bobbitt also understands that the absence of external mediation does not excuse us from the obligation of choice. It is therefore the act of choice itself that defines our values, rather than any external or objective values that require the choice. As Bobbitt eloquently makes the point,

> It is the illusion of our Age, to which we relentlessly cling, that men and women can create tools to solve moral and political problems, much as we have created technologies that solve physical problems. And yet, as ever, when one goes to the room where such tools are kept, one finds only the shards and artifacts of ideas broken in earlier tasks. We are incapable of making something that will obviate (rather than suppress) the requirement for moral decision. Then each person must go back out, armed with what he has found, to defend what he wants to survive ultimately when the one thing he knows for certain is that he himself will not ultimately survive.[35]

If we could confine our activities to raw choice, we might be satisfied with this solution. But Bobbitt's position takes too little account of the fact that we interact with others who have different views from our own. If, as he claims, the tools of moral argument have been "broken in earlier tasks," it is unclear how we are supposed to use them to "defend what [we want] to survive ultimately." Put differently, Bobbitt's views do not help us understand how constitutional argument interacts with community. As we have already discussed, in a large and diverse community such as ours, people do more than simply choose; they also engage in conversation with others about what is to be done.

For example, from a wholly internal perspective, I might be satisfied to define myself as an originalist whose moral values are best actualized from within this framework. But I cannot live within a bubble. There are many others engaged in constitutional practice who are not originalists and whom I would like to persuade. Once we are within the realm of persuasion, rather than action, Bobbitt's solution seems of little use.*

If Leff and Bobbitt are too pessimistic about the possibilities of productive dialogue, then various perspectivist theorists are too ingenuous. Such thinkers as Mari Matsuda,[36] Patricia Williams,[37] and Richard Delgado[38] have seized upon critical insights as a rhetorical tool that might serve the ends of persuasion. Their argument is simple: Because the boundaries between the linked categories that define constitutional law are neither rational nor objective, they do not provide a justification for the outcomes they produce. Instead, they amount to no more than exercises of power over the powerless. Once critical techniques reveal this boundary manipulation for the fraud it is, the way will be clear to end the unjust racial, class, and gender hierarchies that pervade our society.

Perspectivist attack on the boundary between equality and inequality provides a useful example. Mainstream proponents and opponents of affirmative action agree that such programs depart from the presumptive norm of racial and gender nondiscrimination. Proponents argue that this departure should be slotted into the exceptional category, perhaps because they believe in compensation for past wrongs[39] or because competing interests in diversity trump the equality requirement.[40] In contrast, opponents argue that it should be slotted into the ordinary category, perhaps because they believe that nondiscrimination is a moral requirement that should not be violated even to achieve worthy ends[41] or because they think that the race consciousness affirmative action promotes will harm minority groups in the long run.[42]

Despite their disagreement, however, proponents and opponents agree on the presumptive validity of nondiscrimination. Perspectivists reject this premise. In good critical fashion, they attack the very existence of the boundary between equality and inequality. What proponents and opponents alike characterize as discrimination can be characterized instead as nondiscrimination. This recharacterization can be accomplished by focusing on the standards of merit enforced by the nondiscrimination requirement. Perspectivists argue that these standards are neither natural nor neutral. Because they are white,

---

*At least, it is of little use as long as we conceptualize constitutional law as embodying a settlement. Tools broken in earlier tasks will not help us settle an argument. As I argue below, they might help us a great deal if our objective is to keep the argument going. Bobbitt's conceptualization of judging as unfettered moral choice fits better within this framework.

male standards, the decision by mainstream proponents and opponents alike to treat them as the equality baseline from which affirmative departures are measured builds bias into the system from the beginning.[43]

The affirmative action example gets us part of the way toward an understanding of how the conventional building blocks of constitutional argument might help create an unsettled constitution. The ability to flip the categories opens up possibilities for destabilizing any current arrangement. Flipping the equal and unequal categories, for example, uncovers the contingent, contested nature of background assumptions about merit, thereby making us uneasy about current distributions of wealth and power.[44]

Nonetheless, I am doubtful that these efforts have made much headway. The main difficulty is that perspectivists too often ignore the conclusions that seem to follow from their own arguments. They begin with the premise that judgments about merit are inevitably biased and situated, and they ask us to draw from this premise the conclusion that wealth and power should be redistributed. But this is surely a non sequitur. If merit judgments are inevitably contested, then questions of distribution will remain contested as well. Of course, minority communities, applying their merit standard, will complain that they have been short-changed, but majority communities can assert with equal justification that according to *their* merit standard, minorities have received exactly what they deserved. Perspectivists cannot have it both ways. If there is no neutral, unsituated mediating standard, then we must live with a world where we cannot appeal to such a standard to complain about unjust treatment.

This difficulty, in turn, sometimes leads to unfortunate results when perspectivists try to employ critical techniques to build community. Instead of unsettling their audience, the complaints of perspectivists are often translated as special pleading or hectoring.[45] The hollowing-out of our core constitutional concepts means that no one is likely to be persuaded by the argument. Everyone knows that there are competing conceptions available and that the choice between these conceptions is driven by political considerations. The upshot is that constitutional rhetoric is, and is perceived to be, a method by which people try to assert power over other people.

It appears, then, that critical insights have led us to a dead end. If the arguments I have made above are correct, late twentieth-century constitutionalism seems to present us with an unenviable choice between cynical withdrawal on the one hand and hypocritical, ineffective posturing on the other. Neither alternative holds much hope for building the kind of community we seek.

I do not wish to deny that much of modern constitutional law produces these results. For reasons Mark Tushnet and I spelled out at greater length elsewhere,[46] there is a kind of sickness that infects contemporary constitutionalism. The sickness is directly linked to the fact that we seem unable either to abandon the core distinctions of constitutional analysis or to use them in good faith. Still, if the critical argument is correct, then it must be that the category of constitutionalism also lacks fixed boundaries. Like all institutions, it is what we choose to make of it. Constitutional law can create division and disengagement, but, used and understood creatively, it also has the potential to advance ends we share. The question is how to achieve that potential.

The Uses of Contradiction

I have already foreshadowed some of the ways we might make the best of constitutional law. To some degree, making the best of things depends on nothing more complicated than changing our attitude about what we are doing. For example, each of us might simply resolve to stop attacking others with arguments we know to be tendentious. We might see the plasticity of constitutional law not as a tool for besting our opponents but as a reason for skepticism about our own conclusions.

This skepticism is not the same thing as, nor does it lead inevitably to, cynical withdrawal. It is possible to be an engaged skeptic. Using constitutional law to build a just community rests on the ability of most people to maintain the truth of contradictory ideas at the same time. One example is our ability to believe, even fervently, in the truth of a proposition while also understanding on a different level that our belief is contingent and situated.

If I know anything at all, I know that American slavery was barbaric and hideous. Yet I also know that there were virtually no white southern abolitionists in 1855. But how would I have felt if I were a white southerner in 1855? In some sense, this thought experiment, like all counterfactuals, is incoherent, yet many of us are irresistibly attracted to such speculation nonetheless. Moreover, the speculation serves a useful purpose.

I cannot make myself believe that if "I" were such a white southerner, I, uniquely among members of my community, would have opposed slavery. This disturbing thought, in turn, suggests that my present beliefs about slavery are also historically contingent. I believe that slavery is wrong not because it is "really" wrong but because this is what people in my present community believe, just as white southerners were influenced by their community to oppose abolition. Remarkably, I can understand all this and yet still believe as strongly as I believe anything that slavery is wrong.

The fact that my opinion about slavery is not changed by this sort of reflection does not mean that nothing is changed, however. Considering how I might have felt as an antebellum white southerner does change my attitude about these people; I cannot work up the level of hatred for them I would otherwise. One must concede that this is something of a loss. Moral condemnation can be an enjoyable activity, and, perhaps more significant, it can also be a goad to action. When directed at people long dead, it is relatively harmless. But there is a greater downside when it is directed at living people with whom one is trying to form a community. A sense of contingency does not mean that we stop having political arguments with others. It might mean that we stop trying to annihilate those we disagree with.

The example I have used above involves historical flipping, but the same points hold true for the kind of constitutional flipping that constitutional critics have taught us. This flipping need not lead to ineffectual shouting at political opponents. Instead of using the device to persuade others, we might use it against ourselves. We might come to see that the arguments we make, even though we believe them, do not lead inexorably to the conclusions we favor. This realization, in turn, might lead to skeptical engagement with our opponents, rather than self-righteous preaching at them.

My point is not simply that people can and should change their attitude about constitutional argument, however. It is also that the very structure of that argument can assist in this change. In order to see how, we need to return to the "what" and "how" of constitutional law. Our effort will be facilitated by a focus on another internal contradiction and yet another contested boundary, this time in the realm of moral psychology.

Central to understanding the "what" of an unsettled constitution is the distinction between universalist and particularist worldviews. A universalist treats all human beings as entitled to disinterested, equal concern and respect. A particularist treats some people as entitled to special caring to which others are not entitled.[47]

We do not want to fall into the formalist trap of treating these categories as if there were a bright line between them. For example, a perfect universalist might not stop at human beings. Perfect universalism might require equal concern for all sentient beings[48] or even for plants and rocks.[49] Conversely, a perfect particularist might care only about himself. All real people are somewhere between these two extremes, extending the boundaries of their care to a greater or lesser extent.

This distinction, like the others we have discussed, can be deconstructed.[50] Care for others can be recharacterized as care for self if one takes into account a "selfish" taste for altruism.[51] Care for self can be characterized as care for others, if one believes that self-love is a necessary prerequisite for love of others.[52]

We can concede all this yet still recognize that the conflicting pulls toward particularism and universalism play an important role in the practical, moral decisions that are the stuff of everyday life. Moreover, as an internal psychological matter, most of us have not worked out the contradiction between the two positions. Consider, for example, a statement attributed to Clare Boothe Luce:[53]

> Americans identify with America, and increasingly there are people — Poles, Italians, Israelis — who identify with two countries. But I do not know of any other identification that I can make, say, with the conditions of the people of the Sahara. I repeatedly see pictures in the papers of a starving mother and her child holding out its hand. I think it would be hypocritical if I didn't say that I would feel a little more compassion if one of my pet birds had broken a leg in its cage in my own house.

This statement is troubling, to say the least. Luce seems remarkably deficient in the ability to play the game of counterfactual identification I have described above.* Yet if we are to be honest about it — if we ourselves are to take seriously the need to avoid self-righteous condemnation and build empathic identification with our opponents — then we might see that part of why Luce's view is so troubling is that it states an uncomfortable truth about humankind. Anyone who owns a pet and spends money on food for it that might instead be used to feed starving children is acting on the beliefs that Luce so indiscreetly verbalizes. Moreover, one does not have to be a follower of Ayn Rand to see that the very flipping exercise producing the empathic identification Luce lacks requires the self-regard she defends. Imagining myself as living in Saharan Africa produces empathic identification only if I begin by caring specially about the self I am imagining in this new context.

A universalist saint, then, is in some ways a strange and not very admirable figure. Disinterested and equal beneficence for all human beings entails the absence of special caring for any particular human being. It means an inability to love individuals, to form particular friendships, and, at the limit, to have the kind of self-regard that is the necessary prerequisite of regard for others.

---

*Reading the statement in the most charitable light possible, we might claim that Luce is much better at the game than I am. On this view, the problem is not that she is unable to imagine herself as living in the Sahara but that she is able to imagine herself being a canary. This (improbable) reading suggests some of the problems with universalism that I explore below.

Of course, it does not follow that uncompromising particularism is the right answer either. There is little to be said for unadulterated selfishness. Love of self, family, and country are goods, but narcissism, tribalism, and jingoism are not. Particularism can provide the moral sustenance that allows us to go out into the world, but it can also produce fanaticism, intolerance, and violence.

Just as constitutional theorists have attempted to domesticate the critical assaults on the constitutional categories, so too we might attempt to soften the contradiction between conflicting particularist and universalist approaches. One way to do so is to explain one category in terms of the other. For example, it is sometimes assumed that the best way to achieve a world where everyone receives equal concern and respect is for each person to give special concern and respect to his or her own family, friends, and fellow citizens. The empirical support for this claim is dubious, but even if it were wholly convincing, the claim fails to take the contradiction seriously. The difficulty with this approach is that it holds particularist responses hostage to universalist justifications. On this view, particularism is a good only because, and only to the extent that, it advances the universalist agenda. But such an approach is unlikely to satisfy a true particularist. Anyone who has fallen in love will immediately understand. My love for my wife is not based upon what produces the greatest good for the greatest number. It stands on its own footing and has its own justification. A universalist who explains love as a means of advancing universalist ends cannot have fallen in love.

Similarly, as already noted, some particularists have attempted to explain universalism as no more than a means of gratifying particularist preferences. Some people simply have a "taste" for altruism that is no different in principle from a taste for any other good. But this approach, too, fails to take the contradiction seriously. To be sure, one can call unselfishness simply a form of selfishness, but anyone who has been unselfish immediately knows the difference. When I give money to help homeless people, I do so because it is right, not because it gives me pleasure. There may be some who indulge universalist impulses solely as a means of achieving particularist gratification, just as there are some who see particularism as a means of achieving universalist goals. But for most of us, there is an important difference between giving money to the hungry and going to a good restaurant. Someone who does not know the difference fails to understand universalism.

A second response attempts to eliminate the contradiction by arguing for a balance between the two tendencies or for relegating each to its appropriate sphere of life. Advocates of this approach are, in effect, proponents of a kind of constitutional settlement but on the individual rather than the community level. But for individuals, as for communities, settlements are not necessarily good. Another thought experiment helps illustrate the point. Sometimes, I think about how I would react if I discovered that my daughter or son had committed a horrible crime.* Would I call the police? Help them leave the country? Do nothing at all?

Of course, no one can be certain what he or she would do in a such a situation, and I do not intend to argue for one response or another. Indeed, I intend to argue against one response or another. The important point for present purposes is that it would be a strange person who had so successfully worked out the boundaries between universalism and particularism as to feel no conflict about whatever choice he made. As the widespread sympathy for the brother of the "Unabomber," Ted Kaczynski, and the mother of Monica Lewinsky illustrates, most of us understand that these choices are excruciatingly difficult, and most of us would not want them to be easy. Indeed, many of us would say that a person who considered them easy was, in an important sense, not a complete human being.

None of this is to say that we lack intuitions about circumstances where one approach or the other is inappropriate. It is wrong to treat members of one's family with the cold, disinterested beneficence one accords to strangers, and it would be bizarre to suppose that individuals are under a moral obligation to treat all people equally when deciding whom to marry.[54] Conversely, despite much sloppy rhetoric about family, it would be wrong for a teacher to treat students in her class with the kind of deeply personal concern that she extends to her own family members, and it would certainly be wrong to prefer one student over another in the personalized fashion we routinely use when selecting friends or lovers.

But although all of us have these intuitions, they are unstable, and how we think about a problem will often turn on contexts that seem to privilege one obligation or the other. For example, the act of voting makes sense only as a symbolic affiliation with universalist goals. To be sure, people take self-interest into account even here, but as many have pointed out,[55] from a particularist point of view, voting is deeply irrational. Since a single vote is extremely unlikely to make a difference,† and since the time necessary to cast a ballot

---

*A special note to Jessica and Andrew: This counterfactual is even more incoherent than usual. Does my use of these personal illustrations (not to mention personalized footnotes) itself raise troubling questions about the appropriate contexts for and boundary between universalism and particularism? Consider, for example, Al Gore's bathetic references to his sister and son in nomination acceptance speeches. As argued below, the public use of private imagery destroys its private character.

†Even in the 2000 presidential election — the closest in our history — no single voter could have changed the outcome.

interferes in some measure with particularist goals (getting home from work on time, making dinner for the kids), voting makes sense only as a way of expressing solidarity with a broader community. Not surprisingly, therefore, when people vote, they often express universalist preferences that they do not express in other contexts. I regularly vote for candidates who favor raising my tax level, but I never knowingly make voluntary donations to the government when filling out my tax return.

Conversely, markets tend to bring out particularist preferences. On rare occasions (for example, during organized boycotts) people focus on universalist concerns when they buy and consume. The more general pattern, though, is to buy according to particularist norms. As a public citizen, I might believe that environmental racism is wrong, but it does not follow that I would buy a home near a toxic dump. I might vote for candidates who favor giving some of my money to starving children in the Sahara, but I buy presents for my own children.*

It turns out, then, that our choice between particularist and universalist approaches is often context dependent. We feel differently depending on whether we conceptualize ourselves as acting as public citizens or as private individuals. What makes the contradiction ultimately unresolvable is that we have no contextless position from which to choose the right context. This choice must itself be made from a universalist or particularist perspective. For example, I can, if I try, make myself feel guilty about my consumption and purchasing decisions by taking a more universalist stance. And I regularly feel guilty about the cold bureaucratic neutrality with which I treat students for whom I have authentic affection. But one must, in the end, take one stance or the other, and taking either seems to deny something basic.

I must concede that the preceding paragraphs do not so much make an argument as appeal to what I hope are shared intuitions. Because particularism and universalism are incompatible and rival positions, it is hard to know how a formal argument would proceed. Accepting each on its own terms, like not prejudging rival constitutional settlements, means living with the fact that there is no mediating principle by which the two can be reconciled. People who believe in settlements, whether on the constitutional or the individual level, may not share the intuitions I am relying upon. For them what I have already said (and what I am about to say) will beg the question. Taking universalism seriously means not placing universalists beyond our political and empathic boundaries, so it would be wrong to condemn them. Perhaps, then, the

---

*Of course, I give money to charity also. My point is that I am willing to vote for candidates who would take from me more money than I presently give to charity.

only appropriate response is to express regret that not everyone shares these intuitions since, as I argue below, the possibility of creating the sort of unsettled constitution that builds just community largely depends upon them.

In any event, the next stage in the argument is to show how this personal struggle relates to the effort to build an unsettled constitution. There are two areas of overlap. First, the unresolved conflict between particularism and universalism helps explain why and how the boundaries of political community remain contested. As we saw in Chapter 2, an unsettled constitution leaves ambiguous who are the "we" in "we, the people." We can understand this ambiguity on the community level as a reflection of unresolved conflict on the personal level, as we struggle over the boundaries of our empathic identification. Paradoxically, the fact that the boundaries of community are unsettled helps to build community.[56] Community must always be defined against the backdrop of otherness. As particularists understand, a community with universal membership is no community at all. Yet a community defined by any fixed line will leave out people who would like to be in. These individuals are bound to do their best to disrupt the settlement that excludes them. It follows that a contested and uncertain boundary, formed by the unending struggle between particularist and universalist urges, may be the best means of ensuring a just peace.

The second point is more subtle and requires lengthier exposition. The conflict between the particular and the universal parallels the linked pairs that, we have seen, are central to ordinary constitutional practice. The connection is most obvious between universalism and the public and particularism and the private. Our public institutions are designed to treat each individual with impersonal beneficence. Democracy, our system of public conflict resolution, gains its moral force from its claim to treat every citizen equally. In contrast, in the private realm, people need not — and often should not — treat every person with equal and disinterested beneficence. We do not determine choice of spouse by democratic election precisely because most people think that this decision should be made according to particularist, rather than universalist, criteria.

The other contested categories reenforce this distinction. Consider, for example, the distinction between feasance and nonfeasance. If the government were responsible for nonfeasance, it would be impossible to wall off an area for private, particularist decision making. A government failure to prevent a marriage would then be the same as a government decision to permit it. If we believe that all government decisions should be defensible on universalist grounds, it would follow that the government must prohibit marriages that do not satisfy these criteria. But then people could not make particularist decisions about whom to marry.

Similarly, when decisions are free, individuals are justified in making them on a particularist basis. When someone chooses to have a child, affiliate with a religion, or write a poem, we do not require her to explain why this activity produces results that treat every sentient being with equal concern and respect. Conversely, when the government coerces individuals, most of us think that it should not do so for the benefit of some and at the expense of others.

How does the struggle between particularism and universalism intersect with the law-politics distinction? If I am correct that we cannot, and would not want to, finally resolve our conflicting impulses toward particularism and universalism, then the boundaries between constitutional law's paired opposites cannot be resolved according to law. Legal resolutions are nondiscretionary, impersonal, and disinterested. They are, in other words, public and universalist. But we cannot maintain a tension between universalism and particularism if the boundary between them is determined solely by universalist criteria.

And yet the boundary must somehow be determined. It is important to emphasize again that an unsettled constitution does not mean that nothing is ever resolved. Disputes must come to an end. The need for resolution, in turn, produces a dilemma. Must not any resolution be dictated by either particularist or universalist criteria, and must not the use of one set of criteria rather than the other settle the conflict between them?

This problem is especially acute because, in the absence of a lawlike boundary between them, there is a natural tendency for both particularism and universalism to expand to their limits. For example, there is a risk that our public institutions will justify their decisions in ways that satisfy private individuals. This happens when institutions are captured by faction or special-interest groups. When they are so captured, public institutions no longer reflect impersonal beneficence toward all inhabitants but instead exhibit a special caring for some of them. This is what the framers called corruption and what we might call special-interest politics.

Our aim should be to resist this trend — to try to keep our public institutions truly public. But precisely to the extent that we succeed in this effort, we would not want our public institutions to determine the boundary between the public and private. Because these institutions would then be truly public, they are likely to draw the line based upon universalist criteria, thereby paying too little heed to the claims of particularism. The risk here is not corruption, but totalitarianism — the complete obliteration of the possibility of a private life. Instead of universalist values being held hostage to particularism, particularism is now held hostage to universalism.

Just as we would not want individuals to achieve a lawlike, worked-out division between their particularist and universalist impulses, so, too, a society should keep these contradictory impulses in tension with each other. But how can we accomplish this goal if the boundary must be drawn by either a public or a private institution? It is at this point that the "how" of constitutional law becomes relevant. At least in this country, constitutional law is closely associated with judicial review. Judges are given the primary task of drawing and policing the boundaries between the paired opposites. In a different society, we might imagine different sorts of people better equipped for this job. But in the United States the system of judicial review is already in place, and as it happens, we can make use of aspects of it to help create an unsettled constitution.

Courts are well suited to play a mediating role between our public and private impulses because they are the most private of our public institutions. Because judges themselves are on the cusp of the public-private divide, they are better suited than other public officials to maintain a creative tension between the two. Their ambivalent position is built into the way judges are selected, the way they are permitted to lead their lives, and the nature of judging as it has evolved in American legal culture.

The most obvious way judges are caught between the public and private spheres relates to their selection and tenure. Judges are public officials with public responsibilities. Their nominations and confirmations are political events; but there are also constraints, albeit vague and controversial, on the permissible political oversight of the nominating process.[57] Although investigations of general competence (whatever that means) and judicial philosophy (an even vaguer term) are permissible, use of litmus tests based on inquiry into decisions in particular cases is not. The selection process imposes some public check on the type of people who become judges yet leaves judges free of previous, publicly coerced commitments that might interfere with the expression of private values in deciding future cases.

Once in office, judges remain uniquely shielded from the political pressures that undermine the ability of other public officials to balance particularist and universalist values. If the purpose of constitutional law is indeed to provide a platform which losers can use to destabilize ordinary politics, then we would want those articulating it to be separated in some measure from the political outcomes they criticize. It is easy to exaggerate the extent to which judges are actually separated. The romantic vision of a judge who is entirely disconnected from the political culture that surrounds her has been rightly discredited.[58] Judicial review operates on the margin. Still, margins can be important, and they can be expanded when there is good reason to do so. A judge who is both free from ordinary electoral restraints and also restrained by the general political culture may be the best-situated public official to police the boundary between public and private.

Although the point is more speculative, it may be that the private lives of judges also make them well suited to this task. Public officials who run for office must make their private lives public. Private decisions about marriage, schooling, and religion are often influenced and sometimes dictated by universalist criteria. Thus, we read of politicians who seek polling data before deciding on vacation plans[59] or who carefully script their hand-holding with a spouse.[60] Although we are obsessed with the question, that obsession makes it silly to ask what the private lives of such politicians are like. Their private lives have been made public and are therefore no longer private.

In contrast, the fact that judges are to a greater degree exempt from electoral politics means that they are permitted to have private lives. Judges may therefore be able to understand, in a way that elected officials cannot, the pull between universal beneficence and particularized special relationships. Because the conflict between these two impulses is more likely to be a force in their own lives, they may be better equipped to keep in balance a regime of institutionalized conflict between private and public values.

Even if this speculation is wrong, there is no doubt that judges' public responsibilities leave them better equipped to maintain conflict between universalism and particularism. The conflict is built into the very act of deciding a constitutional case. As we have already explored, the tools of constitutional judging strongly resist closure. Because public can always be characterized as private, free as coerced, or nonfeasance as feasance, it is extremely difficult for a judge to work out a comprehensive, fixed theory for distinguishing the universal from the particular sphere.

As the work of David Strauss illustrates,[61] the inductive, common law development of constitutional doctrine further reenforces this tension. The case or controversy requirement means that judges always have the facts of particular cases before them. They are therefore likely to be more resistant to the sterile abstractions that dominate when we try to formulate general rules. This context pushes judges toward an appreciation of private values. Yet the tendency toward particularism is held in check by the norm that judges must be willing to formulate a more general principle that explains the result in the case before them. One of the things that makes this principle general is that it is intended to apply to anonymous individuals without personalities and individualized life stories that might influence intuitions about appropriate outcomes. The requirement therefore pushes judges toward the universalist ideal of equality and impersonal beneficence. Of course, when a subsequent case arises, the judge need not always follow the principle. The particular facts of the new case — the force of particularist values — may cause him to abandon it. But if he does so, he must acknowledge that he has abandoned it and formulate a new principle that takes into account the new decision.

It is true, as many critics have complained, that the neutral principle requirement does not restrain judges with lawlike rigidity.[62] But that is precisely the point. No effort to hold in tension contradictory universalist and particularist impulses can be determined by a rigid theory. Most people simply hold different, contradictory beliefs when they think about issues from particularist and universalist perspectives. One result will therefore seem right if the judge thinks about the problem ex post and cares about doing justice to the particular individuals before him. Another result will seem equally right if the judge thinks more broadly about the ex ante incentive effects of his decision on anonymous individuals and whether the rule to be derived from the case will maximize overall utility. A judge who is trained to think about questions in both ways will be sensitive to the contradictory demands of public and private values. Such a judge will regularly struggle between the desire to do "justice" to particular, real litigants before the court and the desire to formulate a general rule to maximize utility for the multitude. The inability to resolve this struggle helps guarantee a permanently contested boundary between public and private.

But it is one thing to say that the American practice of constitutional review has the potential to create an unsettled constitution, and another to say that the potential has been realized. It is a mistake to idealize the sort of people who currently serve in the judiciary (although, in fairness, it is equally wrong to idealize the inhabitants of the political branches). Judges have the potential to be sensitive to unresolved conflict, but they can also be stolid and arrogant. Judge-made constitutional law can upset and delegitimate entrenched arrangements, yet it can also make these arrangement seem inevitable.

In fact, American constitutional law has, at various times, both settled and unsettled our political disputes. It has been a force for creative conflict and a force for rigid reaction. My only point is that there are strands in our constitutional tradition which, if understood and nurtured, can help us to build the kind of constitutional law that all members of the community have an obligation to respect.

4

The Elusive Goal of Unsettlement

I have suggested that the primary virtue of liberal constitutionalism is its incoherence, which can be put to good use if our aim is to build an unsettled constitution. Unresolvable conflicts between the paired opposites that dominate constitutional analysis can build community by allowing losers to attack entrenched arrangements. Moreover, our own appreciation of these conflicts can help us empathize with our political foes even as we argue with them.

I have also suggested that judges are institutionally well positioned to foment this sort of creative conflict. In a variety of ways, they live and work in the borderland between the paired opposites. They are both linked to the prevailing regime and shielded from it. Their decisions affect real individuals, yet those decisions are also tested against abstract generalities. Judges lead both public and private lives. As such, they themselves straddle and struggle with the contradictions between the universal and the particular that we wish to nurture.

It is one thing to say that judge-made constitutional law has the potential to serve these ends; it is another to say that it has actually done so. In this chapter I consider what it would it mean for judges to implement an unsettled constitution. Do judges deciding constitutional cases in fact behave in the way I suggest they should? If not, what are the obstacles to putting in place an unsettled constitution? For reasons I explore below, it turns out that not only liberal constitutionalism but also the very concept of unsettlement is beset by contradiction. The upshot is that unsettlement is an ever receding goal—a state that always eludes us at just the point when it seems within grasp.

We must begin with a hard fact: The overall historical record of American judicial constitutionalism is little short of dismal. Although there have been a few Supreme Court Justices who were authentically creative, sensitive, and inventive, the majority of the jurists who have populated the Court have been eminently forgettable.* And the record of the lower courts is, if anything, worse. The short of the matter is that throughout most of our history, the judicial branch has been a stolid and unimaginative, if sometimes inept, defender of the status quo.[1]

To be sure, there have been instances where the Supreme Court has served as an important critic of political arrangements. In the twentieth century, the so-called Old Court's conflict with the Roosevelt administration and the Warren Court's forays into race relations, free-speech law, criminal procedure, and political representation provide the primary examples. Some might also cite the Court's invalidation of anti-abortion laws, its defense of gender equality, and even its assault on affirmative action and defense of states' rights. But important recent scholarship suggests that the extent of the Court's departure from political outcomes has been vastly overstated even in these instances.[2] The Old Court was not nearly as reactionary[3] nor the Warren Court as adventuresome[4] as popular myth has it. Even when the Court has tried to make a real difference, its efforts have usually been short-lived and ineffectual. And the difference it has made has usually been in support of an already existing national consensus against regional outliers or of already powerful political elites against the forces of popular democracy.[5]

Still, this record, standing alone, need not discourage us. It reflects no more than what we would expect from the kind of people who have been appointed to serve as judges and Justices. If we appoint different people (or if the people we appoint act in different ways), we shall get different results.

Of course, one might respond that we are unlikely to appoint different people. Perhaps there is something inevitable about the mechanics of judicial selection and behavior that yield these results.[6] But this sort of fatalism is self-fulfilling; it has power over us only to the extent that we believe it. Viewed retrospectively, arguments from historical experience often seem overpower-

---

*To pick names almost at random, consider some of the Justices who have occupied the seat now held by Justice Kennedy. Who among us can name the contributions of Justices H. Brockholst Livingston, Smith Thompson, Samuel Nelson, Ward Hunt, and Samuel Blatchford?

ing. Historical events always have causes, and if we specify enough about the surrounding circumstances, they will always seem inevitable. Given the forces in play, it will seem that the Supreme Court could have done nothing but uphold "separate but equal" in 1896 and nothing but strike it down in 1954.*

If we insist on being historical determinists, then there is indeed nothing to be done. But being a determinist is itself a choice, and a particularly disabling one at that. Just as we have a kind of split vision between universalism and particularism, so, too, most of us have contradictory reactions to determinism. When we look back over the sweep of history, we can see large patterns that make us feel like helpless victims of overwhelming forces. But why should we want to view the world in this way? We might instead focus on how we contemporaneously experience our own lives. Then it will seem that presidents, senators, Justices, and citizens need only make different choices and the world will be different.†

*Consider, for example, the research on presidential elections published in the early 1990s. Ray C. Fair, a respected economist at Yale University, carefully examined past presidential elections and created an elaborate model utilizing a wide variety of variables, including the inflation rate and the per-capita growth rate, to predict presidential elections. The model accounted for sixteen of the past nineteen elections, and those that it failed to account for were extremely close. Utilizing the model, Fair concluded that it was extremely unlikely that Bill Clinton would win the 1992 election. And, indeed, it was — up to the moment when it happened. On the day after this embarrassing outcome, Professor Fair told the *New York Times* that it was possible his model could be "adjusted in a way that preserved its utility." No doubt such an adjustment will make other results seem inevitable until they, too, fail to materialize. *See As for All That Lore about Foolproof Predictors, '92 Made It Look Foolish,* N.Y. Times, Nov. 5, 1992, at B1, col. 1. For the latest fiasco, see *Political Scientists Offer Mea Culpas for Predicting Gore Win,* Wash. Post, Feb. 9, 2001, at A10, col. 1 (reporting that "Political scientists whose 2000 election forecasts all predicted an easy victory for Al Gore have offered explanations for why their elaborate mathematical models were wrong"). According to the *Washington Post,* "Michael S. Lewis-Beck of the University of Iowa and his forecasting partner, Charles Tien of Hunter College, offered a defiant postmortem. 'Gore's vote total should have been much higher than it was' they wrote." Id., at A11, col 4. Indeed.

†Consider in this connection the implications of Newcomb's Problem. The problem was initially invented by William Newcomb, a physicist, and first received widespread attention when discussed in Robert Nozick, *Newcomb's Problem and Two Principles of Choice,* in Essays in Honor of C. G. Hempel (N. Rescher, ed., 1969). Imagine a game devised by an adept social scientist who has made a detailed study of human choice and can make predictions about how people will play the game with a high degree of accuracy. The rules are as follows: There are two boxes, B1 and B2. Box B1 contains $1,000. Box B2 contains either $1 million or nothing. You have a choice between either taking both boxes or taking only the second box. So far, the solution seems easy. Clearly

Determinist pessimism is especially inappropriate in light of the vulnerability of the prevailing ideology of judging. This ideology has required judges regularly to distance themselves rhetorically from their own conclusions. Like the Wizard of Oz, they want us to pay no attention to the little man behind the curtain. They would have us believe that they never reach results because they want to reach them. Instead, they are constantly being forced to outcomes, kicking and screaming as it were, by the good-faith application of impersonal, disembodied principles.

It is true that in many run-of-the-mill cases there is broad agreement about the appropriate outcome (at least among the people who get to be judges). But even thoughtful defenders of the prevailing ideology admit that this consensus

---

the choice of both boxes dominates the choice of only the second. But now suppose that you know that if the social scientist predicts that you will take what is in both boxes, he puts nothing in the second box, whereas if he predicts that you will take only the second box, he puts $1 million in it. It is important to understand that the social scientist makes the prediction and places the money in the boxes before you choose.

On the one hand, it seems that if you take what is in both boxes, the social scientist will almost certainly have predicted this, which will mean that you will not get the $1 million, whereas if you choose only B2, the social scientist will have predicted this, and you will be a millionaire. Yet on the other hand, since the social scientist has already made his prediction and distributed the money, it seems irrational to think that your decision now can influence his prior actions.

The second line of reasoning can be seen as a reproach to social science's predictive and determinist pretensions. Whatever the social scientist thinks, it will seem to the person playing the game that he has a free choice between the two options presented. What can it mean to say that the social scientist to is able to predict future events when any prediction can be frustrated by this current choice? And yet it is very hard to let go of the idea that choices are not uncaused, that they fall into patterns that can be understood, and that these patterns yield probability distributions.

Newcomb's Problem has generated a large literature. For an introduction, see Paradoxes of Rationality and Cooperation: Prisoner's Dilemma and Newcomb's Problem (Richmond Campbell and Lanning Sowden, eds., 1985). As Nozick describes the current state of play, "Despite . . . technical elaborations — backtracking subjunctives, explicit incorporation of tickles and meta-tickles, the ratifiability of decisions, and so forth — and despite attempts to show that the problem is irremediably ill defined or incoherent, the controversy continues unabated. No resolution has been completely convincing." Robert Nozick, The Nature of Rationality 43 (1993). Displaying admirable humility, Nozick sensibly concludes that "the reasoning seems quite compelling on *all* sides" and that "[i]t would be unreasonable to place absolute confidence in any one particular line of reasoning for such cases or in any one particular principle of decision." Perhaps this is simply another way of saying that reasonable people have a choice about what to make of historical determinism.

breaks down in important, politically charged cases.[7] Apparently, then, it is no more than stark coincidence that in these cases, liberal judges regularly perceive our neutral principles as embodying liberal values while conservatives regularly perceive them as embodying conservative values.

This idea is so obviously silly as to make determinist objections seem ridiculous as well. The wonder is not that we should believe ourselves capable of escaping this make-believe world but that it should have had such a hold over us for so long. Why do the Justices cling so desperately to a patently false view of their own work?

There are two possibilities. The cynical view is that the appeal to a disembodied constitutional settlement, coupled with the quasi-religious imagery that surrounds the Supreme Court, is designed to fool people into accepting outcomes they would not otherwise tolerate. Fortunately, this view seems implausible. As discussed above, the Court has not often tried to change political outcomes in significant ways, and when it has tried, it has usually been unsuccessful. Certainly, there is little evidence that the modern Supreme Court has a secret agenda to remake the country in its own image.

The more likely explanation is that the Justices have managed to convince themselves that their power is legitimate only to the extent that it stems from our constitutional settlement. On some level, the Justices understand that we have not one but several competing settlements. Moreover, anyone who has spent even a little time working with or thinking about constitutional law's paired opposites knows that they produce nothing but anomalies and contradictions. As a psychological matter, it must be exceedingly difficult for the Justices to suppress this knowledge as they do their daily work. Yet suppress it they must because, they believe, our constitutional settlement binds the community together and gives legitimacy to the exercise of governmental power.[8] It logically follows that any departure from the settlement risks nothing short of a complete unraveling. Hence, the regular predictions of catastrophic collapse whenever the supposed settlement is breached.[9]

It ought to give the Justices pause that this collapse, like other oft-predicted apocalyptic events, is perpetually just around the corner. In fact, the collapse never comes because the Court has made a simple mistake about its likely cause. Consider in this regard Bush v. Gore. In his dissenting opinion, Justice John Paul Stevens attacked the majority for lending "credence to the most cynical appraisal of the work of judges throughout the land" and warned, "It is confidence in the men and women who administer the judicial system that is the true backbone of the rule of law." Similarly, Justice Stephen Breyer complained of a the majority's "self-inflicted wound" that might "harm not just the Court, but the Nation."[10] Apparently, the majority Justices had similar con-

cerns. In a series of extraordinary extrajudicial statements, they tried to reas-
sure the country that their decision was neutral and apolitical. It is hard to
believe that many people were fooled by these efforts, yet despite their failure,
life seems to have gone on pretty much as before. In the wake of the Court's
decision, there were no tanks in the streets, no raging mobs at the barricades.
Public opinion polls suggested that, even though most people (correctly, I
believe) understood that Bush v. Gore was political, the Court paid no price
for the decision and may have even benefited from it.

This mistake about the source of the Court's legitimacy has, in turn, caused
it to be extremely defensive whenever it describes its role. The plurality opinion in Planned Parenthood of Southeastern Pennsylvania v. Casey,[11] reaffirm-
ing Roe v. Wade,[12] provides an example. The plurality begins sonorously and
portentously with the assertion, "Liberty finds no refuge in a jurisprudence of
doubt."[13] This rhetoric would be bad enough if it were merely pompous. But it
is also profoundly wrongheaded. For reasons we have already explored, the
continuity of a just political community depends on the doubt that an unsettled constitution engenders.

The *Casey* plurality goes on to worry darkly about how the overruling of
Roe "would seriously weaken [its] capacity to exercise the judicial power and
to function as the Supreme Court of a Nation dedicated to the rule of law."[14]
Once in a great while, the plurality asserts, "the Court decides a case in such a
way as to resolve [an] intensely divisive controversy."[15] When this happens, it
has "call[ed] the contending sides of a national controversy to end their national division by accepting a common mandate rooted in the Constitution."[16]
Overruling such a decision "would subvert the Court's legitimacy beyond any
serious question."[17]

All this rests on no more than a mistake, albeit a serious one: the same
mistake that may have motivated the Court's ill-considered intervention into
the 2000 presidential election. "When contending parties invoke the process
of the courts," the *Bush* majority observed, "it becomes our unsought responsibility to resolve the federal and constitutional issues the judicial system has
been forced to confront."[18] But no one "forced" the Supreme Court to grant
certiorari in *Bush,* and it was not the Court's responsibility to "resolve" the
issues posed by the election. Apparently the Justices were motivated by a deep
fear that things would spin out of control if the Court did not save the country
from chaos by settling the issues that divide us. But if the U.S. Supreme Court
had not intervened, the 2000 election would have been settled by the Florida
legislature or, more plausibly, by the U.S. Congress. The process might have
been untidy, difficult, and controversial, but there is no doubt that in the end,
ordinary political processes would have produced some outcome. The appro-

priate role for the Supreme Court is not to "end . . . national division," as the *Casey* Court claimed, or to call together "contending sides of a national controversy." Its proper function is to promote the open texture of fundamental law, and I contend that its legitimacy rests on its embrace of, rather than its resistance to, constitutional change. In short, the obsessive fear of delegitimation that seemingly drives the plurality's opinion is simply a bugaboo. It would seem to follow that all we need to do is make the Justices understand their error, and they will be only too ready to shed the terrible burden of cognitive dissonance, not to mention the perpetual dread of imminent disintegration, that they have borne heroically for so long.

Unfortunately, however, things are a bit more complicated. It is a mistake to be paralyzed by historical determinism but it is also a mistake to ignore real barriers to reform. There is no reason to think that we are stuck with the choices that Justices have made in the past, but it is also foolish to suppose that misunderstanding and failure of nerve are the only obstacles to progress. In fact, even if the Justices could be disabused of their misunderstanding and had the courage to act on their newfound wisdom, it is not obvious how they could act so as to achieve the ends of an unsettled constitution.

The main obstacle to unsettlement is the double effect produced by any effort to implement it. We might call this the paradox of legitimation: anything that constitutional law does to unsettle current arrangements also subtly entrenches them. This paradox poses a problem on three different levels.

First-Level Legitimation: Case Unsettlement

On the simplest level, imagine a judicial decision designed to serve the cause of unsettlement. For the moment, we can put to one side questions about what such a decision would look like. Whatever its substantive content, the decision must end in a judicial decree that orders someone to do something. Such scholars as Barry Friedman[19] and Robert Burt[20] have argued that judicially enforced constitutional law gains its legitimacy from its dialogic quality. Judicial decisions (at least of the right sort) do not finally settle disputes; instead, they are invitations to a continuing conversation. For example, Burt distinguishes between the *Dred Scott* decision,[21] which, he thinks, unwisely tried to impose a judicial settlement on the slavery problem, and the *Brown* Court's "all deliberate speed" approach,[22] which was designed to entice the South into a further discussion of segregation.[23]

But even if this characterization is accurate in some broader sense,* it surely

---

*I shall argue below that even in this broader sense, there is a risk that judicial decrees will close down, rather than open up, discussion.

romanticizes the effect of individual judicial decisions. As Robert Cover eloquently reminded us, individual judicial decrees are not polite invitations to academic discussions. They invoke violence and the threat of violence to achieve their ends.[24] To be sure, decrees are not self-implementing. Because they command no troops, courts must, in effect, negotiate with those who do. In this sense, constitutional decisions leave things unsettled. Unfortunately, though, the very need to negotiate pushes courts toward authoritarian rhetoric. Their lack of power means that they must insist all the more firmly that others are obligated to listen.

A decree by its very nature, therefore, purports to settle the dispute that gives rise to it and demands obedience. The judges issuing the decree are likely to feel the need to justify the implicit violence it unleashes by demonstrating that they are not indulging mere personal preferences. Hence, the regular appeal to the impersonal force of law.[25] The decree is thus settling in a double sense: it creates a winner and a loser, and it suggests that the loser has lost because of some fundamental, community-constitutive principle that reflects more than simply the preference of the Court.

Even on this simplest level, the paradox of legitimation cannot be completely resolved, but there are ways of reducing its force. Perhaps we cannot change the fact that judicial decisions settle the results of individual cases, but we can change the authoritarian voice with which judges regularly speak. Ironically, judges might better command obedience and produce more community if they were more ready to acknowledge candidly that their decisions rested on contested, political premises. They need not pretend that their decisions are the product of a final, impersonal settlement independent of their own political convictions because such a settlement is impossible and because, in any event, the existence of such a settlement is not the source of their legitimacy. Instead, as I have argued in Chapter 3, judicial decisions are legitimate to the extent that judges themselves straddle the contradictions of liberal constitutionalism and embody its open texture in their work and daily lives. A judge who realizes this fact need not be defensive or dishonest about the idiosyncratic or political nature of her decisions. Because the paired opposites around which constitutional law is organized do not yield person-independent outcomes, judicial decisions must inevitably be personal statements. The aims of unsettlement are served so long as judges are candid in acknowledging this fact and do not pretend that people are obligated to obey because judicial decrees follow logically from a neutral settlement.

This point is buttressed if we remember that judges have no alternative to constitutional law and no alternative to violence. If judges do not settle disputes in one way, they will be settled in another. If cases are not resolved by remitting the question to individual, particularist choice (the private sphere), they will be resolved by remitting the question to collective, universalist choice (the public sphere). Either way, there will be people who dislike the outcome and who must be coerced if they resist it.

Thus, a judge who decides a case by deferring to the political branches has not avoided the necessity of settlement. For example, when the Court held in Bowers v. Hardwick[26] that states could prohibit homosexual sodomy, it was not being passive. Its holding amounted to a determination that this sexual conduct belonged in the public sphere, instead of the private, and that this sorting, like any other sorting, could be enforced by public violence.*

Two points follow from this observation: first, since there is no escape from settlement of at least the particular case before the court, judges need not waste their time trying to defend the fact that they are imposing a settlement. The inevitable requires no defense. Second, if there is hope for an unsettled constitution, it cannot be on the level of the individual case. Although judges can change the rhetoric of decision, they cannot change the fact that all such decisions settle the matter before the court. If there is to be unsettlement, it must come from the content of the decision, rather than its existence. The hope is that this content will produce systemic unsettlement even as the individual case before the court is resolved.

Second-Level Legitimation: Systemic Unsettlement

At this point, though, we arrive at the second level of legitimation. Is it possible for a decision's content to produce systemic unsettlement? Consider, for example, the Supreme Court's decision in West Virginia State Board of Education v. Barnette.[27] In the course of invalidating a state law requiring all children attending public schools to salute and pledge allegiance to the flag, Justice Jackson wrote that "if there is any fixed star in our constitutional

---

*It is true, of course, that *Bowers* left the states free to outlaw or permit homosexual sodomy as they chose. The decision therefore left the *status* of sodomy unsettled. But a decision affirming a right to homosexual sodomy would also have left its status unsettled. Obviously, such a decision would not obligate anyone to engage in this activity. Individuals would remain free to engage in the activity or not as they chose. The important point is that a decision either way settles the *method* by which the status of homosexual sodomy will be determined. The Court's decision means that instead of individuals deciding for themselves whether to engage in this practice, the issue is remitted to the political branches. If, as I argued in Chapter 3, our collective institutions should decide questions from a universalist perspective, it follows that *Bowers* slotted the sodomy question in the universalist category. If *Bowers* had come out the other way, the Court would have been slotting the question in the particularist category.

constellation, it is that no official, high or petty, can prescribe what shall be orthodox in politics, nationalism, religion, or other matters of opinion or force citizens to confess by word or act their faith therein."[28]

In the sense we have just explored, *Barnette* is contradictory. The decision itself "prescribe[s] what shall be orthodox" by prohibiting for the entire nation a practice some wished to follow. Yet it might be argued that this settlement is in the service of unsettlement. What is settled in this particular case furthers the cause of systemic unsettlement by outlawing a fixed, official orthodoxy in matters of opinion.

The problem is that the opinion once again produces a double effect, this time on the systemic, rather than individual case, level. The very act of permitting a safety valve for dissenters seems to suggest that they have no just cause for dissatisfaction with our overall settlement. Precisely because their narrow grievance is acknowledged, their broader disaffection seems unjustified. This second-level legitimation is pervasive and troubling. Another example is provided by the Court's occasional efforts to correct defects in political decision making by coming to the defense of "discrete and insular minorities."[29] As Richard Parker has powerfully argued, in the guise of unsettlement, this effort in fact provides potent support for an entrenched status quo.[30] The Court's implicit message is that the problems with American democracy are small and manageable. So long as occasional defects are corrected through the Court's intermittent intervention, political outcomes command our respect. Interstitial and occasional unsettlement produces systemic complacency.*

Perhaps, then, the solution is to remove the safety valve. Paradoxically, the effort to entrench a rigid settlement might be the best method for guaranteeing

---

*We do not want to lose sight of the fact that our ultimate objective is to achieve a certain form of systemic legitimation. Our aim, though, is to produce what might be called "Habermasian" rather than "Weberian" legitimation. *Compare* 1 Max Weber, Economy and Society: An Outline of Interpretive Sociology 31 (G. Roth and C. Wittich, eds., 1968) (associating legitimacy with actor's belief that social order can generate binding maxims) *with* Jürgen Habermas, Communication and the Evolution of Society 200 (1978) (arguing that legitimacy exists when there are *good arguments* for a political order's claim that it is right and just). *See* Alan Hyde, *The Concept of Legitimation in the Sociology of Law,* 1983 Wisc. L. Rev. 379, 399 n. 45 (endorsing Habermasian, but not Weberian concept of legitimacy). Recall that the argument for an unsettled constitution rests precisely on the claim that it provides a good motive for losers to adhere to the political community. But the unsettlement thesis holds that this form of legitimation occurs only so long as the boundaries and nature of the community remain unsettled. The worry about second-level legitimation is that it will foster a false belief that there is no need to question a particular conception of the political community because of the intermittent protection that courts provide for minority rights.

unsettlement. Consider, for example, the effect of the Supreme Court's decision in Pierce v. Society of Sisters.[31] In 1925 a unanimous Court held that the
due process clause prohibited states from barring private education. There is a
sense in which this decision, like *Barnette,* serves the ends of unsettlement.
Public schools are, and are intended to be, a mechanism for inculcating in
diverse groups the national culture that embodies our settlement. Private
schools provide a platform from which this dogma can be criticized and destabilized. Moreover, *Pierce* itself implicitly acknowledges the weakness of the
claim that public education's settlement is objective and neutral. A constitutional right to private education makes little sense unless there is some good
reason why some parents might find public education offensive or defective.

Still, the eighty-year history of *Pierce* suggests that its primary effect has
been to entrench, rather than to destabilize, a settlement. The existence of the
private school safety valve has played an important role in suppressing critics
of public education, who have objected to its secularizing, nationalizing, and
homogenizing mission. The best way to destabilize this settlement might be to
overrule *Pierce* and block the exit option. Without private education, people
who oppose public education would be compelled to stand and fight.[32] But for
reasons we have already explored, it is clear that no resolution of the ideological disputes racking public education can be truly neutral. With no exit option,
the public schools would become a permanent battleground with no prospect
of long-term settlement.

We have important historical examples of how the effort to entrench a
settlement can itself be destabilizing. The Court's ill-conceived effort to settle
the slavery issue in *Dred Scott*[33] galvanized the nascent Republican Party;[34]
Roe v. Wade created the pro-life movement;[35] Bowers v. Hardwick[36] has im-
measurably helped organizing efforts by gay rights advocates. It is clear, as
well, that advocates themselves understand how they can win by losing. For
example, in the 1980s, we were treated to the bizarre spectacle of pro-life and
pro-choice advocates gathered in separate camps on the steps of the Supreme
Court, each arguing to the assembled press that the Court's latest delphic
pronouncement spelled disastrous defeat for its position. Both sides understood that there is nothing like a disastrous defeat to bring a flood of new
money over the transom.

There is no doubt, then, that entrenchment has the potential to create unsettlement. We have already explored the problems with this strategy, however.
For as long as it is effective, rigid entrenchment is the antithesis of the unsettlement we seek. And when it collapses, it is likely to produce the sort of convulsive change that I discussed in Chapter 2. If our ultimate goal is to build a just
community, we hardly want a situation where each side, upon gaining power,

attempts to permanently cement its gains, thereby triggering a violent response from the other side. This is surely a recipe for permanent civil war, rather than community.

Consider, for example, what school board elections would look like in a world without *Pierce*. In a winner-take-all struggle of this sort, the fight would be brutal and the wounds long-lasting. True, the results of any election would be under permanent attack, but so long as those results remained in place, they would amount to the exclusion of the losers. And if the losers managed to reverse their defeat, the upshot would be no more than the substitution of one exclusionary regime for another. It is hard to imagine a state of affairs less conducive to community commitment.

Third-Level Legitimation: Pervasive Unsettlement

Our efforts at unsettlement seem to have reached a dead end. On the individual case level, judicial decisions inevitably purport to settle the dispute that gives rise to them. On the broader, systemic level, occasional and interstitial constitutional criticism of the status quo serves to entrench and legitimate it. This effect might be avoided by eliminating legitimating safety valves, but doing so is likely to produce a recurring pattern of stagnation followed by convulsive change — a pattern that is destructive of the community we seek.

There is yet another option we need to consider: pervasive unsettlement. Justices might seize upon their position astride the public-private divide to destabilize political outcomes in a fashion that was not merely occasional and interstitial but ongoing and generalized. Instead of substituting one entrenched winner for another, they might make every winner perpetually uncomfortable.

As we have already seen, the tools of constitutional law are readily adaptable to these ends. Since any outcome can be characterized as coerced or unequal, a court so inclined can make its own commands impossible to satisfy. As a result, any status quo is subject to ongoing criticism.

Yet even here the danger of legitimating double effect lurks. A regime of permanent criticism is difficult to maintain. Part of the problem is the simple but powerful psychological desire for closure. People who in good faith wish to obey constitutional commands want to know what to do, and courts have a natural desire to tell them. Moreover, the elusiveness of liberal constitutionalism can itself provide an excuse for inaction. Teachers who consistently expect the impossible from their pupils frequently find that their pupils stop trying. So, too, a constitution that *cannot* be satisfied is one that *need not* be satisfied, and a court that engages in endless carping from the sidelines may find itself irrelevant.

These effects might be mitigated if the Court could demonstrate real change as a result of its efforts. Unfortunately, however, producing actual change requires a transformation of the allusive and illusive tools of liberal constitutionalism into formal rules that can be implemented in the real world. As soon as this happens, constitutional law loses its uniquely destabilizing force.

Three famous examples from the Warren period illustrate the dilemma. Consider first Miranda v. Arizona.[37] In a series of cases decided over a thirty-year period between 1936 and 1966, the Supreme Court attempted to regulate police interrogation by deciding whether the suspect's free will had been overborne.[38] These cases were decided against a jurisprudential backdrop that made clear the problem with the freedom-coercion dichotomy. At the very moment the Court was developing the voluntariness doctrine in the confession context, it was dismantling the *Lochner* Court's systemization of the freedom and coercion categories. Legal realists and New Dealers understood that private choice was always made in a context formed by public decisions that always made one choice or another more attractive and that this effect could always be labeled "coercive" if one desired.[39]

Of course, the same criticisms that ultimately doomed *Lochner* ideology can be advanced against dividing confessions into categories of "free" and "coerced." Suspects never confess in a vacuum. Their decisions are embedded in a network of incentives that "cause" them to decide whether to talk or remain silent. Here, as elsewhere, the decision whether to characterize these incentives as coercive is political rather than legal or factual.

Given the ultimate incoherence of the free will–coercion test, it is hardly surprising that the Court never managed to give it any clear, substantive content. As Justice Felix Frankfurter, the test's great defender, conceded at the end of the thirty-year experiment with this approach, the Court had utterly failed to develop a "single litmus-paper test for constitutionally impermissible interrogation."[40]

But this failure served the purposes of unsettlement. For all its problems, a coercion approach is uniquely powerful. There may be no logical way to divide actions between the free and the coerced, but the distinction nonetheless has a powerful grip on us — a hold that no critical argument can loosen. Most people have intuitions about the importance of freedom in their own lives, and the imperviousness of these intuitions to critical attack demonstrates their strength. The upshot is that the free will requirement can neither be satisfied nor abandoned. Whenever a criminal confessed, the argument was always available that the confession had been coerced and that the penalty inflicted upon him was therefore unjustified.

This is not to say that the argument always prevailed. Unsettlement is not the same thing as shutting down the criminal justice system. The availability of the argument is enough to promote unsettlement, even when it is unsuccessful. So long as the argument is plausibly available, criminal penalties can never be fully legitimated. The argument serves as a brake on the self-righteousness that otherwise accompanies punishment. It serves, in other words, as a builder of community by reducing the prospects of fanaticism and violence directed against even the most vulnerable community members.

It might therefore come as a surprise that it was the liberal justices most dedicated to the protection of the vulnerable who ended up dismantling the voluntariness approach to confessions. Yet their motivations for doing so are obvious. The voluntariness approach could make people uncomfortable, but there were limits to the extent to which it could change behavior.[41] Police departments and courts are bureaucracies that respond to clear rules, rather than philosophical musings. Because the Court never succeeded in capturing the voluntariness requirement in a clear verbal formulation, neither the police nor lower federal courts had enough direction about how to handle challenged confessions. Moreover, voluntariness was fatally retrospective in orientation. A court engaged in a voluntariness inquiry was supposed to look at all the facts and circumstances of the particular confession. This highly individualized inquiry might do justice in a particular case, but it had little prospective relevance for future cases with subtly different facts.

Miranda can be seen as an effort to avoid the trap of irrelevant carping from the sidelines by substituting a hard fact for an illusive, metaphysical concept. Custodial interrogation, according to the *Miranda* court, by definition amounts to compulsion. Once this equation was accepted, it followed that statements flowing from the interrogation were subject to the Fifth Amendment privilege against compelled self-incrimination and could not be used at trial unless the compulsion was somehow dissipated. This could be done, Chief Justice Earl Warren maintained, only by administering the now-famous warnings and providing the opportunity for the presence of counsel during interrogation. A defendant who claimed the right to remain silent could not be further interrogated. Once warned, the defendant could relinquish his rights, but the state would have the burden of showing that the rights were relinquished knowingly and voluntarily. Under these conditions, a subsequent confession would no longer be considered compelled, and it could be introduced at trial without violating the Fifth Amendment.[42]

What *Miranda* amounts to, then, is the kind of "single litmus-paper test" to voluntariness that Justice Frankfurter thought impossible. The decision reflects a Faustian bargain. On the one hand, the Court achieved a real-world impact that avoided the risk of irrelevance. *Miranda* warnings could be, and were, printed on cards and carried by every police officer in the country. Courts reviewing confessions had clear directions that could be easily followed. In short, *Miranda* mattered in a way that a handful of reversed convictions based upon involuntary confessions never could.

On the other hand, the Court gave up on the possibility of pervasive unsettlement. The factors which made *Miranda* effective also made it legitimating. The Court's implicit message was that once *Miranda* warnings were given and the rights waived, the confession was by definition free.* Indeed, the Court has recently made the message explicit in United States v. Dickerson,[43] a decision written by Chief Justice William Rehnquist that strongly reaffirms *Miranda*.

It is no accident that conservatives like Rehnquist have come to favor the *Miranda* rule. As Rehnquist noted, "[E]xperience suggests that the totality-of-circumstances test [which *Miranda* superseded] is more difficult than *Miranda* for law enforcement officers to conform to."[44] To be sure, as a theoretical matter, the old voluntariness test remains available to suspects challenging their statements. But, the Chief Justice candidly acknowledged, "Cases in which a defendant can make a colorable argument that a self-incriminating statement was 'compelled' despite the fact that the law enforcement authorities adhered to the dictates of *Miranda* are rare."[45]

---

*A review of the case law through 1992 demonstrated that in the quarter-century following the *Miranda* decision the Supreme Court reversed only two convictions on voluntariness grounds, whereas there had been twenty-three reversals during the comparable period before *Miranda*. *See* Louis Michael Seidman, *Brown and Miranda,* 80 Cal. L. Rev. 673, 945–46 and n. 239. This change might be attributable, at least in part, to improvements in police behavior, but judicial oversight of that behavior has also changed. For example, in Colorado v. Connelly, 479 U.S. 157 (1986), the Court held that personal characteristics of a defendant, including severe mental illness, did not make his statement involuntary in the absence of coercive police activity.

Moreover, even in cases where the police resorted to various forms of coercive pressure, lower courts often admit the resulting statement after finding that under the "totality of the circumstances," the defendant's will was not overborne. These courts have routinely admitted confessions secured through threats of severe punishment, deceptive statements, and promises. They have also upheld the product of interrogations conducted with suspects who were mentally disabled or who were undergoing drug withdrawal or suffering from lack of food or sleep. For an egregious but not atypical example, see Purvis v. Dugger, 932 F.2d 1413 (11th Cir. 1991). As Chief Judge Richard Posner of the Seventh Circuit U.S. Court of Appeals has summarized the current state of the law, "The [voluntariness] formula is not taken seriously. . . . [V]ery few incriminating statements, custodial or otherwise, are held to be involuntary, though few are the product of a choice that interrogators left completely free." United States v. Rutledge, 900 F.2d 1127, 1129 (7th Cir. 1990).

The upshot is that the warning-and-waiver ritual has become a powerful symbol of subjugation and legitimation instead of a means to effectuate unsettlement. *Miranda* "has become embedded in routine police practice to the point where the warnings have become part of our national culture."[46] The elaborate *Miranda* ritual effectively puts to rest the doubts and uncertainties that once prevented us from treating convicted criminals as completely outside of the community.

The Warren Court's encounter with racial segregation provides a second, parallel example of the problems with a pervasive unsettlement strategy. There are important analogies between the pre-*Miranda* voluntariness regime and the pre-*Brown* separate-but-equal regime. Like the voluntariness requirement, the equality requirement could never quite be satisfied. The obstacle to settlement in voluntariness cases was liberalism's commitment to an individualized conception of freedom. In the case of equality, the obstacle was liberalism's commitment to an individualized conception of value.

The problem becomes apparent when one focuses on how a court was supposed to evaluate the equality of two separate facilities. Consider, for example, the NAACP's first Supreme Court victory in a school segregation case. In Missouri ex rel. Gaines v. Canada, the Court was faced with Missouri's desire to operate two state universities — the University of Missouri, open only to whites, and Lincoln University, the black institution. Although Lincoln, unlike the University of Missouri, had no law school, a state statute authorized the board of curators to arrange for black students to attend institutions in neighboring states and to pay reasonable tuition rates for such attendance. Gaines, an African American, was denied admission to the University of Missouri Law School and claimed that his right to equal protection had thereby been denied.[47]

Writing for seven Justices, Chief Justice Charles Evans Hughes agreed. It was "beside the point," in the Court's judgment, whether the out-of-state school provided as valuable a legal education as that provided by the University of Missouri. Nor was it significant that Gaines was the only black student ever to apply to the University of Missouri. "The basic consideration is not as to what sort of opportunities other States provide, or whether they are as good as those in Missouri, but as to what opportunities Missouri itself furnishes to white students and denies to negroes solely upon the ground of color."[48]

Taken alone, this observation hardly explains the result reached by the Court. Of course, the key issue was "what opportunities Missouri itself furnish[ed]." But the state could fairly respond that Missouri "itself" had furnished Gaines with the opportunity to attend law school — albeit in a neighboring state. This opportunity was insufficient to satisfy constitutional standards only if the opportunity to attend law school in another state was not equal to the opportunity to attend law school in Missouri.

In light of the Court's concession that equality in the objective value of out-of-state education was "beside the point," the constitutional violation must stem from the frustration of Gaines's subjective desire to attend the in-state school. Liberalism's individualistic premises meant that Gaines was entitled to an equal right to vindication of this personal desire even if it was shared by no other member of his race.

It is hard to see the stopping point for this sort of analysis. For example, from Gaines's individual perspective, it would not matter if Lincoln had an excellent medical school and the University of Missouri didn't. Nor would it matter if vast numbers of African Americans wished to attend the medical school and Gaines was the only member of his race interested in law school. As long as Gaines wanted to attend law school and Missouri's law school was open only to whites, the equality principle would be violated.

Furthermore, there is no magical reason why the analysis is limited to the division between different disciplines. Suppose, for example, that both Lincoln and the University of Missouri had law schools but that Lincoln Law School offered law review but not moot court, while Missouri offered moot court but not law review. If the Court wished to determine whether the two schools were equal for constitutional purposes, it would have to decide the value of moot court compared to the value of law review. But liberal individualism precludes such an inquiry. Instead, each individual must be allowed to determine for himself the value of these goods. It would seem to follow that if an individual African American student wished to participate in moot court and was uninterested in law review, this hypothetical system of segregated education would deny him equal protection.

The upshot was pervasive unsettlement. No matter what a jurisdiction did to equalize separate black and white facilities, there would always be some difference between them. Advocates for racial justice could seize on this difference to claim that the equality requirement had not been satisfied. At least in theory, this technique could have been utilized to require that massive resources be funneled into black institutions.*

And yet the advocates of racial justice were the ones who chose to forsake

---

*On the eve of *Brown,* South Carolina undertook a program to improve black schools in order to ward off desegregation. The program was pitiful, but it was a start. There might have been much more if the Court had ordered serious enforcement of separate but equal. *See* Richard Kluger, Simple Justice: The History of Brown v. Board of Education and Black America's Struggle for Equality 334–35, 752–53 (1977).

the possibilities of unsettlement. They did so by an equation that converted metaphysics into fact. Just as Miranda v. Arizona equated custody and interrogation with coercion, Brown v. Board of Education equated separation with inequality. The motivation for *Brown*, like the motivation for *Miranda*, is straightforward. The separate-but-equal requirement was no more administrable than the voluntariness requirement. Whatever was true in theory, the fact was that the Supreme Court was not about to make individualized equality judgments for thousands of schools and order massive reallocations of school resources.* The same emptiness of the equality requirement that gave it such destabilizing power also prevented its use as an effective means for forcing change. Faced with a hard choice between unsettlement and progress, the Court again chose progress.

Unsurprisingly, the result has been the same sort of legitimation that accompanied *Miranda*. The implicit message of *Miranda* was that once the warning-and-waiver procedure was satisfied, confessions were unproblematic. So, too, the implicit message of *Brown* was that once facilities were no longer legally separate, they were equal. For at least some, it followed that there was no longer reason to be concerned about the existence of a racially identifiable underclass. Since facilities had been equalized, blacks had no one to blame but themselves for their own subjugation.[49]

Consider, finally, the third member of the Warren Court trilogy. In Baker v. Carr[50] and Reynolds v. Sims,[51] the Court for the first time held that legislative apportionment schemes were subject to judicial oversight. Its technique should, by now, be familiar. The Court converted a complex and enigmatic philosophical concept—this time equality of political power—into a fixed, formal requirement: the one person–one vote test.

Writing almost two decades before *Reynolds,* Justice Frankfurter warned his colleagues to avoid the "political thicket" of redistricting.[52] If the Court had undertaken the task of measuring real political power, this criticism would have been on target. As many political scientists have demonstrated, there is no single, uncontroversial method for fairly aggregating political preferences, and any effort to define or implement majoritarian procedures is bound to produce anomalies and contradictions.[53] But as John Hart Ely has perceptively argued, the one person–one vote formulation was attractive pre-

---

*Indeed, on the eve of its great victory in *Brown,* the NAACP was desperate for funds to continue the struggle. See Richard Kluger, Simple Justice: The History of Brown v. Board of Education and Black America's Struggle for Equality 617 (1977). It is fanciful to suppose that it could have continued to wage an effective district-by-district equalization campaign.

cisely because its formalism avoided the thicket Frankfurter rightly feared.[54] The Court once again substituted a bright-line, administrable test for the messy and contradictory, perhaps even incoherent, goals the test was meant to implement.

We can see the trade-off this choice reflects by comparing the majority's position in *Reynolds* with the position Justice Potter Stewart advocated in his separate opinion. At least superficially, Stewart's approach seems more sophisticated. He was prepared to acknowledge that "no one theory [of representative government] has ever commanded unanimous assent"[55] and that any effort to capture representative fairness would have to take into account "topography, geography, demography, history, heterogeneity and concentration of population, variety of social and economic interests, and [the] operation and interrelation of [a state's] political institutions."[56] But the sophistication of Justice Stewart's approach inexorably leads to paralysis. Because courts could never get to the bottom of so complex a problem Stewart would have had the judiciary defer to political outcomes except in the most extreme cases.[57]

In contrast, by abstracting from the complexities of democratic theory, the majority was able to formulate a test that produced substantial change in the apportionment of legislatures throughout the country. One should not underestimate the impact this change produced.[58] Once again, though, the price the Court paid for this achievement came in the coin of legitimation.

To be sure, at the margin the Court has left open the theoretical possibility of challenging extreme denials of political equality even when the one person–one vote requirement is satisfied, just as it continues to hold open the theoretical possibility of challenging confessions on voluntariness grounds or racial inequalities in legally integrated schools. But for the most part, the one person–one vote requirement has become a safe harbor. The Court has funneled most of its energy into an obsessive preoccupation with precise mathematical equality while paying only intermittent attention to the problem of gerrymandering[59] and ignoring altogether the huge impact on the allocation of political power of wealth and education disparities, agenda control, disparities in intensity of preference, free-rider problems, and winner-take-all systems. Significantly, the one exception to this pattern has been for districting designed to equalize the political power of racial minorities.[60] Here, the Court has relied upon the *Brown* settlement for the proposition that racially conscious districting is constitutionally suspect. Thus, when the *Brown* and *Reynolds* settlements are taken together, they serve as a powerful force legitimating the existing distribution of both racial and political power.

What's Left Unsettled

In the face of these problems, what remains of the unsettlement thesis? The difficulties outlined above demonstrate why we can never implement a version of constitutional law that leaves everything permanently up for grabs. The legitimation paradox means that the effort to produce unsettlement to some degree entrenches social structures and hierarchies. There is therefore some truth to the claim that constitutional law is, by its nature, a conservative and legitimating force.

Still, it does not follow that these difficulties discredit the thesis. We have identified some conservative tendencies in constitutional law, but we have yet to consider how strong these tendencies are or how they might be mitigated. In any event, it is worth emphasizing again that we cannot do without constitutional law. It follows that our only alternative is to think about the double effect produced by constitutional decisions. How can we minimize the risk that these decisions will undermine a just basis for community?

We might begin by reviewing some reforms that are relatively unproblematic. First, judges could stop pretending that their decisions are the product of a disembodied, impersonal rule of law and that those who disagree with them are somehow outside the bounds of rationality. Judicial decisions need not be authoritarian to be authoritative. Judges detract from their own legitimacy when they pretend that liberal constitutionalism's paired opposites yield a single legitimate conclusion. On the contrary, judicial decisions merit respect to the extent that they reflect a good-faith struggle by actors who are themselves caught between contradictory forces and uncertain about their own conclusions.

Sometimes judges who feel or express such modesty end up deferring to the political branches.[61] But this is also a mistake. Judges need to come to grips with the fact that when confronted with disagreement, resolution by private individual decision making and by public collective processes are competing constitutional choices and that the idea of judicial restraint (not choosing) is therefore incoherent. In particular, unsettlement is not produced by automatic deference to collective political institutions, and certainly not by pretending that such deference is no decision at all. Instead, it is achieved by an ongoing, personal struggle between the competing but incompatible values of particularism and universalism. Such a struggle is best resolved by actors who see themselves as located within neither the public nor the private sphere but astride the boundary between them. Good judges must recognize the impossibility of principled choice between these two spheres even as they recognize that they must, inevitably, choose.

To be sure, even if judges did all this, the legitimation paradox would still pose a problem. But the problem should not be overstated. As Alan Hyde has shown, there is reason to doubt the extent to which law serves as a legitimating force. The widespread assumption that it does so ignores the studies showing that the public has little awareness of judicial decisions and that even when the public knows about them, these decisions have little effect on public attitudes toward law more generally.[62]

Moreover, even if law in general can sometimes legitimate, there is also reason to doubt that the reduction of liberalism's contradictory paired opposites into formal rules does so. Often, these contradictions will simply re-emerge to produce what might be called second-generation unsettlement. For example, after *Miranda,* at least some of the concern over the voluntariness of confessions was transmuted into concern over the voluntariness of *Miranda* waivers.[63] Similarly, for at least a time, unsettlement produced by the separate-but-equal formulation was replaced by unsettlement produced by a similarly vague concept — the unitary school system that *Brown* required.[64]

It remains true nonetheless that judges who wish to implement an unsettled constitution face a hard trade-off between progress and unsettlement. We should hardly be surprised by this dilemma. It is a commonplace that a cost of maintaining a diverse community is that no community member will be fully satisfied. For many political theorists, this observation has led to the conclusion that a constitutional settlement must embody compromise.[65] It is perhaps less obvious, but equally true, that *unsettlement* also requires compromise. Ironically, settlement is what is necessary to produce the full and uncompromising implementation of a substantive judicial program. In order to have real impact, doubts and anomalies must be put to rest and a "single litmus-paper test" substituted for endless mediation between paired opposites. A settlement like this can produce some social change — change that itself can be destabilizing in healthy ways. But it does so at the expense of the ambivalence, uncertainty, and unresolved contradiction that are the building blocks of just community.

Judges need to think carefully about this trade-off. They might focus, for example, on how much social change judicial reform actually produces, as compared to the value of the unsettlement being sacrificed. As already noted, recent scholarship suggests that the possibilities of judicial reform are, at best, limited. Holding everything else constant, perhaps judges are better at fostering contradiction than at mandating justice.

The need to make this trade-off, in turn, produces unsettlement at the meta-level: a kind of unsettlement about unsettlement. This effect is especially pronounced because, it turns out, the choice once again reproduces the conflict between particularism and universalism. Consider again the difference between the voluntariness regime on the one hand and the *Miranda* regime on the other. A voluntariness approach focuses on the individual facts and circumstances surrounding the interrogation of each particular suspect. The legal outcome is fine-tuned so as to do justice to each individual. It is, in short, particularistic.

In contrast, the *Miranda* approach is universalistic. *Miranda* clumps individuals into large groups. Personal differences are cast aside in favor of generalizations thought to serve the collective good. Instead of asking whether a particular individual has been coerced, a Court applying the *Miranda* rules acts so as to minimize coercion over the range of cases. Whereas voluntariness is retrospective, focusing on the legal consequences of past actions, *Miranda* is prospective, focusing on the most efficient procedures to prevent future misconduct.

Unsurprisingly, all the other paired opposites follow from the replication of the particularism-universalism conflict. Thus, a voluntariness approach associates coercion, nonfeasance, and the private sphere. On this view, the suspect is free so long as the government does not engage in coercive activity, thereby leaving the choice of whether to confess up to private individuals. The *Miranda* approach associates freedom, feasance, and the public sphere. On this view, the suspect is free only if a government agent acts by going through the warning-and-waiver ritual, thereby establishing a publicly required context for confessions. Even the local-national distinction reproduces itself. Because the voluntariness inquiry is individual, it must be made on the local level, by local fact finders. In contrast, *Miranda* was designed to limit local variation and assert national control over police practices throughout the country.

A moment's reflection makes clear that the same conflict plays out in the context of the *Brown* and *Reynolds* decisions. Although not all the paired opposites align themselves as neatly, there can be no doubt that *Brown* and *Reynolds* replaced a local, particularized regime with a national, universalized one.

The short of the matter, then, is that the unsettling possibilities of liberal constitutionalism are much more robust than they first appear. Indeed, they are virtually irrepressible. Even judicial entrenchment of a formal rule promotes unsettlement through a kind of reversal of our legitimacy paradox: the effort to impose a settlement reinvigorates the contradictory impulses between universalism and particularism that make settlement impossible.

To be sure, the legitimacy paradox means that we can never achieve a completely unsettled constitution. It follows from this failure that no political community will ever be universally inclusive and that there will always be some people on the outside for whom we can offer no just reason to obey. Indeed, if arguments from particularism have any force at all, then it must be that empathic connection is meaningful only if it is somewhere bounded. Yet it is also true that the boundaries will inevitably remain contested. The very effort to fix them triggers universalist worries that push toward expansion.

The upshot is that while unsettlement can, and should, be nurtured, it is not so fragile as to require constant, worried attention. So long as we keep our goals modest, the most serious risk is that misguided adherents of conventional settlement theories will affirmatively try to stamp it out. That risk is important but it is one that we can do something about. Liberal constitutionalism has already provided us with the tools to build a just community. Now we need only learn how to use them.

5

The Constitution of Political Community

The preceding chapters have been dominated by theory. But no theory is worthwhile unless it aids our understanding of the real world. This does not mean that theories must predict real-world behavior. Good theories can be normative as well as positive. Still, any worthwhile theory must provide us with tools for either understanding or criticizing observed behavior. Consequently, I shall now examine discrete areas of constitutional doctrine through the lens of unsettlement theory to demonstrate how this doctrine can be better defended and understood, criticized and reformed.

This chapter focuses on the ways in which constitutional doctrine determines the appropriate boundaries of political community. The Supreme Court's docket is filled with cases that require it to define these boundaries. Consider the following examples:

- A California law prohibited recently arrived residents from receiving welfare benefits that exceed those provided by the state they came from.[1]
- A Texas law eliminated funds to school districts for the education of the children of illegal immigrants.[2]
- Under pressure from the Justice Department, North Carolina created a bizarrely shaped congressional district so as to promote African American representation equal to its proportion of the state's population.[3]
- Without securing a warrant, federal officials participated in the search of the

Mexican home of a Mexican national who was detained in the United States.[4]

- An Oregon law imposed a surcharge on waste deposited within, but generated outside, its borders.[5]

- A Federal law prohibited the possession of a firearm at a place the individual knows, or has reasonable cause to believe, is a school zone.[6]

These cases raise a variety of disparate issues. Yet each of them requires a determination of the boundaries of political community. This task, in turn, necessitates analysis of two separate but closely related questions. First, we must address the question of power. Over what people, territory, or transactions does the jurisdiction of the community extend? Second, we must address the question of voice. Who is permitted to decide how the power should be used?

When we try to answer the first question, we can conceptualize communities in two different ways. Some communities are nested within one another. For example, one version of the American constitutional settlement imagines a series of concentric circles that define communities. The outermost circle separates the federal government from the rest of the world. Inner circles form boundaries between the states and the federal government and between smaller subdivisions and the states. When communities are nested, inner spheres may have a certain autonomy and outer spheres some restrictions, but the autonomy and restrictions are themselves a product of outer-sphere law.

Alternatively, we might imagine separate, autonomous communities. For example, the United States and Canada are usually thought of as separate communities, divided by a boundary that defines spheres of authority. When communities are autonomous, they may nonetheless adopt the law of another jurisdiction. For example, American conflict-of-laws principles may require the application of Canadian law to settle some disputes.[7] But when a community adopts foreign law, its decision to do so is mediated through its own law. The decision is discretionary, rather than required by the law of another community.*

---

*For this reason, the Supreme Court has held that in a diversity case, federal courts must not only apply state substantive law but also state conflict rules that determine the content of state substantive law. *See* Klaxon Co. v. Stentor Electric Mfg. Co., 313 U.S. 487 (1941). The states are sovereign with respect to one another. In contrast, they are nested with respect to federal authority. Diversity courts must therefore apply federal conflict principles to the extent that the Constitution, or law appropriately made under the Constitution, so requires. *See* id., at 496–97 (*"Subject only to review by this Court on any federal question that may arise,* Delaware is free to determine whether a given matter is to be governed by the law of the forum or some other law") (emphasis added).

How do we know whether a community is nested or autonomous? We might suppose that constitutional law provides the answer. The U.S. Constitution establishes the federal and state governments as nested communities. Article I contains a fairly detailed specification of the powers of Congress. Articles II and III contain more general statements of the powers of the other two branches of the federal government. The supremacy clause[8] makes clear that laws made pursuant to these powers preempt inconsistent state law. To be sure, the Tenth Amendment protects inner-sphere law-making, but the protection itself derives from outer-sphere law.

In contrast, the Constitution also seems to establish the autonomous status of the United States vis à vis other communities. True, Article VI provides that "all Treaties made, or which shall be made, under the Authority of the United States shall be the supreme Law of the Land," and Article I grants to Congress the power to "define and punish . . . Offences against the Law of Nations." But these references only emphasize the fact that international law is applicable because domestic law — the Constitution, or statutes enacted by Congress — makes it so.

We have already seen the difficulty with an approach that looks to constitutions to establish the nature of community, however. As outlined in Chapter 1, we have not just one but many potential constitutional settlements, with no metalanguage we can agree on to mediate between them. Part of the difficulty is created by temporal conflict. As we saw in Chapter 2, any argument for respecting the particular textual settlement agreed upon at the founding requires a conception of community that extends over time. Yet the best argument for such a community rests not on settlement but on the sort of unsettlement that gives losers an ongoing reason to affiliate with the group.

Even if we put aside the temporal problem, there is a further difficulty produced by contemporaneous conflict. When we think about constitutional law in terms of nested (outer- and inner-sphere) and autonomous (on the same plane) communities, this aspect of the problem comes to the fore. Suppose, for example, that we somehow managed to explain why the past should bind the future and why, therefore, constitutions extend over time. We would still need to figure out *which* constitution governs conflicts about whether communities are nested or autonomous.

Two decisions by Chief Justice John Marshall rendered early in our history illustrate the problem. In Johnson v. McIntosh,[9] Marshall argued for an autonomous theory. At issue was a dispute between the plaintiffs, whose claim to a piece of land derived from a conveyance by the Piankeshaw Indians, and the defendant, whose claim derived from a grant from the U.S. government. Marshall seemed to concede, at least *arguendo*, that outer-sphere law would favor the plaintiffs if the United States were nested in a larger world community. It might well be true, he suggested, that the Piankeshaw Nation deserved to prevail under "principles of abstract justice, which the Creator of all things has impressed on the mind of his creature man, and which are admitted to regulate, in a great degree, the rights of civilized nations, whose perfect independence is acknowledged."[10] Nonetheless, Marshall felt duty bound to obey inner-sphere law. This obligation arose because the American political community was autonomous, rather than nested. It followed that judges were obligated to follow "those principles . . . which [their] own government has adopted in the particular case." Marshall maintained that "[c]onquest gives a title which the Courts of the conqueror cannot deny, whatever the private and speculative opinions of individuals may be, respecting the original justice of the claim which has been successfully asserted. . . . Courts of this country [have no right] to question the validity of this title, or to sustain one which is incompatible with it."[11]

Compare *Johnson* to Marshall's much more famous opinion in McCulloch v. Maryland,[12] upholding the constitutionality of the National Bank and invalidating a state tax levied against it. *McCulloch*, like *Johnson*, ends up giving primacy to federal law. Unlike *Johnson*, however, it contains a powerful defense of a theory of nested communities. On the one hand, federal legislation establishing the bank took precedence over conflicting state law because

> the government of the Union, though limited in its powers, is supreme within its sphere of action. This would seem to result, necessarily, from its nature. It is the government of all; its powers are delegated by all; it represents all, and acts for all. Though any one state may be willing to control its operations, no state is willing to allow others to control them. The nation, on those subjects on which it can act, must necessarily bind its component parts.[13]

On the other hand, state law adversely affecting the federal bank stood on a different footing from federal law adversely affecting state institutions.

> The people of all the states, and the states themselves, are represented in congress, and, by their representatives, exercise . . . power. When they tax the chartered institutions of the states, they tax their constituents. . . . But when a state taxes the operations of the government of the United States, it acts upon institutions created, not by their own constituents, but by people over whom they claim no control. It acts upon the measures of a government created by others as well as themselves, for the benefit of others in common with themselves. The difference is that which always exists, and always must exist, between the action of a whole on the part, and the action of the part on a whole.[14]

Taken together, *Johnson* and *McCulloch* neatly pose the dilemma of choosing between theories of nested and autonomous community. When communities are autonomous, the local sphere claims the allegiance of those within it because, as Marshall asserts, they are obligated to obey the principles of their own government. When communities are nested, people within the inner sphere are also within the outer sphere. Outer-sphere law therefore takes precedence because, as Marshall also asserts, it is "action of a whole on the part" rather than "action of the part on a whole." How do we decide which way to conceptualize the relation?

The difficulty comes into focus if we examine instances where the autonomous status of the United States and the nested status of individual states has been challenged. Consider first Filartiga v. Pena-Irala,[15] where the U.S. Court of Appeals for the Second Circuit upheld federal jurisdiction to entertain a suit between Paraguayan nationals concerning acts of torture committed in Paraguay. In the court's view, the case "arose under" federal law as required by Article III because customary international law was a part of federal law and, therefore, binding on federal courts. Scholars like Curtis Bradley and Jack Goldsmith have made powerful arguments against *Filartiga*.[16] In some ways, though, both Bradley and Goldsmith on the one hand and the *Filartiga* Court on the other begin by assuming away the hard question. Both start their analysis with the premise that the domestic status of international law is itself a question for domestic law. They disagree only as to the content of this domestic law. Some international law scholars have labeled this position "dualist" because it treats international and domestic law as separate, autonomous systems.[17]

Dualism is so deeply ingrained in American legal thought that it may seem bootless to question it.[18] It would be wrong, though, to dismiss monism out of hand. Monists ask why we should view local law as autonomous, rather than nested within international law. After all, they argue, the purpose of international law is to govern decisions made by nation states.* How can it serve that

---

*See Louis Henkin, International Law: Politics and Values 64 (1995). There may be less at stake here than first meets the eye. As *Filartiga* illustrates, dualists do not necessarily deny that domestic courts have an obligation to enforce international law. Their claim is merely that the enforcement is mediated through a domestic requirement. Monists claim that international law is binding even in the absence of such a requirement, but not all monists think that domestic law must therefore give way to international law. For example, Hans Kelsen, a leading monist, nonetheless argued that domestic law that conflicted with international law was valid under international law. See Hans Kelsen, Principles of International Law (1952). Moreover, a positivist might question what it would mean for international law to have primacy in the absence of a means of enforce-

purpose if it does not trump nation state decisions? These arguments are not merely theoretical. At least in Europe, transnational legal bodies are on the ascendancy; American intervention in Yugoslavia was based on the primacy of international norms even with regard to intranational disputes.*

The important point for our purposes, though, is not whether monists or dualists are correct. Rather, the problem for settlement theories is that the correctness of either position cannot be established by examination of a domestic constitution. For example, Bradley and Goldsmith point out that some other constitutions, unlike the U.S. Constitution, provide by their own terms for the supremacy of international law.[19] Article 25 of the German constitution states that rules of international law "shall be an integral part of federal law" and that "[t]hey shall override laws and directly establish rights and obligations for the inhabitants of the federal territory."[20] But this provision does not establish monism. On the contrary, it merely incorporates international law into domestic law, just as the *Filartiga* court did. The German constitution does not, and cannot logically, displace domestic law. The German constitution is itself domestic law and for it to establish the primacy of international law it would have to displace itself. It would seem to follow that no domestic constitution can ever establish its own subservience.

Nor can a domestic constitution establish its own supremacy. Consider, for example, the dispute over "interposition" — a view most closely associated with John C. Calhoun in the nineteenth century[21] and revived by southern politicians in the mid-twentieth century.[22] Calhoun in effect argued for a dualist position with regard to state and federal law. The states, he claimed, had a right to "interpose" themselves between "oppressive" federal law and the people. Opponents of interposition responded that a declaration of state equality counted for nothing because states were "in fact" nested within the American political community.[23] If they were "in fact" nested, it followed that the announcement of state law primacy, even in a state constitution, must yield to a contrary assertion by the broader community of which the states are a part. Proponents of state sovereignty responded by claiming that states were

---

ment. I am indebted to my colleague Carlos Vazquez for helping me to understand these points.

*Saying that American intervention is premised on the primacy of international law is not the same thing as saying that American interpretation of international law is correct. Opponents of American intervention argue that international law prohibits intervention in a domestic dispute, especially when the use of force is not authorized by the United Nations.

not "in fact" nested. If they were right, then the federal assertion of supremacy must yield.

The intractability of the problem becomes even clearer when we think about the second aspect of the boundary difficulty — the question of voice. Perhaps the people themselves should decide on the status of their own communities. But which people?

Suppose that a majority of people living in Northern Ireland wish to remain nested within the United Kingdom. Does a constitutional settlement based upon majority rule require this outcome? Only if the relevant community is Northern Ireland, which is, of course, the very issue to be settled. Irish nationalists might claim that we have bounded the community in the wrong way because Northern Ireland is nested within the Republic of Ireland. Perhaps, then, the right question to ask is whether a majority of people living in the Republic of Ireland and the six northern counties favor unification. Unionists, in turn, might respond that we need to broaden the community still further. What if a majority of people living in the six northern counties, the rest of the United Kingdom, and the Republic of Ireland favor the status quo? And of course a starry-eyed advocate of world government might contend that even this boundary is insufficiently inclusive. Why shouldn't citizens of the world determine the outcome?*

Finding a solution to these problems is crucial to settlement theories. As our example demonstrates, even when people agree on a procedural settlement, we cannot know the result it requires unless we know the relevant unit whose

---

*This problem is a subset of a still more pervasive difficulty — that of defining the units of aggregation around which virtually all law is organized. Consider, for example, the Fourth Amendment requirement that warrants be issued only upon probable cause. Suppose that a reliable eyewitness sees someone place drugs in one of a bank of fifty lockers in an airport but has no idea which of the fifty lockers is the right one. Should a magistrate issue a warrant? If the appropriate unit of aggregation is the entire bank, then there is probable cause to believe that the drugs are located somewhere within it and the magistrate should allow a search of the bank which, of course, entails a search of each of the lockers within it. On the other hand, if the unit of aggregation is each individual locker, then there is no probable cause with respect to any individual locker and no search of any part of the bank should be permitted. Taken to the limit, this reasoning can allow or disallow virtually any search: There is cocaine somewhere in Washington, D.C., so if the entire city is conceptualized as the object of the search, probable cause exists to search the entire city. On the other hand, if each movement of a police officer's eyeballs is conceptualized as a separate search, then probable cause is lacking to search any part of any location even if the police are certain that drugs are located somewhere within that location.

disputes have been settled.* Yet settlement theories seem to lack the resources to answer this question. In our hypothetical, we cannot take a vote on the boundaries of the community unless we first know what those boundaries are — the very question to be decided by the vote. The nature of the settlement depends on which unit of aggregation we utilize, but we can only determine the unit of aggregation by reference to the settlement.

It seems to follow that the status of and membership in various communities cannot be settled by constitutional law. How should they be determined? Legal positivists claim that this status amounts to no more than a social fact. A crude version of Austinian positivism might ask whether one entity or another has the raw power to back up its commands with force.[24] On this view, it was the victory of the Union army in the Civil War, rather than abstract argument, that established that the states were nested within the United States. The absence of an effective international army means that the United States and the world community are autonomous. In contrast, the version of positivism associated with the work of Hans Kelsen and H. L. A. Hart would inquire into the content of the rule of recognition — the norm by which people decide what counts as legal norms. As a matter of social fact, Americans today seem to treat the states as nested within the United States, and the United States as autonomous from the rest of the world.[25]

This is not the place for a full-blown discussion of the strengths and weaknesses of legal positivism. For present purposes, it is sufficient to say that, whatever their merits, positivist approaches do not respond to the core problem we are addressing. Our concern is not with how an outside observer would characterize our current practices but with what practices we ought to choose.[26] For example, if there is to be a plebiscite on Irish unification, someone must decide who will be allowed to vote. It is hard to see how positivist theories help answer that question. Rather, we must develop a normative theory. Our aim should be to select a version of constitutional law that provides good reasons for individuals to affiliate themselves with a community that has just claims over them. Facts on the ground are always relevant to that choice, but they can never dictate it. Insiders must always decide how to respond to the facts.

If neither facts nor law can answer the power and voice questions, how should they be answered? My strategy in the sections that follow is to focus on a functional approach. Just as we asked in Chapter 1 what kind of constitu-

---

*Our example shows that this is so even when putatively different communities agree on the decision mechanism. The problem becomes still more acute when the different communities have competing procedural settlements.

tional law best accomplishes its aims, we can now ask what size and type of communities best serve the purposes for which communities are established in the first place.

Settling Political Boundaries

A functional approach might begin by combining the two dilemmas we have so far discussed. On this view, communities function best if power and voice are aligned with each other. The first step is to determine who is affected by a legal decision. If a group is affected, it should be deemed part of the political community with regard to that decision. Conversely, if the group is excluded from the political community, then we should take measures to prevent it from being affected.

An approach such as this appeals to fundamental intuitions about fairness, but it also has functional virtues that are clarified by thinking about the economic concept of "externalities." To maximize overall welfare, people must be made to bear their own costs and allowed to capture their own gains. If these conditions are not met, they will choose activities or activity levels that benefit them even though these result in an overall welfare loss produced by costs exported to outsiders or forgo activities that create an overall welfare gain produced by benefits captured by outsiders. It would seem to follow that voice and power should be aligned. People who bear the costs and realize the benefits of a decision should be allowed to participate in making it to ensure that all the costs and benefits will be taken into account.[27] Perhaps, then, citizens of both the Republic of Ireland and the United Kingdom should vote on Irish reunification, but citizens of Bangladesh should not.

This intuition helps explain a great deal of our law defining political communities. For example, some Supreme Court decisions concerning voting rights suggest that individuals have a right to vote on an issue if, but only if, decisions by the governmental unit will affect their lives.[28] Similarly, due process and standing rules require that an individual be allowed to invoke a community's judicial power if, but only if, she can demonstrate "injury in fact."[29] Conversely, equal-protection doctrine treating with "suspicion" laws directed against "discrete and insular minorities" is designed to regulate the impact of law on people who are excluded from the process of making it.[30] Jurisdictional limits on the extraterritorial effect of state laws are designed to accomplish a similar objective.[31]

Standing alone, however, a settlement based upon the avoidance of externalities will not solve our problems. There are three difficulties. First, nothing we have said so far determines whether we should avoid externalities by regulating power or voice. We can bring the two into alignment either by expand-ing the scope of community franchise or by restricting the reach of community law. Large consequences turn on the choice we make. The first option pushes us toward very large communities that will inevitably leave individual citizens removed from sources of power and that must attempt to combine diverse and perhaps incompatible ethnic, national, and religious groups. The second pushes us toward small, fragmented entities with little power to deal with problems that transcend community borders.

A second problem is that current law has in fact adopted neither solution and is unlikely to do so any time in the foreseeable future. Political entities regularly take actions affecting citizens of other entities without giving them a chance to participate in the decision.[32] No voters in Mexico participated in an election determining American immigration policy. Citizens of Ohio did not vote on whether Maryland would build a new, multimillion-dollar sports complex, which would lure their beloved Browns away from Cleveland.*

The second problem is aggravated by a third: in order to make our solution workable, we would need an uncontroversial standard for "externality." Sup-pose, for example, that some citizens of Bangladesh are really unhappy be-cause Ireland is not united? What if Cleveland Browns fans in Los Angeles oppose the move to Maryland?[33]

A simple hypothetical both illustrates this third difficulty and points the way toward a possible solution for all three of our problems.[34] Imagine a railroad car occupied by a group of passengers who disagree about whether smoking should be permitted. If we assume a constitutional settlement that requires a voting procedure, what is the appropriate unit of aggregation? An analysis based on avoiding externalities would conclude that the franchise should be limited to people who have a stake in the decision. We can see immediately that there will be difficulties in determining who these people are. On the narrowest view, they might be only the people riding in the car. Unfortunately, however, the effects of the decision cannot be so narrowly confined. On the one hand, if smoking is permitted the decision could affect close relatives or friends of people within the car as well as those who might bear some of the

---

*One might respond that Ohio citizens did vote for representatives in the U.S. Con-gress, which could have passed legislation regulating the movement of sports teams. *See,* *e.g.,* Professional Sports Team Community Protection Act, S. 287, 99th Cong. (1985) (proposed legislation that would have regulated movement of professional teams). We might say, in other words, that the externalities problem argues in favor of large, rather than small communities. Still, requiring Ohio citizens to resort to a federal remedy places the considerable burden of inertia on them in a way that a vote in Maryland elections would not.

cost of medical bills for illnesses caused by smoking. On the other hand, if smoking is banned in one car it might increase the incidence of smoking in other cars.

We can put these difficulties aside and, perhaps arbitrarily, cut off the lines of causation at some point. We might say, therefore, that people in the adjoining car — or, if you will, in another train, or in another train in another country, or in another train in another country in another century — should have no say in the decision. To be sure, these people may have *views* about the appropriate outcome, but they have no *stake* in it and therefore should not be allowed to participate.

Even this arbitrary line-drawing does not resolve the problem, however. We can begin to see the difficulties when we examine the types of people within the relevant car who will be allowed to participate. One group of individuals wishes to smoke. It will seem to members of this group that they are adversely affected by a "no smoking" rule.* A second group does not want to breathe secondhand smoke and will therefore be adversely affected if the first group gets its way. The problem arises because there may also a third group of passengers in the car who neither wish to smoke nor care whether they breathe secondhand smoke. Although these people have no personal stake in the decision, they may nonetheless have opinions about it. They may believe in some abstract sense that it is right or wrong for people to smoke. Since these people are also in the car, surely they should be enfranchised. It is, after all, "their" car. The problem is that these people seem identical in relevant respects to people in the adjoining car, who also have abstract opinions about the issue but who are not permitted to vote. Why can't they claim that it is "their" train?†

We can make some headway in understanding our intuitions about this problem if we focus on the artificiality of the hypothetical. People who happen

---

*I put to one side the large problem of addictive and metapreferences. For a sophisticated discussion, see Cass R. Sunstein, *Legal Interference with Private Preference,* 53 U. Chi. L. Rev. 1129 (1986).

†In its crudest form, a Coasian approach suggests that we need not be concerned about the legal rule because whatever the rule, in the absence of transaction costs the parties will ultimately bargain to an efficient outcome. *See* Ronald Coase, *The Problem of Social Cost,* 3 J. L. & Econ. 1 (1960). But the plausibility of a Coasian solution depends upon a settlement of the externalities question raised in text. If we define externalities narrowly, then perhaps the parties could bargain to an efficient outcome. As externalities are defined more broadly, the obstacles to bargaining grow, and the assignment of the initial entitlement becomes correspondingly more significant. *See generally* A. Mitchell Polinsky, An Introduction to Law and Economics 11–13 (1983).

to be riding in one car or another do not constitute a "real" community. Precisely because they are not an organic group but only people who happen to be in a car at a given time, it is easy to destabilize our intuitions by comparing them to another serendipitous group—the people who happen to be in an adjoining car.

Advocates of settlement theories might claim that real communities are not like this. They are not random collections of people temporarily gathered together for a single decision but groups who are united over time by a common history, culture, ethnic identity, or set of beliefs. This sense of group identity, in turn, means that it is coherent for members of the group to think of decisions as affecting their community rather than someone else's. Put differently, we can begin to construct a functional settlement theory by reversing our assumptions about the primacy of individual and community preferences. Perhaps the constitution of community is a problem only because we have started with the assumption that communities need to be constituted. On this view, we should not begin with disembodied individuals who have preexisting and freestanding preferences who must somehow be formed into groups. Perhaps community identity comes first and helps to form the preferences.

How does this idea of organic community fit with a functional approach? Suppose that we started out with a world without political boundaries.[35] In such a world, all decisions would be made by a central administration governed by a single political settlement. There are obvious respects in which a world government of this sort would be inefficient. Larger governmental units inevitably incorporate more people who dissent from the constitutional settlement, thereby creating the legitimacy problems we have already discussed at length. Moreover, a centralized administration charged with ruling a vast territory and huge numbers of people would find it difficult to control activity within its jurisdiction or to respond to regional differences. From a functional perspective, it seems clear that there would be great efficiency gains if the large entity were broken into smaller units—units that could realize further gains by competing with one another for population and resources. Moreover, once we have made this decision, there are also obvious efficiency gains in making the units correspond to preexisting language, cultural, and ethnic divisions.

By itself, though, this argument does not explain why we should choose autonomous, rather than nested, communities. After all, a central administration could achieve the gains of localism by delegating authority to regional governments while still maintaining for itself ultimate authority to overrule decisions when the need for coordinated action is pressing. Why should we insist instead on community autonomy that may prevent this sort of compromise?

As Jules Coleman and Sarah Harding have argued,[36] autonomous communities are capable of creating another good—political membership. Individuals associated with autonomous communities have a sense of belonging and rootedness. Such communities are not simply random collections of people but organic entities constitutive of individual identity. As we have already seen, the development and recognition of such communities not only satisfy deep human needs but also provide the only hope for explaining how constitutional decisions can be binding over time.

There is an obvious connection between the recognition of such communities and the conflict between universalism and particularism. The demands of universalism suggest that every individual is entitled to membership in some community. On the other hand, once established, the membership itself is always particularistic. It must be constituted against the backdrop of non-members. What being a member means—what makes it constitutive—is having a special relationship with fellow members. By their very nature, special relationships cannot be universally shared. It follows that constitutive communities cannot be nested. Such communities must have the freedom to judge their own members against their own norms and cannot be held to account to standards promulgated by a larger group.

With this conception of organic community as background, we are now in a position to address the questions we have left hanging. If we want to bring power and voice into alignment, how should we decide whether to expand voice or restrict power? A functional approach argues for power and voice boundaries that correspond to preexisting cultural, ethnic, and affective groupings. This is so not just because shared language, mores, and beliefs make coordination more efficient, although that is surely an important good in itself. It is true, as well, because an important function of community is the creation of the good of membership. True membership is more than the simultaneous cohabitation of the same physical space by an adventitiously created group. True membership requires the linking together of an organic group.

Once we have accomplished this goal, we are also in a better position to make judgments about what should count as externalities. Within the boundaries of a community, every community member should be entitled to a voice. The concept of full membership implies an ability to influence community decisions. Membership also implies that members should be permitted—indeed encouraged—to use this entitlement to express what we might call bounded universalism. Certain strands of communitarian theory, most prominently associated with Michael Sandel, suggest that within the confines of the community, the sense of belonging that we wish to recognize and foster entails concern by each member for every other member.[37] Hence, in an organic community (as opposed to a railroad car) it is perfectly appropriate for me to have preferences that are not grounded in my personal, narrowly defined needs or desires. Indeed, it is the ability to transcend such needs and desires and identify with group welfare that transforms a random collection of individuals into a community.

In contrast, people in one community have no right to impose "mere" opinions on other communities. Within their boundaries, community members must be universalists, but community autonomy is grounded in particularism. It follows that community decisions should not be judged by standards developed outside the community. Thus, within communities, power and voice are aligned by treating all community members as having a stake in the character of the community, even if they have no personal stake in the outcome of a particular dispute. Between communities, power and voice are aligned by granting each community autonomy to determine its own character.

The Contradictions of Functional Community

The preceding discussion illustrates some of the attractions of a functional definition of community that takes the good of membership seriously. Does it follow that functionalism can settle community boundaries? No. Functionalism in fact leads to boundaries that are permanently contested rather than settled.

This becomes apparent when we renew a question left over from the previous section: Why is it is that our current practices so seldom align voice and power, as a functional settlement seems to require? The answer is that the conflict between particularism and universalism cannot be resolved by the strategy of bounded universalism. The creation of a universal right to particularistic communities only reintroduces the conflict, which, in turn, results in the inevitable failure to align voice and power.

Functionalism concedes two points to universalism. First, every person is entitled to membership in some community. Second, within each community, every community member is entitled to equal concern and respect. However, the communities themselves are particularistic: the right of membership has meaning only if equality of concern and respect does not extend to noncommunity members. If outsiders were treated in the same manner as insiders, communities would lose their particularistic character. True, people in one community have no right to implement their opinions about how members of another community should live. This limitation is built into the universal right to membership in an autonomous community. Suppose, though, that each community feels its autonomy threatened by the other? It would seem that precisely because everyone has the right to community autonomy, communities can take measures to protect themselves, even when these measures have an adverse effect on outsiders. Because there is no universalized duty of empathic connection across community boundaries, people who are harmed by extracommunity decisions designed to protect autonomy need not be given a voice in the community that harms them.

This argument provides a reason why the United States need not allow Mexicans to vote on American immigration policy. The problem is that if outsiders need not (should not) be given a voice in such decisions, it would seem to follow that the rightness of such decisions will not be judged by universal standards. Instead, these judgments will be community specific, with different communities reaching conflicting judgments based upon particularistic norms. And if this is so, the boundaries between communities will not be settled in the way settlement theory requires. A universal right to community autonomy simply cannot be reconciled with particularistic judgments about whether autonomy has been invaded. Instead, the two claims will be in permanent war with each other.

This problem arises even if we assume that it is possible and desirable to maintain purely particularistic communities. A second problem for functional settlements becomes apparent as soon as we challenge this assumption. Some of the difficulties are practical. Community is based not just on affective ties but on physical territory. Just as our railroad-car hypothetical is unrealistic because it treats a randomly constituted group of people as if they were a community, so too a model built upon organic community is unrealistic because it fails to account for the adventitious groupings of people within a given geographical territory.

When political boundaries are linked to geography, the cost of creating and maintaining organic community becomes very high. Most of the extraordinary violence and suffering that have marked the twentieth century have been triggered by various efforts to settle community boundaries by creating ethnic or cultural "purity" in a given geographical area. Moreover, even if this homogeneity could somehow be achieved, it can be maintained only if borders are effectively sealed. The problem is not simply intercommunity migration. Even if everyone stays put, modern trade and communications pose the risk of cultural migration. Communities are not static. They change over time as different influences are brought to bear on them. Maintaining community cohesion in the face of these influences is no easy matter.

This plasticity of communities poses a third challenge. The argument so far has assumed that political boundaries must be built around preexisting cultural differences. But political boundaries also have the capability of forming a common culture. People located in the same railroad car for long enough may begin to share common habits, beliefs, and mores.[38] In fact, there is a dialectical relation between politics and culture, with each influencing the other. Indeed, an optimistic view of the American experience suggests that it may be possible to form a common culture out of an agreement to tolerate different cultures.

The phenomenon of community change is closely linked to the difficulty of community definition. Our discussion above has unrealistically assumed that the defining characteristics of a particular community are uncontroversial. In fact, though, different community members may define the community in a variety of ways. Consider, for example, the centuries-long argument over who is a Jew. It is wrong to suppose that there is a natural, permanent, uncontested answer to this question. The nature of Jewishness has shifted over time, influenced both by internal struggle and external pressures. The paradox, to which we shall soon return, is that communities of this sort retain their identity even as they engage in unresolved struggle over what that identity is. Indeed, it is the struggle that produces the identity.

Finally, even if all these problems could be resolved, there is a still deeper difficulty. Although a sense of particularistic belonging and identity is fundamental, it is not the only thing most people want. This sense is under pressure from both directions. From one side, communitarianism's bounded universalism is challenged by liberalism's insistence on recognizing still more particularistic claims of individual rights. Membership in a group can satisfy deep human needs, but it can also be oppressive. Concern about the character of the group as a whole, which communitarian membership encourages, can threaten the freedom of individual group members who dissent from majority norms.

From the other side, particularistic membership is challenged by the irrepressible urge toward an unbounded universalism. Most people want to retain their group identity, but they also want to transcend it. When they are in the mood to transcend, they can sometimes see that they have been blinded by their membership in a particular culture, that more unites than divides people, and that all particularistic communities are nested within a world community. Viewed from this perspective, the random people in a railroad car are in some sense a true community, linked by a common humanity rather than by artificial distinctions of culture and ethnicity.

From this cosmopolitan, universalist perspective, political boundaries seem arbitrary and unjust. Perhaps a sense of membership is a good, but this good is unevenly distributed. Membership in some communities is more beneficial than membership in others, and, in any event, we must not lose sight of the fact that there are goods other than membership. The particularistic claims of membership can provide a rationalization for ignoring suffering and deprivation just across the border.

For these reasons, it is neither practical nor desirable to maintain purely particularistic communities. This conclusion should come as no surprise. It is no more than another application of the more general argument against constitutional settlements. As we have already seen, the attempt to fix boundaries inevitably excludes some who cannot be given a just explanation for their exclusion. It is the permanent and unresolved conflicts at our borders, rather than the final settling of those conflicts, that makes our communities just.

It does not follow that a purely universalist regime is a desirable alternative, however. I have argued that an unsettled constitution provides the best means for building a just community. But for the boundaries of a community to be unsettled, there must be a community in the first place, and there can be no real community in the absence of particularistic commitments. The special attachment that makes community must always be formed against the background of an otherness that is not special.

The upshot is that in order for communities to serve their function, they must rest on a permanent, unresolved contradiction. A just community requires an affective commitment to an entity whose nature remains contested and unclear. Such a community must be bounded in some way if it is to elicit the commitment and, indeed, if it is to be a community at all. But it is wrong to think that the boundaries must be settled. On the contrary, they must always be under attack if we are to provide a just reason why putative members should respect community decisions. Fortunately, this contradiction corresponds to contradictions in human psychology. Most of us are appalled by Clare Boothe Luce's indifference to suffering in sub-Saharan Africa but, if we are honest, most of us recognize similar impulses in ourselves. Ironically, the inability to work out these contradictions provides the best hope of stable and lasting political membership.

Drawing Contested Boundaries: Legislative Districting

What remains is to examine the extent to which American constitutional law promotes the unsettlement of community boundaries by navigating between particularism and universalism. Before we get down to cases, however, it is necessary to explain the limitations of what follows. I make no claim that unsettlement theory provides a "correct" answer to these disputes. Only constitutional settlements purport to do that. An unsettled constitution leaves us free to struggle with contradictory impulses toward particularism and universalism. Answers are correct only to the extent that they are made by people who themselves embody this struggle and do not purport to have a worked-out resolution of it. Consequently, my ambition for what follows is radically different from that in most case analysis. To be sure, unsettlement theory can help us develop insights about the cases. It provides a platform from which to both criticize and sympathize with certain results. But instead of trying to find solutions to contested cases, my hope is to make the cases seem harder than they might at first. No doubt, some readers will find this ambition perverse. What good is a theory that makes an already difficult task harder still? My response is grounded in the core claim of unsettlement theory: only by unset-tling constitutional law — by understanding why cases are hard and their reso-lution indeterminate — can we maintain the dynamic tension that makes just community possible.

One way the Supreme Court has attempted to build an unsettled constitu-tion is by adopting what we might call the "railroad-car" model of political community. Instead of settling boundaries through the recognition of organic communities, it has sometimes tried to unsettle them by insisting upon arbi-trary geographical lines.

Consider, for example, Shaw v. Reno.[39] Under pressure from the Justice Department, North Carolina created a bizarrely shaped congressional district that would have a majority of African American voters within its borders. The district comported with *Reynolds'* one person–one vote requirement, and there was no claim that the white vote had been diluted on a statewide basis. Nonetheless, the Court held that, at least under certain circumstances, race-conscious districting could violate the equal-protection clause. The majority reasoned that a

> reapportionment plan that includes in one district individuals who belong to the same race, but who are otherwise widely separated by geographical and political boundaries, and who may have little in common with one another but the color of their skin, bears an uncomfortable resemblance to political apartheid. It reinforces the perception that members of the same racial group — regardless of their age, education, economic status, or the community in which they live — think alike, share the same political interests, and will prefer the same candidates at the polls. We have rejected such perceptions elsewhere as impermissible racial stereotypes. . . . By perpetuating such notions, a racial gerrymander may exacerbate the very patterns of racial bloc voting that majority-minority districting is sometimes said to counteract.[40]

In spite of this passage, the majority conceded that race might legitimately play a role in reapportionment decisions. As the Court explained in a later case, the test is whether race is "the predominant factor motivating the legislature's decision to place a significant number of voters within or without a particular district. To make this showing, a plaintiff must prove that the legislature subordinated traditional race-neutral districting principles, including but not limited to compactness, contiguity, respect for political subdivisions or communities defined by actual shared interests, to racial considerations."[41]

Shaw and its progeny have been subjected to harsh criticism by the commentators,[42] and there is, indeed, much that is troublesome in the Court's approach. Yet it must also be said that the Court is on to an important insight, which can be elucidated through unsettlement theory. What the Court has done, in effect, is to reverse the relation between geography and ethnicity presupposed by functional settlements. The functional settlements described above attempt to draw political boundaries that coincide with ethnic or cultural divisions so as to promote the good of membership. In contrast, a railroad-car model might take advantage of the arbitrariness of geography to build ethnically diverse communities. Arbitrary lines promote overlapping identities that encourage conflict between universalist and particularist impulses. On the one hand, no political boundary can eliminate cultural identities. African Americans who live in New York or Mississippi or California have something in common and see themselves as a socially relevant group. Yet on the other hand, geographical proximity, coupled with political boundaries drawn without regard for organic community, can create alternative loyalties.[43]

I am told that until fairly recently, undergraduates at Yale selected their own residential college. Through this process of self-selection, the various colleges developed distinctive identities. Then the university switched to a random-assignment system. Yet despite this randomization, the colleges still seem to retain their identity over time. Although everyone knows that college membership is purely arbitrary, it nonetheless continues to make sense to generalize about the kind of people who are in one college or another. Despite their arbitrariness, the lines between colleges take on meaning and serve as an alternative locus for loyalty and group identity.[44]

So, too, arbitrary political lines might serve to compete with and unsettle cultural groupings. People thrown together into a political unit will of necessity have to negotiate with one another to find common ground. The hope is that this process will produce a constructed sense of membership that competes with, but does not displace, organic group identification. Moreover, the fact that the membership is constructed rather than organic makes it easier to contest and unsettle the empathic boundaries that membership creates.[45]

A natural response to this argument is that whether or not it is correct, it is certainly contestable, and it is not constitutionally compelled. After all, the Court concedes that neither bizarrely shaped districts nor racially motivated districting is independently unconstitutional. Since the Constitution says nothing about these matters, what justification do courts have for intervention?

This objection fails to come to grips with insights derived from unsettlement theory. As we have already seen, any attempt to resolve this issue by reference to a constitutional settlement leads us in a circle. Such a resolution requires a determination of how votes are to be aggregated, yet the method of aggregation is the very matter in dispute. The only way to get leverage on the problem is to think about what functions districting should serve. If one believes that railroad-car districting best promotes contested boundaries and multiple identities that, in turn, best build just community, then arbitrary requirements like compactness and contiguity are justified on functional grounds.

The difficulty with *Shaw* is not the Court's failure to tie the result to a constitutional settlement but its failure to take a consistent position on the relation between organic groups and districting. As we have already seen, the Court is suspicious of efforts to draw district lines that respect racial groupings. Yet the passages quoted above also seem to endorse the recognition of other kinds of organic communities. Indeed, it is the failure of North Carolina to recognize these other groupings based upon "actual shared interests" that the Court finds objectionable. Why, we must ask, do African Americans lack "actual shared interests?"[46]

More troubling still is the Court's treatment of the North Carolina district as if it were not racially diverse. An argument for railroad-car communities might be used to criticize racially homogeneous communities, but in fact, the district challenged in *Shaw* was integrated.[47] Why doesn't it count as a railroad-car community? The Court seems untroubled by districts that are entirely white as long as the district lines are not drawn in a race-conscious fashion. What seems to bother the Court is not racial homogeneity but the sort of race consciousness that produces black majorities.

When *Shaw* is viewed against the backdrop of the Court's encouragement of other sorts of organic communities, it suggests not unsettlement but a particularly ugly sort of settlement. The Court's message seems to be that Americans are entitled to government recognition when they form themselves into organic communities as long as those communities do not give expression to racial nationalism. Facially, this opposition may appear neutral as between minority and majority racial identification, but against the backdrop of a culture that is pervasively white, it is not neutral at all. Black culture is perceived as particularistic and threatening while white culture is taken for granted. What is effectively settled, then, is the primacy of a particular ethnic identification that is so freed from external challenge as to seem universal to those who embrace it.

A defender of *Shaw* might respond that once you permit race consciousness, you risk triggering a virulent form of particularism that will swamp universalism. This is true for two reasons. First, concentrating blacks into a few districts so as to give them proportional representation dilutes their strength in other districts. Without the need to negotiate with a substantial African American minority, representatives of these districts are more likely to identify solely with the interests of white voters.[48] In order to counteract polarizing racial block voting in the electorate, a system of race-based districting may reproduce it among representatives chosen by the electorate. Second, the more general worry is that Black Power inevitably begets White Power and that racial antagonism is so deep and so dangerous that this process must not be allowed to begin. Precisely because racial interests are so deeply shared, law can never acknowledge them.

At this point, though, the argument begins to contradict itself. Disapproval of race-based districting is itself an acknowledgment of racially shared interests. As Justice John Paul Stevens has argued, white voters in a predominantly African American district are injured by this districting only to the extent that the Court acknowledges the race-based interest that, it claims, cannot be acknowledged.[49] The assertion that we cannot notice these differences draws attention to them.

There is no easy way out of this dilemma, but the course the Court has taken is at least defensible as an imperfect compromise. Imagine two polar positions. First, suppose that a state abandoned geographical districting altogether in favor of race-based proportional representation. Under such a scheme, the jurisdiction would conduct separate elections for the "black," "white," "Hispanic," and "Asian" seats, with each group given a share of the total seats proportional to its percentage of the population. This solution settles political boundaries wholly by reference to particularistic community membership. For obvious reasons, which we have already explored, it is quite unattractive. Such a solution assumes that membership is fixed, static, and reducible to a small number of groups whose nature is uncontested. It also assumes that individuals are completely constituted by these groups and have no ability to transcend them. Few would find these assumptions palatable. Yet it is worth noting that a system of race-based districting is not far removed from this alternative, differing only because geographic constraints inevitably lead to the inadvertent capture of a few "outsiders" in an otherwise racially identified district.

Now imagine the alternative extreme: a purely universalist system. In such a system, community membership is completely constructed. District lines are drawn without regard to group membership, perhaps by a computer programed to produce "random" outcomes. This system, too, is a settlement, only now the settlement is based upon the universalist ideal of neutrality, as opposed to the particularist ideal of group identification.

A solution like this may have more intuitive appeal, but it too is unsatisfactory. When superimposed on a world where there actually is group identification, it is bound to produce inequities. For example, some groups may be more geographically concentrated than others. Why should geographically concentrated groups be able to elect their own representatives while dispersed groups are swallowed up in districts where they cannot form a majority? And even if the system somehow avoided these inequities and worked precisely as intended, it raises questions we have just addressed as to the legitimacy of government obstruction of group solidarity. In a recent lawsuit, Orthodox Jewish students argued against their random assignment to Yale residential colleges. They claimed that in a number of concrete ways, the construction of this artificial community interfered with their particularistic religious practices.[50] Their objections illustrate the broader point that insistence on bland, lowest-common-denominator politics bleaches out particularistic conflicts, promotes the primacy of majority culture, and perpetuates the myth that it is universalistic.

What the Court has done is to steer between these two extremes.* A critic might claim that it has done so by, in effect, endorsing group solidarity for other minority communities but denying this possibility to African Americans. As I have already indicated, there is some force to this criticism, but it is also somewhat unfair. In fact, the Court has never denied that race can be a factor in districting decisions. It has said only that race cannot be the *predominant* factor.[51] This formulation is bound to leave a doctrinal purist unhappy, but it does have the virtue of indeterminacy. It is hard enough under the best of circumstances to make factual judgments about the intent of collective institutions such as legislatures. It becomes well-nigh impossible when the judgment is complicated by deciding whether a particular intent is "predominant" as opposed to merely subordinate. And even this fudge word does not fully capture the indefiniteness of the inquiry the Justices have mandated. Although its language is subject to different interpretations, the Court has also suggested that a legislature can use race as a proxy for other types of interests. For

---

*This is not to say that the Court has chosen the only or the best way of avoiding the unattractive poles. For example, a system of cumulative voting and supermajority requirements within integrated districts might more effectively encourage voters to form shifting coalitions. *See* Lani Guinier, *Groups, Representation, and Race-Conscious Districting: A Case of the Emperor's Clothes,* 71 Tex. L. Rev. 1589, 1617 (1993).

example, it could rely on empirical data showing that most African Americans vote for Democratic candidates. Armed with this data, it could then draw district lines deliberately concentrating African American voters, as long as the purpose was to create a Democratic seat, rather than an African American seat.[52]

Distinctions such as these are so diaphanous that they are extremely unlikely to produce a settlement. On the contrary, what we are left with is a situation not unlike that prior to *Brown, Miranda,* and *Reynolds,* discussed in Chapter 4. Without the establishment of clearer lines, there is little risk that the Court will try to mandate a fixed rule to resolve all cases. Instead, the vagueness of the Court's approach leaves any settlement vulnerable to constitutional attack. The Court seems likely to respond to such attacks with interstitial and occasional intervention, as it did before *Brown, Miranda,* and *Reynolds.* Such intervention is designed to ward off the most destabilizing threats of racial polarization while still recognizing the reality of racial identification. In other words, viewed most charitably, the Court's approach promises an unstable and unsettled balance between particularism and universalism in an area where the explosive possibilities of settlement are especially worrisome. Perhaps this is the best we can expect.

Drawing Contested Boundaries: The States

As complicated as the districting problem is, the analysis becomes more complex still when we are dealing with putatively nested communities, such as the states of the United States. We might think of the states as providing a functional, organic settlement. On this view, there is a universal right to membership in particularistic, organic state communities. Every person (at least within the United States) has a right to state citizenship, but citizens of one state need not extend equal concern and respect to citizens of another state. Alternatively, we might treat states as nested within a broader federal community. If we treat states as nested, state autonomy risks the obstruction of universalist solidarity within this broader community. Somewhere between these two positions is a conceptualization of states as constructed, railroad-car communities. Viewed in this way, states provide a locus for membership, but that membership is constructed, rather than organic. As with legislative districts, states provide a source of membership that competes with ethnic or cultural identities.

In fact, on different occasions the Court has viewed states in all three ways, thereby creating a confusing doctrinal hodge-podge whose one certain effect is to leave the constitutional law of state sovereignty unsettled.

Consider first Saenz v. Roe.[53] In this case, the Court seems to have imagined states as particularist communities creating the good of particularistic membership, and the United States as guaranteeing the universal right to such membership. A California law imposed a durational residency requirement before new citizens of the state were eligible for full welfare benefits. Long-time residents received amounts established by a state schedule of benefits. In contrast, newly arrived residents received either this amount or the amount granted in the state they came from, whichever was smaller.

California argued that this regime, unlike previous statutory schemes that had been invalidated by the Court,[54] did not penalize the constitutionally protected right to travel, since newly arrived residents did not receive smaller payments than they would have received had they remained in their home state. The Court responded by shifting the doctrinal ground for decision. Instead of analyzing the right to travel between states, the Court relied on the Fourteenth Amendment's guarantee of the privileges and immunities of national citizenship. One privilege of national citizenship, the Court said, was the right to full state citizenship.[55] The Court held, in effect, that this right created the bounded universalism of functional settlements. State discrimination between new and old residents was unconstitutional because states are obligated to treat all citizens with equal concern and respect.

It is important to notice that one consequence of this way of thinking is that universalist obligations stop at state boundaries. Thus, although California must treat all California citizens with equal concern and respect, it need not extend this empathic connection to non-Californians. The Court nowhere suggests, for example, that California must provide welfare benefits to non-Californians, even if they are within California's geographical boundaries.[56] Moreover, the Court distinguished its own earlier decision in Sosna v. Iowa,[57] upholding a durational residency requirement for divorce, on the ground that persons seeking divorce might utilize Iowa's courts and then return whence they came, whereas newly arrived California welfare recipients were likely to spend their welfare money in California.[58] This distinction implies that a state can take measures to ensure that it is not exporting benefits to out-of-staters by, for example, opening its divorce courts to people who will not remain within the jurisdiction. It was only because the Court thought that such benefit exportation was unlikely that it invalidated the California statute.

If the earlier discussion in this chapter is correct, then this effort to treat the Constitution as creating a universalist right to particularist membership is bound to produce contradiction. As we have already seen, one set of contradictions arises when claims of state sovereignty conflict. When communities feel their autonomy threatened, their particularistic character will mean that there is no universalistic way of settling the dispute.

Consider again Sosna v. Iowa. The *Saenz* Court distinguishes *Sosna* on the ground that Iowa was legitimately preferring members to outsiders by granting members access to its divorce courts, while restricting access to those unlikely to remain within the state. Perhaps there is something to this view, but there is also a more charitable explanation for the exclusion. Instead of discriminating against residents of other states, there is a sense in which Iowa's durational residency requirement protects their autonomy. Other states, for reasons that seemed good enough to them, enacted more restrictive divorce laws than Iowa. Were Iowa to open its courts to new residents likely to return to their home state, it would undermine the autonomy of these other states.[59]

If we read *Sosna* in this way, it can be reconciled with *Saenz* by distinguishing between "mere" opinion and "actual" impact, as functional settlement requires. As already discussed, particularistic communities are entitled to act on mere opinion within their own borders but can defend themselves only from an actual impact coming from the outside. Thus, California is entitled to its own opinion about the appropriate levels of welfare, so long as it extends these benefits to all its members. Iowa is entitled (required?) to prevent its mere opinion about divorce law from interfering with the opinions of other communities.

We have already seen that this distinction between opinion and impact is difficult to maintain. Because communities are particularistic, there can be no universal standard against which we can measure the difference. For example, although the Court is unwilling to allow different welfare benefits for newly arrived and long-established residents of California, it is prepared to tolerate different benefit levels for citizens of California and Utah. Indeed, such differences are a necessary consequence of Utah's autonomy and its correlative right to determine welfare levels for its own citizens. Yet it is obvious that Utah's decision to provide lower benefit levels affects California. It makes California a potential "welfare magnet" for poor people from Utah. Precisely because California is a particularist community that cares more about its members than its nonmembers, the threat of becoming a welfare magnet, in turn, risks depressing the benefit levels that it would otherwise be able to provide for its own citizens. Why should California be precluded from protecting its autonomy from this threat?*

---

*Perhaps this argument seems fanciful, but the Court has accepted a closely analogous position with regard to regulation of interstate highways. When Iowa imposed strict limits on the size of trucks traveling on its highways, the Court held that the decision had

Conversely, Utah has an interest in preventing California from providing higher welfare benefits. Recall that Iowa was justified in discriminating against new arrivals in *Sosna* so as to avoid undermining sovereign decisions by its neighbors. So, too, California might justify its two-tier system to protect Utah's sovereignty. Suppose, for example, that Utah decides that the best way to alleviate poverty is by investing additional funds in education rather than welfare. Its particularistic attachment to its own citizens and lack of similar empathic identification with outsiders means that this investment will seem undesirable unless Utah citizens can capture the benefits. California's high welfare levels may prevent this capture by "buying off" Utah residents after they have already been educated. Utah, in turn, will not want to expend money educating its citizens if, once educated, they immediately leave for California. The result is a suboptimal level of educational investment from Utah's point of view.

These difficulties might be mitigated by subjecting state particularism to a universalist check. Institutions might be arranged in such a way as to promote resolution of these conflicts in a fashion that took the welfare of all citizens into account. The Court has promoted such a check in two ways. First, *Saenz*, like *Shaw*, can be read as defending railroad-car rather than organic community. If states were truly organic, they could limit membership to people with particular characteristics. California might say that it is not enough for people to live within its geographical boundaries. Rather, potential members must demonstrate that they are true Californians—that they have the attributes which make California membership special.* *Saenz* squarely rejects this view. True, it provides a universal guarantee of state membership, but it is a watered-down membership. Because California is constitutionally obligated to accept all comers once they have established residence, state community does not pose the same threat to universalism that an organic community would. On the contrary, indiscriminate state membership encourages universalism by requiring members within geographical boundaries to negotiate across cultural and ethnic boundaries.

Second, state particularism is held in check by universalist federal intervention, justified by the states' nestedness within a federal union. This interven-

---

an unconstitutional impact on surrounding states by diverting truck traffic to those states. See Kassel v. Consolidated Freightways Corp. of Del., 450 U.S. 662 (1981). Why isn't California entitled to similar protection against low welfare benefits in surrounding states?

*With some reluctance, I shall resist the temptation to specify what those attributes are.

tion might be either legislative or judicial. Legislative intervention occurs when Congress overrides particularist state laws to impose a universal solution. For example, the congressional decision to establish a national bank preempted local decisions that were in conflict with it. As Chief Justice Marshall explained in *McCulloch,* the federal action prevailed precisely because it is universalistic. Since the interests of all citizens of the United States (at least theoretically) are represented in Congress, the congressional decision establishing the bank was an action by the whole on the parts, rather than the parts on the whole.

Even in the absence of legislative intervention, the Court sometimes applies a universalist check through application of a complex of doctrines, including the so-called dormant commerce clause, the equal-protection clause, and Article IV's privileges-and-immunities clause. Consider, for example, Oregon Waste Systems v. Department of Environmental Quality,[60] where the Court invalidated an Oregon statute imposing a surcharge on imported solid waste. Relying on a long line of previous cases, the Court held that the tax violated the commerce clause because it discriminated without sufficient justification against out-of-state interests. Since Oregon failed to demonstrate a relevant difference between in-state and out-of-state waste, the Court reasoned that there was too great a risk that the measure was a regulation of interstate commerce "designed to give [Oregon residents] an advantage in the marketplace."[61]

If there were no limits on this universalist check, state particularism might be swamped. But there are limits, albeit contested and poorly defined ones. Consider first the legislative check. In *Saenz,* Congress itself had enacted a statute which authorized California's durational-residency requirement.[62] Surely this congressional action, taken by a body where all states are represented, satisfied the demands of universalism. But the majority brushed off the federal legislation with the observation that "Congress may not authorize the States to violate the Fourteenth Amendment."[63]

This explanation is less than satisfactory. The Fourteenth Amendment creates a federal right to state citizenship. As the Court correctly observes, Congress cannot constitutionally interfere with this right. But when Congress itself differentiates between citizens of a state, its actions have nothing to do with state citizenship, which defines the relationship between citizens and their state governments. Presumably, then, federal legislation directly establishing different welfare levels for people in different states and durational-residency requirements before individuals could receive increased benefits would not interfere with state citizenship. It is hard to see how federal ratification of a state decision to do the same thing is meaningfully different.

The result in *Saenz* is more understandable if we focus again on the Court's special role in enforcing an unsettled constitution. As discussed in Chapter 3, there is a fundamental difficulty in keeping particularism and universalism in tension with each other. The choice between particularism and universalism must itself be made according to either particularist or universalist criteria, but measuring one approach against standards provided by the other fatally biases the result. The only solution to this problem is to vest the choice in an institution designed to straddle the boundary between the two. For reasons explored in Chapter 3, judges have the potential, if they will only use it, to embody the ambivalence between approaches that makes an unsettled constitution possible.

A similar defense might be offered for the Court's much-discussed decision in United States v. Lopez,[64] where, for the first time in several generations, it invalidated a federal statute on the ground that Congress had exceeded its commerce clause powers. There is much in Chief Justice Rehnquist's majority opinion that suggests a yearning for constitutional settlement. If Congress can constitutionally criminalize the possession of a firearm near a school, Rehnquist complains, then "we are hard pressed to posit any activity by an individual that Congress is without power to regulate."[65] This rhetoric suggests the insecurity that regularly accompanies the frightening realization that things have not been finally worked out. Sixty years of judicial laxity, the Court seems to say, have left us with a situation where everything is up for grabs. If the political branches are free to do whatever they want, then the Constitution settles nothing, and if it settles nothing, then the old hobgoblin of unrestrained political conflict rears its ugly head.

When one turns from the rhetoric to the Court's holding, however, *Lopez* can be easily accommodated within an unsettled constitution. It is important that the Court says virtually nothing about the appropriate test for the legitimate exercise of federal power. It makes no effort to work out fixed boundaries. We are told that the Gun-Free School Zones Act went too far, but it is unclear whether the addition of a jurisdictional element (requiring that the gun, or some portion of the gun, move in interstate commerce, say),[66] a clearer showing of interstate effect,[67] or a regulation of a commercial portion of the transaction (buying the gun to use near a school)[68] would have sufficed.

Thus, instead of erecting fixed and settled limits on congressional power, *Lopez* can be understood as a reminder of the Court's power to unsettle. Indeed, Rehnquist acknowledged as much. As he put the point, "[S]o long as Congress' authority is limited to those powers enumerated in the Constitution, and so long as those enumerated powers are interpreted as having judicially enforceable outer limits, congressional legislation under the Commerce Clause always will engender 'legal uncertainty.' . . . The Constitution mandates this uncertainty by withholding from Congress a plenary police power that would authorize enactment of every type of legislation."[69] The case stands for the proposition that Congress cannot be the final judge of its own authority, for to leave it in that position would mean that the appropriateness of a universalist check should be determined by universalist criteria. In order to prevent this outcome, the Court sits astride an uncertain and contested boundary, intervening occasionally and enigmatically so as to remind us that our universal and particular urges can never be wholly reconciled.

Dormant commerce clause decisions, unlike the decisions in *Saenz* and *Lopez,* are subject to congressional revision.[70] At least theoretically, Congress could reverse the outcome in *Oregon Waste Systems.* As a practical matter, however, Congress has rarely utilized its authority,[71] and, for reasons explained below, dormant commerce clause jurisprudence also contributes to the unsettled Constitution. The difficulty here is in sorting out when the states are permitted to act as particularistic defenders of their own citizens and when they must act as nested within a broader universalist community.

There is a sense in which both *Saenz* and *Oregon Waste Systems* are consistent along this dimension. Both stand against protectionism and therefore in favor of universalism. Whereas *Saenz* supports free interstate movement of people, *Oregon Waste Systems* supports free interstate movement of goods. At least according to conventional economic theory, free trade may create individual losers, but from a universalist perspective it will produce the best outcome overall.

But there is another sense in which the two cases seem impossible to reconcile. *Saenz* prohibits discrimination between California citizens, but it makes clear that California has no obligation to noncitizens. In contrast *Oregon Waste Systems* condemns Oregon's favoritism of its own citizens over outsiders.

In this context, the Court has produced unsettlement by utilizing one of liberal constitutionalism's paired opposites discussed in Chapter 3. The difference between *Saenz* and *Oregon Waste Systems* is the difference between freedom and coercion. Since there is no right to welfare, a discretionary offer of welfare benefits expands the domain of freedom. California can therefore offer this benefit to its own citizens without coercing outsiders. For similar reasons, benefits like public education can be reserved for insiders,[72] and the so-called market-participant exception to dormant commerce clause restrictions serves to insulate other choice-expanding subsidies from judicial attack.[73]

On the other hand, taxes, like those imposed in *Oregon Waste Systems,* restrict the domain of freedom. They stand with criminal penalties and tariffs as coercive measures that harm outsiders, instead of merely failing to benefit them. In this way, the freedom-coercion dichotomy is linked to the other paired distinction. Whereas taxes actively impose a burden, the failure to provide welfare is no more than nonfeasance. Taxes amount to public intervention, whereas failure to provide welfare merely leaves private outcomes intact. Taxes are therefore under national control, while welfare is local.

Of course, critical theories have little difficulty in making a hash of these distinctions. Sometimes their incoherence is embarrassingly obvious. Consider, for example, West Lynn Creamery, Inc. v. Healy,[74] decided during the same term as *Oregon Waste Systems*. Massachusetts levied a nondiscriminatory tax on all milk sales in the state. This tax, in turn, funded a subsidy whose proceeds were distributed solely to Massachusetts milk producers. When viewed in isolation, both halves of this program seem constitutionally permissible. To be sure, the tax is a coercive burden, but it is nondiscriminatory. The subsidy discriminates against out of staters, but it is no more than a failure to benefit. Yet when the two programs are taken together, their economic effect is identical to a discriminatory tax. The distinction between coercion and freedom collapses under this sort of pressure.

But to complain about the incoherence of the paired opposites is to miss the point. It is their very failure to produce fixed boundaries coupled with their stubborn hold on our way of seeing the world that makes them ideally suited for destabilizing the border between particularism and universalism. A Court that struggles to decide cases on the basis of this distinction is certain to produce an unresolvable conflict between the special claims of particularism and the general obligations of universalism.

Drawing Contested Boundaries: The Nation

Whereas American law is unsettled about the status of states as particularist communities, the status of the federal government is relatively uncontroversial. Without thinking much about it, we expect the federal government to embody the bounded universalism of a particularist community. On the one hand it should treat all American citizens with equal concern and respect. On the other it does not and should not treat foreign citizens with the same regard that it accords American citizens. The United States, unlike California, can choose which new members to accept.[75] We may be unclear about whether states must treat citizens of other states with equal concern and respect, but virtually no one expects the United States to consider the welfare of foreign citizens equally with its own when it formulates national policy.

Yet as familiar as we are with this view of national government, there are powerful forces that threaten it. Indeed, when one considers the long term, the future of nation states as important units of government is far from certain. Around the world, they are squeezed between the still more particularistic forces of regionalism and the homogenizing, universalizing forces of transnational capitalism.[76] What seem to matter today are entities like Bosnia, northern Italy, and various remnants of the Soviet Empire on the one hand, and NATO, the European Union, and the International Monetary Fund on the other. If nations are to play an important role, it will be because of their ability to mediate between these two forces. Their survival depends on their ability to create a locus for membership that is universalist enough to incorporate diverse local populations but particularist enough to resist incorporation into a much larger, transnational community. In other words, their survival depends upon their ability to foster unsettlement.

Of course, a natural response is to wonder why we should care about the survival of the nation state. If regional and transnational governments better serve their people, why maintain a sentimental attachment to an outmoded governmental unit? In fact, there is much more than sentimental attachment at stake. It has become a commonplace that neither regional nor transnational governments have been very successful at maintaining the social safety net that nation states have traditionally provided to temper the most virulent effects of unregulated markets. This is no coincidence. Our discussion of state boundaries has already illustrated the difficulties regions have in insulating their markets from outside forces. Without such insulation, interregional competition is bound to defeat efforts at market regulation.[77] Transnational governments might succeed in accomplishing this end, but the populations of such units are too large and diverse to maintain political support for redistribution. National governments are ideally suited to serve as market regulators precisely because they occupy the middle space between balkanized particularism and anonymous universalism.

So far American constitutional law has played a relatively minor role in promoting this mediation, but even here, our unsettled constitution has had some effect. Compare, for example, the Court's decision in Plyler v. Doe[78] with United States v. Verdugo-Urquidez.[79] In *Verdugo-Urquidez* the defendant, a Mexican citizen, was suspected of helping to smuggle drugs into the United States. He was arrested by Mexican police, who handed him over to American officials. While he was detained in the United States, American law-enforcement officers assisted in the warrantless search of his home in Mexico. The Supreme Court held that the Fourth Amendment placed no limitations on the search. Writing for the majority, Chief Justice Rehnquist held that the "people" referred to in the Fourth Amendment "refers to a class of persons who are part of a national community."[80] Although the defendant was physically present in the United States at the time of the search, he was not part of the community. This was because his presence, although legal, was involuntary and because at the time of the search, he had been in the United States for only a matter of days.

Verdugo-Urquidez stands in sharp contrast with the Court's earlier decision in *Plyler*, where it held that Texas had violated the equal-protection clause when it withheld state funds from local school districts for the education of children not "legally admitted" into the United States. Justice William Brennan's majority opinion holds that "Aliens, even aliens whose presence in this country is unlawful" are "persons" guaranteed Fifth and Fourteenth Amendment protection.[81] Concluding that the state had failed to demonstrate a substantial interest supporting the exclusion of undocumented alien children from public schools, the Court held that the law was unconstitutional.

Verdugo-Urquidez and *Plyler* are both, in their own ways, anomalous. One might make sense of *Verdugo-Urquidez* in circumstances where a party is entirely outside the jurisdiction of the United States. If the United States and Mexico are each autonomous, the United States might simply have no authority within Mexican borders. For example, in Skiriotes v. Florida,[82] the Supreme Court reviewed the conviction of a defendant charged with violating a Florida statute prohibiting the use of diving equipment in the Gulf of Mexico. Although the Court assumed that Skiriotes was diving in international waters, it nonetheless upheld the conviction on the ground that as a citizen of Florida and the United States, he was subject to American authority even when outside its territorial jurisdiction. However, the Court made clear that the result would have been different if Florida attempted extraterritorial enforcement of its law against a foreign national.[83]

As we have already seen, refusal to apply domestic law in circumstances such as these can reflect respect for the autonomy of particularist communities. Just as Iowa's insistence on application of its liberal divorce law might impinge on the autonomy of other states, so too, the application of American law to Mexican nationals might, in some circumstances, impinge on Mexican autonomy. No such argument is available on the facts of *Verdugo-Urquidez*, however. The defendant's Fourth Amendment claim arose in the first place only because the United States was asserting that the defendant's activities produced what I have referred to as an "actual impact" on the United States and that it was therefore not asserting a "mere opinion." Perhaps "impact territoriality" is a sufficient basis for this jurisdiction, even though Verdugo-

Urquidez was a foreign national whose activities occurred in a foreign country,[84] but it is hard to see why the government should be allowed to have it both ways. If the defendant's activities were sufficient to bring him under American jurisdiction for purposes of our criminal laws, then why are they insufficient to make him subject to the constitutional protections that accompany those laws? As Justice Brennan put the point in dissent, the Court's holding amounts to a statement that "although foreign nationals must abide by our laws even when in their own countries, our Government need not abide by the Fourth Amendment when it investigates them for violations of our laws."[85]

Yet Justice Brennan's opinion in *Plyler* is equally mysterious. The difficulty can be stated succinctly: Because the *Plyler* plaintiffs were in the United States illegally, their rights would not have been violated if they had been deported. Moreover, if they had been deported, their rights would not have been violated had they been deprived of access to American schools. Yet somehow their rights were violated when they were allowed to remain but denied access to American education. How can this outcome violate their rights, when an alternative outcome (deportation without education) would have placed them in a worse position, yet not violated their rights? Two wrongs may not make a right, but somehow two "no rights" do add up to a right.*

Thus, even when considered separately, *Verdugo-Urquidez* and *Plyler* are more than a little puzzling. When we consider them together, the outcomes are completely mysterious. Both Verdugo-Urquidez and the *Plyler* plaintiffs were physically present in the United States and both owed their presence to the violation of American law. Although the property searched in *Verdugo-Urquidez* was located in Mexico, the Court's decision does not turn on this fact.

---

*It would be an overstatement to claim that this sort of logic is unique to *Plyler* or that it is always misguided. For example, if the police have probable cause to believe that a suspect has committed a crime, his rights are not violated by an arrest. If the suspect is arrested, his rights are not violated by a search incident to the arrest. Yet the Supreme Court has held that a defendant's rights are violated when he is searched without being arrested. *See* Knowles v. Iowa, 525 U.S. 113 (1998). But problems like this are analytically different from *Plyler*. There is no doubt that a criminal suspect, whether arrested or not, is an appropriate rights bearer. He is a member of our political community, and the government may not deprive him of that status. He has a right not to be searched if he is not arrested, even though he has no right not to be arrested, because the arrest provides the reason for the search — a reason that is lacking when the police elect not to execute the arrest. In contrast, it is not the deportation that provides the reason for denying an illegal alien the right to an American education. Such an alien is not a legitimate member of our political community in the first place; he has no right to have rights.

Instead, its holding is that the defendant was not part of the "people" whose rights are protected by the Fourth Amendment. This was true even though his presence in the United States was entirely legal. In contrast, the *Plyler* plaintiffs are the kind of "persons" referred to in the Fourteenth Amendment even though their presence is illegal. To be sure, Verdugo-Urquidez's presence was involuntary, but the *Plyler* Court treats the possible involuntariness of the plaintiffs' presence as a point in their favor.[86] And while it is true that Verdugo-Urquidez's physical presence in the United States was brief, nothing in *Plyler* remotely suggests that the Court would have permitted a durational-residency requirement for school attendance by illegal aliens.[87] Why, then, are the *Plyler* plaintiffs part of the relevant community while Verdugo-Urquidez is not?*

The tension between *Plyler* and *Verdugo-Urquidez* is an inevitable by-product of the mediating role of national government. *Plyler* reflects the universalist pole. It emphasizes the artificiality of geographical boundaries and the duty to accord equal concern and respect to all. The fact that these boundaries are artificial creates a railroad-car community, where people are accorded at least some rights of membership regardless of the circumstances that place them within our territorial boundaries.

As attractive as it is, *Plyler's* universalism inevitably raises anxieties. Bounded universalism is always unstable because universalism by its nature pushes against bounds. Thus, if borders are in fact artificial, why pay any attention to them? If we owe a duty to aliens who are only within our borders because they have broken our laws, why do we not owe a similar duty to aliens who remain in foreign countries because they have respected those laws? The anxiety created by *Plyler*, in turn, leads to results like *Verdugo-Urquidez*. Nation states can remain a focus for particularist membership only if membership counts for something, and it can count for something only if not everyone

---

*One other distinction between the cases requires mention. In *Plyler*, state officials engaged in the constitutionally questionable conduct, whereas federal officials were implicated in the *Verdugo-Urquidez* search. There are intimations in *Plyler* that it is the federal government, rather than the states, that is vested with authority to regulate immigration, and that the outcome might therefore have been different if a federal law had deprived illegal aliens of access to public education. But these observations do little to reconcile *Plyler* with *Verdugo-Urquidez*. The Court's observations about federal power relate to substantive equal-protection analysis. Having decided that the equal-protection clause was applicable to the plaintiffs, the Court was faced with assessing the legitimacy and strength of the state's interest in excluding them. In contrast, Verdugo-Urquidez was defeated at the threshold. The Court had no need to investigate the analogous question — whether the search was "reasonable" — because it concluded that the defendant was not a member of the "people" to whom the Fourth Amendment applied.

is a member. There must be limits somewhere, the Court seems to be saying, and a person who is in this country only because he has been brought here against his will for violating our laws is surely outside those limits.

I make no claim that *Plyler* and *Verdugo-Urquidez* establish the right balance between particularism and universalism or even that the two decisions are consistent with each other. On the contrary, an unsettled constitution rests on the belief that there is no permanent and fixed "right" balance, and any temporary balance that the Court establishes is bound to be unstable and contradictory. What deserves celebration, then, is not the results in these two cases, but the uncertainty that they engender — an uncertainty upon which our ability to maintain a just political community ultimately rests.

6

The Structure of Unsettlement

If the constitutions of just communities produce fluid and contested boundaries, how do these communities make decisions? In this chapter, I argue that decision-making structures cannot achieve political settlement. Even readers who have been sympathetic with what I have said so far may find this claim implausible. Much of the U.S. Constitution consists of a detailed specification of these structures. The Constitution establishes terms of office for various officials,[1] allocates power among different branches of government,[2] sets forth procedures by which bills become laws,[3] and establishes rules for succession in the event of the death or disability of a president.[4] Should all these matters be up for grabs?

It might be thought that a political community based upon ongoing and unresolved conflict over foundational issues must nonetheless entrench the institutions best suited to maintaining this conflict. How, then, can we have unsettlement all the way to the bottom?

Perhaps we cannot. In the previous chapters I myself have supported certain decision-making structures. For example, I defended a role for judges employing the standard tools of liberal constitutionalism as a structure that can promote unsettlement. (I shall return to this problem in the Conclusion.) Before we confront this vexing problem, however, we need to discuss a simpler one. Most advocates of fixed, constitutional structures have defended them not because they unsettle but because they resolve community conflict. They do so through the specification of the sort of public, political process described in Chapter 1. The basic idea is that people who continue to disagree about ordinary political issues will be reconciled to an outcome if agreed-upon processes are employed to reach it. This idea is fundamentally flawed. Structures cannot settle. On the contrary, the goal of an inclusive community is best realized by conflict, even on the structural level.

Most constitutional theorists who have supported something resembling unsettlement theory have nonetheless assumed that the central purpose of constitutional law is to establish fixed decision-making structures. These theorists have defended their structures as politically "neutral," leaving to future generations the choice of substantive policies to pursue. For example, James Madison can be read as arguing for the Constitution on the ground that it would produce unsettled political outcomes.[5] One might defend the baroque system of overlapping powers and constituencies that the Founders created on the ground that it prevents any one faction from gaining all the levers of power and so entrenching a particular substantive settlement. Yet Madison also argued for entrenching this structure precisely because it was likely to produce outcomes that were not entrenched.

So, too, defenders of democracy sometimes argue that this form of government is uniquely flexible and open. Democracy establishes no a priori truths. It gives each generation the power and responsibility to create the kind of society that meets its needs and desires.[6] Yet democracy's defenders insist on fixed, democratic structures just because such structures will create fluid political outcomes.

It is important to understand at the outset that these efforts to defend settled structures on the ground that they produce unsettled results are unsuccessful. Even a superficial reading of the Federalist Papers makes clear that its authors favored particular structures because they thought that they were likely to produce the "right" substantive outcomes. Their central concern was the risk of government tyranny. True, they favored unsettled government in the sense that they feared that a single faction might seize control. But unsettlement in the public sphere was designed to produce insulation for the private sphere. The complex system of overlapping powers in a large republic, which Madison defended, was meant to make vigorous government intervention difficult, thereby entrenching a settlement that supported status quo private distributions against public attack.[7]

Conversely, democracy entails a system for aggregation of public preferences. It, too, biases the system toward certain outcomes. True, in its idealized form democracy leaves things unsettled in the sense that it is neutral as between different potential majorities that compete for power. We have already seen that real democratic structures can never achieve this ideal of neutrality. Any instantiation of democracy will inevitably favor one group over another. Moreover, even if we could somehow establish democratic structures that were neutral as between potential majorities, these structures would nonetheless privilege majorities over minorities. Democracy favors public, collective decision making over its individual, private rival. For what would democracy amount to if it were not a system whereby majorities generally prevailed over minorities, who would prefer to settle the matter for themselves? Majority rule, by its very nature, is in tension with a system under which disputes are resolved on the individual level.

Settlements as Rules of the Road

A more convincing defense of structural settlements concedes that they inevitably have substantive impacts, yet nonetheless defends them on the ground that it is more important to settle these structures one way or the other than to settle them the "right" way. Even a suboptimal or contested settlement of these issues allows us to devote time and energy to our substantive disagreements.

A simple and familiar analogy provides powerful support for the argument. Suppose that the government of Erewhon is building its first roads. The government might well leave unsettled the destination that individual drivers will choose. It might even leave unsettled whether individuals or groups should be permitted to make this choice. But no government would leave unsettled the side of the road on which motorists drive. People might have different opinions on the subject, and any settlement will produce some losers. Yet the gains produced by coordination outweigh any losses caused by the "wrong" choice. Indeed, without this coordination, the roads become unusable — which is itself a kind of settlement.

So, too, political structures might be thought to provide necessary rules of the road that allow the rest of our politics to remain unsettled. Consider, for example, Article II, section 1, which sets the presidential term at four years. This provision leaves our politics entirely open with regard to who the president should be and what policies he should follow. Surely, this openness would not be enhanced if a president, after completing a four-year term, announced that the length of his service was unsettled and that he therefore planned to remain in office for an additional year. We know something about societies where presidents regularly make such pronouncements, and they are not famous for their political cohesiveness, justness, or stability. If we were starting over, we might conclude that a four-year term is not optimal. Still, now that it is established, agreement on this fundamental rule of the road is what permits losers to accept outcomes they detest. The old Brooklyn Dodgers could not have cried, "Wait 'til next year," if the New York Yankees had been permitted to cancel the next World Series.

Despite the intuitive appeal of this argument, I think it is wrongheaded. I offer two interlocking refutations: a normative claim about the function that constitutional law should serve, and a positive claim about the function it does serve.

The Problem of Contested Structures

The normative claim begins by quarreling with the analogy. The "rules of the road" example gains its power from the fact that almost nothing turns on the choice. Because almost no one cares about which side of the road she drives on (and almost everyone cares about avoiding head-on collisions), it is plainly desirable to settle the question one way or the other.

The four-year presidential term is a hard case for unsettlement theory because it, too, has no strong political valence.* Of course, it is not completely politically transparent. At the limit, departures from the four-year rule could have a profound effect. Some of the framers favored a life-time presidential term.[8] Had they prevailed, our politics would look very different indeed. Still, there is no clear way in which the balance of power between, say, conservatives and liberals would be altered if the president served five or three, rather than four, years.

It is worth noting at the outset that most issues of constitutional structure are not like this. Decisions about the form of representation in the House and the Senate, the method of electing the president, or the division of authority between different branches of the federal government are not substantively transparent. They affect political outcomes in obvious, foreseeable, and controversial ways.† Even here, many might believe that it is better to settle the question, even wrongly, than to continue to argue about it. But because these

---

*At least it has no such valence if it is consistently followed over time. Strategic departures from the rule might have a strong valence. I discuss this problem below.

†For example, during the post-Vietnam period, liberals tended to favor a strong executive in the domestic arena and a strong Congress in the foreign arena. We can surmise that they did so not solely because of a disinterested reading of constitutional text and history but also because this alignment was thought to promote redistributive policies at home while discouraging interventionist policies abroad. Conservatives tended to favor the opposite configuration for complementary ideological reasons.

structures are much more likely than literal rules of the road to produce constitutional losers, there is more risk that any settlement will leave these losers unreconciled to their loss.

Suppose, though, that we focus on the hardest type of case for unsettlement theory. Does the theory really require that the president's term of office remain undetermined? If we can establish the virtue of unsettled structures in this situation, where the argument for a resolution is strongest, then we will have gone a long way toward establishing the desirability of unsettling constitutional structures more generally.

At first, no doubt, it will seem downright wacky to suppose that a just constitution must leave the presidential term up for grabs. Even if there are some people who are not completely happy with the four-year term, we are surely all better off with a fixed term than with periodic struggles over presidential succession.

Of course, if everyone really agrees that we are better off, then there would be no need for a constitutional settlement. People would follow the four-year rule because of their unanimous, all-things-considered judgment that following the rule produces the best long-term outcome.

To be sure, there is always the risk of strategic defections from the rule. People who secretly believe that the four-year rule is best over the long run might nonetheless depart from it so as to gain short-term advantage. But as game theorists have demonstrated, in a repeat game of this sort, there are sound reasons grounded in self-interest not to defect.[9] Perhaps more significant, for this argument to be convincing, we would need to discover something about constitutional settlements that prevents such defections. It cannot be that constitutions deprive people of the raw power to defect. The great claim for liberal constitutionalism is that it creates a community based upon law rather than force. If constitutions worked by depriving people of raw power, we would have collapsed the distinction between law and force. Put differently, once such a constitution was installed, the constitutional rule would always be identical to whatever people with power wanted to do. It follows that if constitutional law is to be something other than force, it must serve its purposes by convincing people who otherwise would defect to play by a particular set of rules. What we must do, then, is to imagine a plausible situation where not everyone will agree with the rules and to ask whether, *in this situation*, a constitutional settlement can produce agreement that would not otherwise exist.

Suppose that on the day before the presidential inaugural, a nuclear blast destroyed most of Washington, D.C. The sitting president survived, but the president-elect and vice president-elect were killed, as were all members of the outgoing cabinet and many members of Congress, including the Speaker of the House and the President Pro Tem of the Senate. It is a moment of supreme national crisis, and the nation cannot afford to be without a leader.*

Given this context, some sensible people might argue that the sitting president should serve for at least long enough to see the country through the crisis and perhaps long enough for new elections to be organized. To be sure, others might claim that it is wrong to change the rules in midstream and that we should simply soldier on and do the best we can. The fact remains that as long as there is a plausible and reasonable disagreement of this sort, the outcome will be unsettled.

It is hard to see how constitutional law can resolve this disagreement once it emerges. Perhaps it would be better in the long run if all of us were somehow conditioned to follow the existing rule blindly without thinking about the consequences. But we can never fully suppress the knowledge of our own freedom. Thus, it will inevitably occur to someone that it would be fairer, more sensible, or even essential to extend the president's term. As soon as it does, there will be an argument about whether to follow the constitutional

---

*Section 3 of the Twentieth Amendment provides as follows: "If, at the time fixed for the beginning of the term of the President, the President elect shall have died, the Vice President elect shall become President. If a President shall not have been chosen before the time fixed for the beginning of his term, or if the President elect shall have failed to qualify, then the Vice President elect shall act as President until a President shall have qualified; and the Congress may by law provide for the case wherein neither a President elect nor a Vice President elect shall have qualified, declaring who shall then act as President, or the manner in which one who is to act shall be selected, and such person shall act accordingly until a President or Vice President shall have qualified." Surprisingly, although the amendment makes provision for situations where neither the president-elect nor the vice president-elect has been chosen or qualified by the beginning of the term, it makes no provision for the death of the president-elect and vice president-elect. Despite this gap, the U.S. Code specifies a list of persons, beginning with the Speaker of the House of Representatives, followed by the President Pro Tem of the Senate and including members of the Cabinet, to serve as president "[i]f by reason of death, resignation, removal from office, inability or failure to qualify, there is neither a President nor Vice President to discharge the powers and duties of the Office of President." *See* 3 U.S.C. sec. 19. Since the Twentieth Amendment does not authorize Congress to establish a line of succession, the statute is arguably unconstitutional insofar as it specifies who shall serve as president if both the president-elect and vice president-elect die. To simplify matters, I have taken the liberty of killing off not only the president-elect and vice-president elect but also all the officers in the statutory line of succession.

settlement. Or, to put the matter more precisely, there will be an argument about *which* settlement to follow — the one embodied in the constitutional text or a rival settlement that says something like "follow the constitutional text except when there are nuclear disasters" or more generally, "follow the constitutional text except when it is very impractical or unfair to do so." Once this argument begins, it cannot be resolved simply by invoking one of the competing settlements, since they are what the argument is about. It follows, then, that a constitutional settlement is ineffectual in this context.

I do not understand the most sophisticated advocates of constitutional settlements as disagreeing with any of the above. How could they? Constitutional settlements establish rules for those already committed to the settlement. A settlement can never defend itself from within against external challenges. Whatever a particular constitutional settlement requires, there will always be an irrepressible question about whether we should follow that settlement as opposed to a competing one.

Still, defenders of settlement theory are likely to have two responses to this argument. First, a natural reaction is to object to my use of an extreme hypothetical. Of course, they will say, if one tries hard enough, one can always imagine extraordinary emergencies where it no longer makes sense to obey the settlement, but there has not (yet) been a nuclear disaster. In more normal circumstances, it obviously makes much more sense to play by the rules.

Unfortunately, this argument is persuasive only so long as we are willing to give up our ambition to form an inclusive political community. To see why this is so, we must first isolate the reasons disobedience to the settlement seems to make sense in the nuclear-attack example and then see whether there are good arguments for cabining this example. The answer to the first question is clear enough. Rule-following has undeniable virtues, but they are not the only virtues. Even strong advocates of rule-following like Justice Scalia are prepared to concede that there will be occasions, perhaps rare, when the value of having a fixed rule is outweighed by the value of avoiding a substantive evil.[10] At least some people will believe that as important as a fixed, four-year term is, it is more important to have a leader at a moment of national crisis.

But once this much is conceded, the argument cannot be cabined unless we are willing to give up on the claim that constitutional law is politically neutral. Imagine, for example, that there are others who believe with equal fervor that unanticipated changes occurring since 1787 make it unjust to have a four-year presidential term or that the election of Al Gore rather than George W. Bush at a particularly grave historical moment is bound to produce a catastrophe. These people, too, are prepared to admit that there should be a strong presumption in favor of rule-following. They nonetheless believe that the problems with a four-year term in general—or with Al Gore in particular—are every bit as severe as the problem of making crucial decisions following a nuclear attack, and that these problems outweigh the virtue of rule-following.

Most of us will disagree with these people, but the disagreement rests on contested political judgments. The debate will not be about rule-following per se, since both sides agree that sometimes rules should be broken. Rather, the debate will be about the strength and validity of various reasons offered for breaking the rule. It follows that there will be no agreement on whether to obey the constitutional settlement as long as there is no resolution of these political disputes. Since settlement theories claim that constitutional settlements are *the way* we resolve political disputes, we are caught in a circle.*

To make the same point in a different way, once we concede that any deviation from the settlement is justified, we cannot give reasons independent of

---

*This problem overlaps with, but is not identical to, the much debated problem for rule utilitarians of preventing their theory from collapsing into act utilitarianism. *See, e.g.,* David Lyons, Forms and Limits of Utilitarianism (1965); *and* Donald Regan, Utilitarianism and Co-operation 94–104 (1980). It also bears some similarity to the dispute between advocates of rules and advocates of standards. For a discussion, see Kathleen Sullivan, *Foreword: The Justices of Rules and Standards,* 106 Harv. L. Rev. 22 (1992).

Philosophers who have argued that rule utilitarianism collapses into act utilitarianism claim that whenever a rule is inconsistent with its purposes, it will always be possible to formulate a narrower rule that brings them back into line. Eventually, the rule that one is left with amounts to nothing more than "do the right thing," which is not a rule at all. Defenders of rule utilitarianism have responded by arguing that some value attaches to rule-following itself. Thus, the "right thing" may include not just the substantive outcome but also the value of having a rule to follow. *See generally* Richard B. Brandt, A Theory of the Good and the Right 286–305 (1979).

The dispute between defenders of rules and defenders of standards raises a similar set of concerns. Rules often fail to correspond to their purposes but have the virtues of clarity and low administrative costs. Standards provide more flexibility but at the expense of greater risks of discriminatory application and higher administrative costs.

There is an obvious similarity between the problem I address in text and these disputes. However, they are not identical. My claim is not just that there will always be a conflict between broader and narrower rules or between rules and standards. Often we will have to choose between competing rules of similar breadth. A rule that says "The president shall serve four years" and one that says "The president shall serve five years" are no different with regard to their generality. More significant, my claim is that whether we are faced with a choice between broader or narrower rules or between different rules of similar generality, the choice will inevitably be influenced by our conflicting beliefs about the purpose we wish to achieve and the weight we attach to achieving it. Hence, neither the choice between rules and standards nor the choice among different rules or different standards can be apolitical.

contested political positions for why other deviations are not justified as well. Because the reasons we offer are tied to political positions, they will not be comprehensible to people with a different set of political commitments. Our refusal even to consider new deviations from the settlement excludes from our community the people who favor them and entrenches their loss at a foundational level.

Consider in this regard, the Supreme Court's decision in Bush v. Gore.[11] In his concurring opinion, Chief Justice William Rehnquist cited NAACP v. Alabama ex rel. Patterson[12] and Bouie v. City of Columbia[13] as precedents for the proposition that the U.S. Supreme Court can undertake an independent analysis of state law. Justice Ruth Bader Ginsburg, in a dissenting opinion, criticized Chief Justice Rehnquist's "casual citation" of these cases, which, she claims were "embedded in historical contexts hardly comparable to the situation here." *Patterson* and *Bouie* arose out of the civil rights struggle in the segregated South. According to Justice Ginsburg, the Florida Supreme Court of 2000 "should not be bracketed with state high courts of the Jim Crow South."[14]

Justice Ginsburg's argument cuts in a direction different from the one she intends. As she comes close to acknowledging, the Warren Court, faced with an overwhelming moral imperative, adjusted ordinary principles of law in order to deal with that imperative. These adjustments extended far beyond the two cases she discusses. As Lucas A. Powe demonstrates in his incisive history of the Warren Court, the Justices regularly reached outcomes that were not legally defensible so as to vindicate their moral and political views regarding racial justice.[15]

Justice Ginsburg thinks that these outcomes were wise and that the need to eradicate segregation is "hardly comparable" to the need to avoid a recount in Florida. Many of us, no doubt, will agree. But it is important to see that this is a political, rather than a legal, judgment. It is possible to imagine people whose political objections to the Florida recount were every bit as strong as Justice Ginsburg's political objections to racial inequality. Her explanation of *Patterson* and *Bouie* amounts to a concession that sometimes political judgments should take precedence over legal ones. I have argued above that this concession is entirely appropriate, but once it is made, it cannot be limited to judgments with which we agree.

What sort of political judgment might have influenced the result in Bush v. Gore? The most obvious and problematic one is a naked desire to see George W. Bush elected president, but there are other, less overtly partisan, judgments that could also have influenced the majority. For example, an important strand in conservative thought emphasizes the importance of formal mechanisms for dispute resolution. Conservatives oppose statistical readjustments of census data not (just) because the readjustments would help the Democratic Party but also because of a fear that such adjustments are subject to manipulation. Similarly, conservatives had legitimate concerns that, as imperfect as machine counts were, they were less subject to manipulation than hand recounts. Closely linked to formalism is a desire for order. At some point the election has to come to an end. When the candidates are separated by a tiny number of votes, the election will never end if we insist on the unattainable goal of complete accuracy. Instead, the process will spin out of control, producing bitterness and chaos that benefits no one. Better for the Supreme Court to shut it down, they might argue, than to go down this path.

My point is not that these political judgments are correct. Indeed, I disagree strongly with them. Moreover, even if they were correct, I believe that it is wrong to equate their seriousness with the need for racial justice. But they are legitimately contestable judgments and therefore cannot be settled by constitutional law. Thus, the problem with Bush v. Gore is not legal. Rather, the Court made (by my lights) an odious political judgment and was not candid about the political character of that judgment.

For present purposes, the issue of candor is more significant. Why did the Court invent obviously frivolous legal arguments in an effort to conceal its political judgment? Almost certainly for the same reason that the Warren Court relied upon a different set of frivolous arguments almost a half-century earlier. Both Courts thought that their role was to settle disputes by appeal to a set of principles that everyone was bound to accept. Both were afraid that their legitimacy would be questioned if they admitted the political character of their decision making. Both Courts failed to realize that political decision making is inevitable and that, so long as there is political disagreement, constitutional arguments cannot and should not be settled. If only the Court understood that its role is not to settle arguments over racial justice, presidential elections, or anything else, it could tell us the truth about the contestable assumptions that in fact motivate its decisions.

The issue of candor plays a central role in the second counterargument defenders of settlements might advance. This argument concedes that whenever we are faced with a putative settlement that produces outcomes with which some people disagree, there will be a dispute about whether to adhere to the settlement. It also concedes that sometimes departure from the settlement may be the wisest course. Nonetheless, judges in particular and constitutional law in general should be aligned on one side of this dispute. Oddly, on this argument an inflexible judicial stance is justified by the possibility that it may be unsuccessful. Judges have an obligation to pretend that they are insisting on the sanctity of our constitutional settlement precisely because they know that they may not prevail. If their appeal to constitutionalism ultimately fails, the failure will occur because the forces of exigency are so powerful as to overcome their stubborn insistence on legality. And we can only know that the forces are this powerful if there is a stubborn insistence to overcome.

Justice Robert Jackson defended something like this position in his justly celebrated opinions in Korematsu v. United States[16] and Youngstown Sheet and Tube v. Sawyer.[17] In *Korematsu*, Jackson, along with Justices Frank Murphy and Owen Roberts, dissented from the majority's decision upholding the exclusion of Japanese Americans from the west coast during World War II. But whereas Murphy and Roberts engaged in fairly standard constitutional analysis, Jackson's opinion was radically different. He started by acknowledging that it would be "impracticable and dangerous idealism"[18] to expect constitutional law to govern in areas like this. "When an area is so beset that it must be put under military control at all, the paramount consideration is that its measures be successful, rather than legal."[19]

Next Jackson observed that Supreme Court Justices are in a poor position to judge whether military measures are necessary or not. "The [limitations] under which courts always will labor in examining the necessity of a military order are illustrated by this case. How does the Court know that these orders have a reasonable basis in necessity?"[20]

One might suppose that these observations would lead Jackson to side with the majority. But at this stage of the analysis Jackson made a subtle and remarkable point. Unlike Murphy and Roberts, he did not claim that Courts can or should stop unconstitutional action by military commanders. On the contrary, he recognized that unconstitutional actions should on occasion be taken and that, in any event, it was foolish to suppose that courts would be in a position to stop them. But if the military commanders continued with their actions, they ought to do so without the Court's permission. When courts intervene, they should enforce the law. They should not decide whether law ought to be enforced, an inherently nonlegal, and therefore nonjusticiable, question. Thus, it might be right in some ultimate sense for the government to expel Korematsu from his home, but it is not right for a court to *say* that it is right.[21]

Jackson's *Youngstown* concurrence has the same essential structure and makes the same essential point. President Harry Truman had seized the steel mills to avoid a strike in the middle of the Korean War and was being sued by the owners of the mills. Once again, the other Justices made fairly standard arguments for and against the constitutionality of the seizure. In contrast, Justice Jackson seemed to step outside of these arguments. He emphasized the distinction between the president's paper powers, which the other Justices expounded upon, and his real powers. The paper powers are defined by the Constitution and by the cases interpreting the Constitution. In contrast, the real powers are extralegal — they are determined by politics.[22] It is through this political process that the president will decide whether a particular situation constitutes an "emergency" and whether the emergency, if it exists, merits use of his real powers. It is foolish to suppose that a court, standing alone, can stop the president from using his real powers. But part of the politics that determines what his real powers are is the assertion by courts that the president is limited to his paper powers.[23]

Thus, although Justice Jackson voted with the majority in *Youngstown*, it did not follow for him that President Truman actually ought to return the steel mills, any more than it followed that the government should refrain from relocating Japanese Americans. Instead, the point was that the Court should tell President Truman that he must return the mills because this would be one contribution to the constellation of political forces that would ultimately determine what he does.

There is much that is appealing about Justice Jackson's position. It seems to uphold the special moral force of rule-following while nonetheless recognizing the reality that sometimes rules should be broken. It also has the potential to close what Larry Alexander has called "the Gap."[24] Alexander argues that even though rule-following may be desirable ex ante, there is no plausible strategy for enforcing rules ex post. This is because rules are never coextensive with their purposes. Whenever there is a gap between the rule and its purpose (which is the only occasion on which the rule has independent force), it will seem sensible after the fact to ignore the rule. To be sure, we could attempt to precommit ourselves. Like Dr. Strangelove, we could announce in advance that we will punish violations of the rule even when it is not sensible to do so. But unless we create an automatic doomsday machine, this strategy, too, is bound to fail. The problem is that the announcement itself is a rule that it will also seem irrational to follow ex post when there is a gap between this rule and its purposes.

Justice Jackson's opinions can be seen as an effort to utilize role morality to close the gap. His argument has the same structure as the familiar argument for another rule of the road — the fifty-five-mile-per-hour speed limit. It would not be desirable for someone driving a critically ill person actually to go only fifty-five miles per hour on a deserted road while heading for the hospital. Still, it may be desirable to *say* that the speed limit should be obeyed. Only by insisting on obedience can we force drivers to internalize the cost of their choice, thereby achieving the optimal level of disobedience.* So, too, judges can close the gap by adhering to their proper role. They can insist on rigid obedience to the constitutional settlement, confident in the knowledge that this insistence will produce something less than the rigid obedience they insist upon.

But as clever as it is, Justice Jackson's argument cannot rescue structural settlements. There are three problems. First, Jackson's argument is coherent only as long as it is not articulated. According to his *Korematsu* and *Youngstown* opinions, the Supreme Court should insist on obedience to the constitutional settlement because this will produce the optimal level of disobedience. But as soon as he articulates this theory, he is no longer insisting on obedience to the constitutional settlement. Perhaps Jackson was relying upon what Meir Dan-Cohen, years later, called "acoustic separation."[25] Because most people do not read Supreme Court opinions, he can articulate his real position for the benefit of a small elite, while not being "overheard" by the rest of his audience, which will continue to believe naively that the Supreme Court really expects them to obey. However, a strategy of this sort is unlikely to work forever.†

Cf. United States v. Dougherty, 473 F.2d 1113, 1134 (D.C. Cir. 1972) (analogizing sixty-mile-per-hour speed limit to jury instructions that preclude jury nullification on the ground that in both cases "the danger of the excess rigidity that may now occasionally exist is not as great as the danger of removing the boundaries of constraint provided by the announced rules").

Some utilitarian theorists of criminal law generalize this point. These theorists claim that the criminal law is designed to make criminals internalize the full costs of their crimes. If they have done so, then the benefit of their activities exceeds the costs, and the crime is socially optimal. *See, e.g.,* Frank Easterbrook, *Criminal Procedure as a Market System,* 12 J. Legal Stud. 289, 292 (1983) ("The optimal price for the offense is just high enough to require offenders to pay for all of the harm their crimes inflict on the rest of us"). This theory leads to the odd consequence that all criminals are in some sense "innocent." The very fact that they engage in criminal conduct in the face of the risk of punishment demonstrates that the crime "should" occur. Yet they must be punished nonetheless because only by punishing them can we be certain that the benefits of their activity outweigh the costs.

There are some criminal law doctrines — most prominently the necessity defense — that exculpate defendants when they can show that their putative crime does more good than harm. As George Fletcher has shown, these defenses lead to a paradox. Defendants are exculpated because we believe that their actions were necessary; yet their knowledge ex ante that they will be exculpated make their claim of necessity less plausible. For a discussion, see George P. Fletcher, *Paradoxes in Legal Thought,* 85 Colum. L. Rev. 1263, 1280–84 (1985).

†It plainly does not work with regard to the fifty-five-mile-per-hour speed limit.

Eventually, the acoustic separation is bound to break down. Moreover, to the extent that it can be maintained, it once again raises disturbing questions, which we have already discussed, about the desirability of achieving civic peace through what amounts to manipulation and dishonesty.

A second problem arises even if one is unconcerned about the problem of candor. As Jackson poses the issue, judges are faced with a choice between obeying and disobeying the terms of the constitutional settlement. But we have already seen that this mischaracterizes the real choice that judges face. The issue is not *whether* to obey the settlement, but *which* settlement to obey. The statement "the president shall serve for four years" and the statement "the president shall serve for four years unless there is a nuclear disaster" both use the syntax of rules. Our choice, then, is not between following the rules and failing to follow them, but between following one set of rules and following a competing set.

Once this point is grasped, the role-morality argument appears in a very different light. Jackson's point cannot be that it is the role of judges to insist upon obedience to the constitutional settlement. Any decision that he renders will enforce some settlement. Instead, his point must be that judges are obligated to insist upon a particular kind of settlement — presumably, the settlement embodied in constitutional text or original intention, as opposed to the many other possible settlements that we might imagine. But why should this settlement be privileged? Unfortunately, nothing in Jackson's opinions argues for its primacy. On the contrary, as we shall see, his *Youngstown* opinion ends up defending a strikingly flexible approach to separation of powers that has little to do with textual interpretation or original intention.

Still a third problem with Jackson's position arises when we focus on the role to be served by constitutional, as opposed to political, argument. No doubt, there is something to be said for settling structural issues and sticking to the settlement even in emergencies. But why should the settlement be constitutional, and why should it be enforced by courts? Even without constitutional law, political actors have strong incentives to work out their differences. As we have already noted, repeat games substantially reduce the advantage to be gained by selfish, strategic behavior.

We have numerous examples of instances where political actors have created structures settling their differences without the intervention of constitutional law.* The United Kingdom has no written constitutional provision

---

*For example, before 1951 nothing in the Constitution prohibited the president from serving for more than two terms, but this limitation was strictly observed for 150 years. Nothing in the Constitution prohibits the majority party in either house from assigning

settling the length of a prime minister's term, yet it does not regularly collapse into paroxysms of violence over questions of political succession.* Similarly, there was little risk that disputes like those adjudicated in *Youngstown* and *Korematsu* would somehow have degenerated into a war of all against all had the Supreme Court not intervened.† Precisely because people wish to avoid lives that are solitary, poor, nasty, brutish, and short, we can more or less count on them to resolve their differences. The real risk is that some will perceive the resolution as unjust. The problem, in other words, is not that the political branches will leave matters unsettled but that the settlement will leave some people out.

---

all committee seats to its own members or refusing to recognize minority members when they seek to speak on the floor. Although the extraconstitutional accommodations that have developed do not work perfectly, they do prevent the sort of chaos that advocates of constitutional settlement most fear.

*The prime minister's term is established by a statute which enjoys quasi-constitutional status. *See* Septennial Act of 1715, 32 Hashbury's Statutes 680 (4th ed., 1996), *as amended by* Parliament Act of 1911, id., at 713 (providing that "all Parliaments that shall at any time hereafter be called, assembled, or held, shall and may respectively have continuance for five years, and no longer"). Perhaps an effort to repeal this statute would trigger a "constitutional" crisis as severe as an effort by an American president to extend his term beyond four years, although it should be noted that during both World War I and World War II, Parliament was in fact extended beyond the five-year period by ordinary legislation. *See* id., at 680 (note). In any event, to the extent that the five-year rule is entrenched, this fact only demonstrates that ordinary political institutions are able to establish relatively fixed structures without the aid of a judicially imposed settlement or a formal system of constitutional law.

†The initial evacuation of the Japanese Americans from the west coast was in fact settled by Hobbesian force. By the time the Court got around to "settling" the matter legally, ordinary political processes had more or less resolved the issue. On the day before *Korematsu* was decided, Public Proclamation No. 21 rescinded the evacuation and exclusion orders and restored to most, although not all, Japanese Americans "their full rights to enter and remain in the military areas of the Western Defense Command." *See* Peter Irons, Justice at War 276, 345 (1983).

In *Youngstown* it was far from clear that there had ever been a conflict that needed to be settled. There was no evidence that Congress and the president had disagreed in the first place over the seizure of the steel mills. When he announced the seizure, President Truman committed himself to obey any instructions Congress provided. *See* Maeva Marcus, Truman and the Steel Seizure Case 94 (1977). Moreover, there is good reason to think that the union and the steel companies would have reached an agreement resolving the entire controversy had not the Supreme Court intervened, thereby causing a strike that would not otherwise have occurred. *See* id., at 147–48.

Perhaps, then, the role of the Supreme Court is to prevent exclusionary settlements. In fact, I believe that this is an appropriate role for the Court, but it does not perform it in the way that most people think—that is, by using constitutional structures to put to rest destabilizing political disputes. It should be clear that displacing a political with a constitutional settlement only makes the exclusionary problem worse. It is one thing to lose a political fight. It is another to be told that the loss is irreversible and foundational. When the Supreme Court uses constitutional rhetoric to shut down an argument by imposing one potential settlement rather than another, it is doing something more than announcing the outcome of a political struggle. It is attempting to constitute the community in a fashion that excludes the losers for reasons that cannot be explained in a fashion comprehensible to them.

It follows that Justice Jackson's argument from role morality has things backward. Yes, there is some virtue to rule-following and yes, it is valuable to have someone whose role is to insist on the rules just because, in a true emergency, we may ignore this advice. But the proper locus for settlement is the political branches. Except in extraordinary circumstances, politicians can be counted upon to find a modus vivendi. Usually, this modus vivendi will involve a continuation of current practices—that is, following the rule. Of course, any resolution that politicians devise will make some people unhappy. An institution like the Supreme Court, which stands outside this settlement, can best take advantage of its outsider status by providing tools with which these people can attack the settlement.

Even if all this is persuasive, there remains a mystery as to how the Court might accomplish this goal. As we saw in Chapter 4, there is little possibility of establishing unsettlement at the level of individual cases. Any judicial decision will rest on some version of the constitutional settlement and, to that degree, entrench the version that is chosen. A Court faced with our hypothetical nuclear-attack problem must either choose the "four-year-term" rule or the "four-year-term-except-in-cases-of-extreme-emergency" rule. Either rule reflects some sort of constitutional settlement. As we have seen, even judicial deference imposes a settlement—in this case, a settlement based on political outcomes.

There are nonetheless two methods by which the Court can promote more pervasive unsettlement. First, judges could candidly acknowledge that their choice between settlements is politically driven and contestable. Instead of pretending they are implementing a neutral structural frame that everyone will approve of, they might concede that any structure biases outcomes in some direction and that the choice between structures will therefore be determined by politically controversial preferences for outcomes.

In fact, Supreme Court Justices often behave in just this way when they make structural decisions. For example, in United States v. Curtiss-Wright Export Corporation,[26] Justice George Sutherland, speaking for the Court, defended presidential authority to conduct foreign affairs on the ground that a vigorous foreign policy requires a single voice and an ability to maintain secrets — attributes that Congress conspicuously lacks.[27] Similarly, consider Justice Scalia's much-celebrated dissent in Morrison v. Olson,[28] where the Court upheld the Independent Counsel Act. Much of Justice Scalia's opinion is devoted to a seemingly apolitical formal attack on the Court's reasoning, but at the conclusion of his opinion, he switches gears and argues that prosecutors who are not constrained by resource scarcity are unlikely to exercise their discretion wisely.[29]

Unfortunately, however, the Justices rarely, if ever, acknowledge that they are articulating contested political positions. Apparently, it did not occur to Justice Sutherland that an isolationist might welcome structures that prevent the country from pursuing a vigorous foreign policy. Nor does Justice Scalia exhibit any awareness that there is a tension between his reliance on his personal conception of what produces the best prosecutorial decision making and his attack on the majority, a few paragraphs later, for an "ad hoc approach to constitutional adjudication" that is not bound by "the judgment of the wise men who constructed our system."[30]

There is little mystery about why the Justices do not own up to the political nature of their structural decision making. Such an admission raises the old bugaboo of judicial legitimacy. If the Court is just playing politics, critics will say, why not leave the decisions to the political branches? But this concern is even less trenchant in the structural context than it is more generally.

First, it is hard to know what it could *mean* to leave the question to the political process when the issue in dispute is the structure of that process. For example, the argument in *Youngstown* was about whether the president or Congress had the power to decide whether to seize the steel mills. The Court could hardly defer to the political branches without deciding which branch it was obligated to defer to.*

Second, it bears repeating that deference itself imposes a settlement — a settlement that privileges the outcome of ordinary political processes as a

---

*The statement in text requires some qualification. On the facts of *Youngstown* itself, it can be argued that there was no disagreement between the president and Congress. *See* Jesse H. Choper, Judicial Review and the National Political Process 272 (1980). Still, to the extent that the *Youngstown* Court confronted a disagreement, a deferential stance could not resolve it.

means of resolving our disputes.* Some members of the community will no doubt favor such a settlement because they believe that as an empirical matter, over the range of cases ordinary political processes are more likely to produce just results than decisions by judges. But this judgment, too, is premised on a contested conception of justice that others will not share. It follows that a deferential stance is no different from any other settlement that disregards the considered judgments of some community members.†

There is therefore no escape from politically contestable decision making when the Court resolves an issue of constitutional structure. Simply in the interests of candor, the Justices would be well-advised to acknowledge as much. Perhaps more significant, such an acknowledgment would itself be unsettling. When the Court confronts losers with a decree that purports to be a fully objective, neutral, and rational declaration of the law, it is trying to shut down further contestation. A Court that acknowledges the political contingency of its judgments invites the sort of ongoing conflict that makes just community possible.

Even if the Justices fail to acknowledge the political character of their structural decisions, there is a second method by which they could promote unsettlement. As I have already argued, the standard tools of liberal constitutionalism tend more or less automatically to promote unsettlement even when individual Justices are trying their best to impose a settlement. Indeed, they sometimes promote unsettlement most effectively precisely *when* individual Justices are attempting to impose a settlement. To see how these tools work in the context of structural settlements, we must turn from our normative inquiry to a description of how the Court actually behaves when confronted with a structural dispute.

Formalism and Functionalism

Most contemporary discussion of constitutional structure is organized around a debate between formalists and functionalists.[31] The Justices who follow a formal approach are transfixed by the value of rule-following. In-

---

*This formulation brackets the first point—that the issue in dispute is the nature of those processes.

†For example, my colleague Girardeau Spann has forcefully argued that ordinary political processes are more likely than judicial intervention to produce outcomes favorable to African Americans. *See* Girardeau Spann, Race against the Court 85–103 (1993). His argument may be convincing for an audience composed of people who share his conception of racial justice. It will cut just the other way for people who have an opposing conception.

deed, on occasion they seem to positively revel in the absurdity of the results they reach. This very absurdity is taken as a virtue because it advertises the work that the rules are doing.

A good example is Chief Justice Warren Burger's majority opinion in INS v. Chadha,[32] invalidating the so-called legislative veto. With the growth of the administrative state, Congress became increasingly concerned about the discretion exercised by administrative agencies. In order to deal with the problem, it developed the practice of coupling delegation of administrative authority with provisions that allowed one or both houses of Congress to "veto" various administrative actions. By the time *Chadha* was decided, a lively debate had developed in the academic literature about the wisdom and efficacy of these measures.[33] Significantly, Burger treats this debate as beside the point. Burger was prepared to concede, at least *arguendo,* that the legislative veto was "a useful 'political invention.' "[34] He conceded as well that respect for the constitutional settlement "impose[d] burdens on governmental processes that often seem clumsy, inefficient, even unworkable"[35] and produced "the obvious flaws of delay, untidiness, and potential for abuse."[36] Nonetheless, he thought, the legislative veto could not stand because "policy arguments supporting even useful 'political inventions' are subject to the demands of the Constitution."[37] Here "[e]xplicit and unambiguous provisions of the Constitution"[38] were enough to make the veto invalid even if it was in some sense desirable to permit it.

Burger's formalism might usefully be contrasted with Justice Jackson's concurring opinion in *Youngstown.* Writing for the Court, Justice Hugo Black adopted a formalist approach similar to Chief Justice Burger's. For Justice Black, one had to look no further than the rule established by clear constitutional text to resolve the dispute:

> [T]he seizure order [cannot] be sustained because of the several constitutional provisions that grant executive power to the President. In the framework of our Constitution, the President's power to see that the laws are faithfully executed refutes the idea that he is to be a lawmaker. The Constitution limits his functions in the lawmaking process to the recommending of laws he thinks wise and the vetoing of laws he thinks bad. And the Constitution is neither silent nor equivocal about who shall make laws which the President is to execute. The first section of the first article says that "All legislative Powers herein granted shall be vested in a Congress of the United States."[39]

In contrast, Justice Jackson took a much more flexible view. Whereas Black and Burger thought that a straightforward application of the constitutional rule was sufficient to resolve legal issues, Jackson expressed surprise

at the poverty of really useful and unambiguous authority applicable to concrete problems of executive power as they actually present themselves. Just
what our forefathers did envision, or would have envisioned had they fore-
seen modern conditions, must be divined from materials almost as enigmatic
as the dreams Joseph was called upon to interpret for Pharaoh. . . .

The actual art of governing under our Constitution does not and cannot
conform to judicial definitions of the power of any of its branches based on
isolated clauses or even single Articles torn from context. While the Constitution diffuses power the better to secure liberty, it also contemplates that practice will integrate the dispersed powers into a workable government.[40]

If standard legal tools are of little use, as Jackson claimed, how should a
Court approach the constitutional question it has been asked to decide? In an
often cited portion of his opinion, Jackson divided such cases into three categories. At one extreme were cases where the president acts "pursuant to an
express or implied authorization of Congress."[41] Here the president's power is
at its zenith, since he possesses all the power the Constitution gives him in
addition to any power that the Congress can delegate. In the middle was a
"twilight zone" where the president "acts in absence of either a congressional
grant or denial of authority."[42] In this situation "congressional inertia, indifference, or quiescence may sometimes, at least as a practical matter, enable, if
not invite, measures on independent presidential responsibility. . . . [A]ny
actual test of power is likely to depend on the imperatives of events and
contemporary imponderables rather than on abstract theories of law."[43] At
the other extreme were cases where the president violated "the expressed or
implied will of Congress."[44] Here, his power is at its nadir, since "he can rely
only upon his own constitutional powers minus any constitutional powers of
Congress over the matter."[45]

In *Youngstown* itself, Jackson concluded that Truman's seizure fell into the
third category because of "three statutory policies inconsistent with this seizure."[46] Applying "the severe tests under [this] third grouping,"[47] he found
that presidential claims of inherent executive authority to deal with an emergency failed. Even here, though, his approach is strikingly flexible and antifor-
mal. As already noted, Jackson's conclusion rested on the distinction between
paper and real powers. In an odd and paradoxical conclusion to his opinion,
Jackson linked his homage to the rule of law with a warning that "[if] not
good law, there was worldly wisdom in the maxim attributed to Napoleon
that 'The tools belong to the man who can use them.' "[48]

What are we to make of this methodological dispute between formalists and
functionalists? On the simplest level, one might be tempted to align formalists
with the effort to settle political disputes through constitutional law and func-

tionalists with the unsettlement approach. Formalism tries to separate the constitutional settlement from the political disputes it purports to resolve and to resolve those disputes permanently by reference to a rigid rule. In contrast, functionalism emphasizes the contingent and flexible nature of any settlement and, at least implicitly, recognizes that the settlement cannot be completely disentangled from the underlying political dispute. Formal opinions cut off further debate by fiat. Functional opinions are invitations to further conversation.

The Court's unwillingness to choose one methodology or the other itself promotes unsettlement. Whichever way the Court resolves a case, the losers are bound to have precedential ammunition that they can train on the resolution. We have already seen the reasons why the Court must continue to vacillate between these two approaches. Ex ante, it will always seem that there are large advantages to be captured if only we could agree on rules of the road. Ex post, we can never disentangle arguments over whether to make exceptions from the political disagreements that divide us in the first place. Because there is no way out of this dilemma, both methodologies, together with the unsettlement that the struggle between them promotes, are likely to be permanent features of the constitutional landscape.

Moreover, formalism and functionalism also interact to produce unsettlement in a second, more subtle fashion. It is probably true that advocates of formal and functional approaches are motivated by their respective attachments to settlement and unsettlement. Chief Justice Burger does seem to yearn for an apolitical rule of law that will authoritatively and permanently resolve disputes. In contrast, no sensitive reader of Justice Jackson's opinions can miss his love of irony, paradox, and open texture. But one of the strengths of liberal constitutionalism is that it produces certain results regardless of the motivations of the people who administer it. Contrary to our intuitions and to the probable intent of those who advocate functionalism, it has settling as well as unsettling tendencies. In contrast, formalism can check the settling tendencies by undermining functional settlements without substituting any settlement of its own.

We can begin to understand how functionalism settles by examining Justice Jackson's three categories with greater care. When we do so, his conceptual scheme becomes subject to the following objection. Justice Jackson claimed that the president's power is at its weakest when, as in *Youngstown* itself, Congress implicitly or explicitly disapproves of his conduct. In contrast, when Congress remains silent, we are in a twilight zone where the president is more likely to prevail and where the outcome will turn "on the imperatives of events and contemporary imponderables."[49]

Why should there be different tests for these two situations? After all, either the president's Article II executive power encompasses the act in question (the seizure of the steel mills) or it does not. If it does, then any effort by Congress to deprive the president of this power would be ineffectual. The power-granting provisions of the Constitution would be meaningless if Congress had the authority to amend them by simple statute. In contrast, if it does not, then a congressional effort to deprive him of the power would be unnecessary. The negative implications of Article II accomplish this goal of their own force. Even if Congress had done nothing, the president would lack the constitutional authority he claimed.

We can make more sense of Justice Jackson's conceptual scheme if we return to some of the distinctions discussed in Chapter 1. Jackson's opinion is best interpreted as answering the "how" rather than the "what" question. The discussion above assumes that all reasonable people reading Article II would come to the same conclusion as to its meaning. Recall, though, that for Jackson, the constitutional materials are "almost as enigmatic as the dreams Joseph was called upon to interpret for Pharaoh."[50] Because the text is indeterminate, focusing on the "what" of constitutional law leads to a dead end. Instead, Jackson can be read as focusing on the "how." The differences between categories make more sense if one takes him as saying that when reasonable people disagree about the meaning of the text, the disagreement should be resolved by Congress. Thus, it is not that Congress somehow has the authority to move particular presidential actions into and out of Article II by simple statute. Instead, these statutes should be read as congressional *interpretation* of Article II. If Congress validates the president's action, it is in effect offering its opinion that the Constitution permits it. If it invalidates his action, it is in effect interpreting the Constitution to prohibit it. If Congress remains silent, the Court must look to "the imperatives of events and contemporary imponderables" to determine how Congress would have interpreted the Constitution if it had spoken.

Although Jackson does not say any of this explicitly, modern functionalists often behave in a manner consistent with this interpretation. Significantly, functionalists rarely look to function in order to invalidate a congressional choice. Instead, functional opinions usually grant Congress discretionary authority to interpret the structural provisions as it chooses. There are many examples. The modern Supreme Court has upheld extremely broad delegations of congressional power to administrative agencies,[51] permitted the creation of "Article I courts" that do not comport with the life-tenure requirement of Article III,[52] and validated such experimental governmental structures as a hybrid sentencing commission[53] and an independent counsel shielded from executive control.[54] In none of these cases has the Court suggested that functionalism *mandates* a particular outcome. Instead, the Court has used functional techniques to validate discretionary congressional judgments.

Viewed from this perspective, we can see that "functionalism" is something of a misnomer. The Court is not, in fact, judging the legitimacy of various structures against criteria derived from function. If it were, it would invalidate structural experiments when they are not functionally justified and impose structures that functionalism requires. Instead, its decisions seem focused on the "how" question. In other words, they enforce a procedural constitutional settlement providing that structural disagreements should be resolved by the legislative branch.

The attractions of such a settlement are obvious. Given the open texture of functional analysis, the Court is uncomfortable imposing its views on the country. Precisely because it is unable to point to unambiguous constitutional text, functional analysis looks more like policy than law. We should nonetheless recognize this type of functionalism for what it is — a settlement, with all the disadvantages of any other settlement. The settlement in effect provides that when there is reasonable disagreement about constitutional structure, the disagreement should be settled by ordinary political processes. Such a settlement is unlikely to be satisfactory to people who dislike the probable outcomes of ordinary political processes. Moreover, as we have already seen, this settlement is especially question-begging in the structural context, where the very issue in dispute is the shape of the political institutions to which functionalists wish to defer.

If even functionalism leads to settlement, how can it be said that liberal constitutionalism undermines settled structures? In contrast to functionalism, formalism is often motivated by the desire to settle destabilizing disputes. Surprisingly, in actual operation it can nonetheless serve as a counterweight to the settling tendencies of functionalism. Formalism provides tools that losers can use to destabilize the political outcomes that might otherwise settle disputes. Moreover, it accomplishes this objective without erecting settling structures of its own.

Recall that unsettlement theory reverses Justice Jackson's argument from role morality. It maintains that we can count on the political branches to resolve our disputes and that the proper role for courts is to undermine these resolutions. When Chief Justice Burger resorts to the formal requirements of constitutional text to invalidate the legislative veto, he is doing just this. Whereas a functional approach would remit this question to the political branches for final resolution, Burger uses "[e]xplicit and unambiguous text"[55] to undermine this resolution.

At first one might suppose that formalism simply substitutes one final resolution for another. Instead of settling the dispute by reference to a political decision, it settles it by reference to constitutional text. No doubt formalists would like to accomplish this substitution. But whatever their desires, contradictions in liberal constitutionalism, discussed in Chapter 3, prevent final resolution. They do so in three ways.

First, in many cases, functionalists are right when they argue that constitutional text does not resolve the dispute. Chief Justice Burger's *Chadha* opinion provides a powerful example. What, precisely, is the "explicit and unambiguous" constitutional text that outlaws the legislative veto? Burger makes repeated reference to the "bicameral requirement of Art. I, §§ 1, 7,"[56] which he paraphrases as "providing that no law [can] take effect without the concurrence of the prescribed majority of the Members of both Houses."[57] It is telling that Burger never actually quotes the relevant text, however. There is a straightforward, if embarrassing, reason for this failure: there is no relevant text. Remarkably, the explicit and unambiguous language he relies upon simply does not exist. The dirty little secret is that the Constitution contains no "bicameralism clause," if by that phrase one means a clause requiring that statutes be enacted by majorities of both houses. Although Article I provides that the Congress "shall consist of a Senate and House of Representatives,"[58] it says nothing about how these bodies should allocate between themselves the responsibility for enacting legislation.*

To be sure, Article I goes on to provide that "Every Bill which shall have passed the House of Representatives and the Senate, shall, before it becomes a Law, be presented to the President of the United States."[59] But this presentment requirement is obviously inapplicable to the one-house veto at issue in *Chadha*. Indeed, the *Chadha* Court rejected the veto precisely because it had not "passed . . . the Senate."[60] As Chief Justice Burger himself acknowledges, one house of Congress often acts so as to change legal rights without presenting its actions to the president for possible veto. Burger cites the cases of impeachment, trials of impeachment, confirmation of presidential appointments, and treaties.[61] He might also have cited the subpoenaing of witnesses — a particularly damning example, because it is nowhere authorized by the

---

*The Constitution does divide up congressional power in some discrete areas. For example, it provides that revenue bills must originate in the House (U.S. Const., art. I, sec. 7, cl. 1), that the House shall have the impeachment power (id., at art. I, sec. 2, cl. 5), and that the Senate shall have the power to try impeachment (id., at art. I, sec. 3, cl. 6), to give advice and consent on the appointment of civil officers (id., at art. II, sec. 2, cl. 2), and to ratify treaties (id.). Given this specificity, one might read constitutional silence on other matters as granting flexibility to the political branches to allocate power as they choose.

Constitution's text.* Moreover, it has been clear since the founding that proposed constitutional amendments need not be presented to the president, even though they are enacted by *both* houses of Congress.[62] Given all this, it is incomprehensible why anyone would think that constitutional text makes the one-house veto illegitimate.

Of course, nontextualists will probably find much of this argument silly. Whatever the literal text says, they will argue, any workable interpretation of the text would place some limits on Congress' power to delegate authority to some subsection of itself. But formalists are precluded from relying on arguments of this sort. They reject the notion that the text should be embroidered upon simply because it may "often seem clumsy, inefficient, even unworkable."[63] Ironically, the commitment to formalist methodology means that the formalist project can never achieve closure. Constitutional text, like the dreams Joseph was called upon to interpret for Pharaoh, often leaves contested questions unresolved. And what could unsettlement amount to if not an insistence on resolving these questions solely by reference to a methodology incapable of resolving them?

Formalism also promotes unsettlement in a second way: the very rigidity of formal rules invites efforts to circumvent them. In part, this will be true simply because in a culture where functionalism has some purchase, formal results will strike many as silly. But even if there were no functionalists, formalism, by its very nature, is vulnerable to circumvention.

Consider, for example, Clinton v. City of New York,[64] where the Court invalidated the so-called line-item veto. The statute in question responded to the widespread belief that "pork" inserted in omnibus spending bills could best be removed by allowing the president to disaggregate the bills, eliminating some budget lines without vetoing the entire measure. By its terms, the Line Item Veto Act authorized the president to "cancel in whole" any items of new spending or any "limited tax benefit."[65]

Justice Stevens' majority opinion relies entirely upon formal structure to invalidate the act. Whatever its other merits, the Court held, the measure meant that the president could "cancel" or repeal a statute without securing a majority vote of both houses before doing so.[66] Because the line-item veto was "not the product of the 'finely wrought' procedure that the Framers designed,"[67] it could not stand.

The difficulty with this position is that, precisely because it is formal, it is

---

*Strikingly, Chief Justice Burger himself wrote an opinion granting Congress extraordinarily sweeping subpoena power. *See* Eastland v. United States Servicemen's Fund, 421 U.S. 491 (1975).

vulnerable to being undone by a simple recharacterization of the act's terms. According to Justice Stevens, although the court was "favored with extensive debate about the scope of Congress' power to delegate law-making authority, or its functional equivalent, to the President," the delegation question "does not really bear on the narrow issue that is dispositive of these cases."[68] It would seem to follow that if Congress could achieve the same objective through delegation, it would avoid the "narrow" problem that concerns the Court.[69]

It hardly requires an expert to see how this recharacterization could be accomplished. Congress could simply change the wording of the act. Instead of permitting the president to "cancel" or "veto" items in a bill, it could delegate to him discretionary authority to decide whether to expend certain appropriated funds. Such a delegation does not authorize the president to repeal legislation. A president who exercises his delegated authority is implementing, rather than repealing, the statute that grants him this authority. For this reason, Justice Scalia is surely right when he asserts in his dissenting opinion that "[t]he title of the Line Item Veto Act . . . has succeeded in faking out the Supreme Court."[70]

"Fake outs" of this sort pose a real problem for formalism. On the one hand, *Clinton* illustrates how formalism's rigidity risks making its commands meaningless. If it really takes no more than a change in title to evade its dictates, why bother? Yet on the other, formalism lacks the resources to respond to evasive maneuvers. A functionalist Court, attentive to how structures actually work rather than what they are called, might penetrate formal characterization to get at the common policy concern raised by both "cancellations" and "delegations." But an analysis of this sort sacrifices the rule-based rigidity that is formalism's chief attraction. The upshot is that formalism can destabilize political outcomes but lacks the resources to entrench substitutes.

There is still a third way in which formalism can unsettle: through exploitation of the ambiguity of liberal constitutionalism's paired opposites, discussed in Chapter 3, many formal decisions can be flipped. *Chadha*, once again, provides a useful example. In this case, the feasance-nonfeasance and freedom-coercion distinctions provide methods for reversing the decision's thrust.

In *Chadha*, the one-house veto overturned a decision by an administrative-law judge in the Department of Justice to grant Chadha a hardship exemption from deportation. The Court characterized the House decision as feasance, which effectively changed Chadha's legal status. But, as Justice Byron White demonstrates in his brilliant dissent,[71] it is easy to reverse the feasance-nonfeasance distinction. Suppose we start with the baseline (established by the statute) that Chadha is subject to deportation. It is common ground that a single house can, by nonfeasance, prevent a change in the status quo, since the putative "bicameralism" requirement mandates approval by both houses. Thus, the House decision to "veto" Chadha's exemption might be characterized as nonacquiescence, blocking a change favored by the executive and the Senate. Put differently, a change in Chadha's status from deportable to nondeportable required the acquiescence of the House, the Senate, and the executive, just as the majority's reading of constitutional text requires. The veto is therefore not functionally different from a statute making people like Chadha automatically deportable, subject to the possibility of the result being countermanded by a private bill, which would have to be enacted by both houses and signed by the president.

Another way to undermine *Chadha* is to exploit the incoherence of the freedom-coercion distinction. Suppose that in the wake of *Chadha*, Congress enacted a statute with three sections. The first section authorized the Justice Department to grant waivers from deportation. The second section established a one-house veto of these waivers. The third section made the grant of authority under section 1 nonseverable from the veto provision in section 2.

How would such a law work in practice? So long as the Justice Department did not grant a waiver, or Congress did not attempt to utilize its veto, there would be no difficulty. Under modern constitutional doctrine, there is nothing constitutionally problematic about the bare delegation of administrative discretion to grant hardship waivers. Of course, any attempt by Congress to utilize the veto would be unconstitutional. But if a court were to invalidate the veto, the invalidation would sweep away not just the veto itself but the grant of Justice Department authority as well. The upshot would be the functional analogue of a veto. The authority of the Justice Department to grant waivers could be countermanded by the action of either branch of Congress — an action that would not have to be presented to the executive for veto.*

---

*It might be argued that this trick would work only one time. Once Justice Department authority was swept away, perhaps future waivers would be invalid. Recall, however, that the severability question turns on congressional intent. A congressional decision to make the grant of authority nonseverable is motivated by an unwillingness to allow the Justice Department to exercise its authority in cases where one house of Congress disagrees with this result. It is hard to imagine that Congress would not want the Justice Department to possess this authority when there was no congressional objection to its use in a particular case. In any event, standing requirements might well shield the veto from judicial scrutiny: in any case where the veto was exercised, a plaintiff harmed by the veto would have no stake in the outcome of the suit, since invalidation of the veto would also destroy the administrative authority to grant him the benefit he seeks.

In *Chadha* itself, the Court held that the veto provision was severable from the grant of

The secret behind this legerdemain is that the legislative veto has the same structure as a conditional offer. As with all conditional offers, it can be characterized as either a constitutionally problematic threat limiting freedom or a constitutionally unproblematic offer expanding freedom. Suppose, for example, that a prosecutor offers to allow a defendant to plead guilty to a lesser offense in exchange for the defendant's waiver of her right to a jury trial. There is a sense in which this "offer" is really a threat that pressures the right to a jury.[72] We might characterize the prosecutor's stance as threatening to charge a greater offense unless the defendant gives up her constitutionally protected jury right.

This is how the *Chadha* Court saw the legislative veto. The legislative veto allows a single house of Congress to control legal outcomes by threatening to countermand an administrative decision. But the problem with this characterization is that the threat is tied to a discretionary offer. A prosecutor who is denied the ability to bargain for a waiver of the jury right might insist upon the greater penalty. There is a sense, then, in which the bargain, taken as a package, is an "offer" that increases the defendant's possibility of choice.[73] After all, she does not have to accept the plea deal. If we start from the baseline of the higher charge, she has something to gain and nothing to lose when the offer is made.

In the legislative-veto context, our hypothetical nonseverability clause makes an analogous linkage explicit. Congress grants administrative discretion to the Justice Department on the express condition that the grant is linked to the legislative veto. Like the prosecutor who would insist on the harsher penalty if prevented from bargaining, Congress would not grant the discretion if it were not conditioned by the veto. Thus, when viewed as a package, Chadha, like the plea-bargaining defendant, is made no worse off by the delegation-veto combination. He is offered the possibility of a hardship exemption that would not exist but for the legislative veto. And far from increasing congressional power, the provision grants the executive some discretion it would otherwise not have had.

The point of this discussion is not that any of these arguments would neces-

---

authority. *See* 462 U.S. 919, at 934. It made clear, however, that severability was a question of statutory interpretation and that Congress therefore had authority to make the provisions nonseverable. *See* id. The Court proceeded on the assumption that if the provisions were nonseverable, Chadha would have lacked standing, although it did not so hold. Justice Rehnquist's dissenting opinion argued that the grant of authority was not severable from the veto provision. *See* id., at 1013. He did not address the standing question.

sarily satisfy the Supreme Court. Indeed, Justice White's dissent confronted the Court with an attack on the feasance-nonfeasance distinction, and we know that the attack did not prevail. Instead, the point is that formalism, standing alone, will not settle the dispute in a dispositive way. *Chadha* resolves the case before the Court, but it cannot permanently resolve the argument. Opponents of the outcome are left with something more to say. Without dissociating themselves from our standard constitutional discourse, they can use the very tools the Court relies upon to undermine the outcome the Court reaches. Ironically, the rigidity of formal rules makes them vulnerable to the "lawyers' tricks" that can be used to get around them. And as long as these tricks remain available, those who resort to them can be enticed to stay within an inclusive legal community.

The upshot, then, is that although the Supreme Court might do more to take advantage of our unsettled constitution by candidly acknowledging the political base for its structural decisions, even when it fails to do so these decisions retain their unsettling potential. The unresolvable argument between functionalists and formalists provides rhetorical resources for losers to mount plausible constitutional challenges to outcomes they dislike. Moreover, even when functionalism tends to settle, formalism retains the potential to destabilize functional outcomes without substituting stable outcomes of its own.

7

The Right to Unsettlement

In Chapters 5 and 6 I discussed constitutional law as the specification of a framework that generates political decisions. Framework theories aim at producing a just political order, but they pursue this goal through indirection. Instead of explicitly specifying a set of results, they rely upon structures and boundaries to generate just outcomes more or less automatically. These approaches stand in opposition to theories that attempt to mandate particular substantive outcomes by, for example, listing a set of rights that the polity must protect. This chapter discusses this rival, substantive-specification approach.

Some constitutional theorists have claimed that the framework approach is the most that constitutional law should attempt.[1] For example, federalist defenders of the new Constitution resisted the addition of a bill of rights on the ground that fixed community boundaries and structures, standing alone, would guarantee freedom.[2] Federalist resistance emphasized one horn of the dilemma posed by substantive specification. The federalists feared that any attempt to create a list of substantive rights would be ineffectual. This criticism, in turn, can be broken down into two separate worries. At best, the list of rights would be merely hortatory because there would be no mechanism for enforcement.[3] At worst, the list was bound to leave out some unanticipated methods of oppression, and the enumeration of some rights without the mention of others might imply government power to invade the rights not listed.[4]

This obstacle can be avoided by vesting in some government body the power to enforce, define, and expand the substantive rights. Enforcement solves the "dead letter" problem by backing up hortatory injunctions with the threat of government coercion if the injunctions are violated. Definition and expansion solve the underspecification problem by granting power to a government body to embroider upon the specified rights in order to deal with new or unanticipated forms of oppression and changing social conditions.

Unfortunately, however, avoiding the first horn of the dilemma leaves us on the second: effective and enforceable withdrawal of power from one branch of government can be achieved only by vesting power in another to enforce the withdrawal. For example, if we choose judicial review as the enforcement mechanism, then we have done no more than trade the risk of abuse by the political branches for the risk of abuse by the judicial branch.* To be sure, the judicial branch might be more protective of liberty — it might be the "least dangerous," to use the famous phrase that Alexander Bickel borrowed from the Federalist Papers.[5] But notice that now our specification approach has collapsed into a framework approach. Even if constitutional frameworks can reduce the risk of oppression by shifting power between the branches, no listing of rights can withdraw power from government altogether. The upshot, on this pessimistic view, is that the substantive-specification approach has no satisfactory answer to the "can" question discussed in Chapter 1: any attempt to guarantee freedom through the constitutional guarantee of rights is doomed to failure.

This argument has considerable force, but it has not carried the day, at least within mainstream constitutional discourse. We can trace its decline to James Madison's change of heart during the ratification period. Initially a vigorous opponent of a bill of rights, Madison came to see the wisdom of the substantive-specifications strategy, perhaps at first under the political necessity of satisfying anti-federalist opponents. Eventually, he became an enthusiastic and apparently sincere advocate of a rights approach and was the principal author of the

---

*The Ninth Amendment provides a powerful illustration of the problem. The amendment, which states that "[t]he enumeration in the Constitution, of certain rights, shall not be construed to deny or disparage others retained by the people," was obviously inserted to avoid the underspecification problem. Read strongly, it does so quite effectively, but only because it shifts broad power to the judicial branch. Precisely because the rights it protects are not enumerated, judges are left free to enforce their contested political preferences by reformulating them in the vocabulary of rights.

Bill of Rights enacted by the first Congress.[6] Since then, the rights approach has all but eclipsed the framework conception. At least for the second half of the twentieth century, the Constitution's substantive specification of rights has held center stage.

Yet despite this historic victory over framework approaches, the initial dilemma of substantive specification has never been satisfactorily resolved. Indeed, modern constitutional theory is dominated by unsuccessful efforts to come to grips with it. The controversies over "judicial activism" and the "countermajoritarian difficulty" can be understood as generated by contradictions that occur when one branch of government is granted power so as to restrain other branches. For example, critics of "judicial activism" claim that when the Supreme Court decided Roe v. Wade,[7] it was not merely restraining the other branches from invading a realm of freedom; it was also exercising power of its own. On this view, *Roe* does no more than trade the putative oppression of women by the political branches for the putative oppression of fetuses ("unborn children," if you will) by the courts.[8]

Traditional theories lack the resources to solve this problem. If the Constitution's substantive specifications are to have meaning, enforcement and expansion mechanisms are essential. Yet as soon as these mechanisms are in place, our constitutional guardians will themselves wield power that can be used for oppressive purposes.

In this chapter, I argue that unsettlement theory provides a way out of this dilemma. I grant that judges who decide contested policy questions under the guise of constitutional law are exercising power. As we have already seen, however, there is no escape from this fact. Any decision a court makes, including the decision to defer to political outcomes, amounts to the enforcement of some contestable specification of just outcomes (for example, a specification that outcomes produced by the political system are just). Judicial power is legitimate in part because it is unavoidable and in part to the extent that courts take advantage of their special position to unsettle the outcomes generated by the political process without imposing a settlement of their own. In order to demonstrate how they might pursue the latter alternative, I begin by examining a fundamental tension within the tradition of rights specification.

Two Conceptions of Rights

The argument for unsettlement begins with the observation that when people talk about "rights" they are referring to two very different things. Sometimes they mean the ability to keep things private, other times, the ability to make things public.* Perhaps most often they mean both at the same time, even though the two contradict each other.

To illustrate the point, consider the following thought experiment. Suppose that Shelley and Kelly engage in some form of illegal "nonstandard" sex in the privacy of their own bedroom. Frankie and Johnnie engage in the same activity, but they arrange to have the activity photographed so that the picture can be posted on an Internet site protesting government regulation of the activity. If the government takes action against both couples, which has the better claim that their rights have been violated?

American constitutional law is hopelessly ambivalent on this question. Shelley and Kelly can invoke the part of our rights-specification tradition that is private-regarding. They can rely on cases such as Stanley v. Georgia,[9] Griswold v. Connecticut,[10] and Roe v. Wade,[11] which, broadly speaking, protect a zone of privacy around home, family, and sex. On this view, the right is protected only so long as the act is, in fact, private.† Familiar principles of Fourth Amendment law illustrate the limitation: a person has a "reasonable expectation of privacy" in things that are shielded from public view but has no such expectation when they are exposed to the broader community.[12] The military's "don't ask–don't tell" policy with regard to homosexuality is premised on a similar intuition.

Frankie and Johnnie can invoke the strand of our rights tradition that is public-regarding. They will cite cases such as New York Times Co. v. Sullivan[13] or Justice Louis Brandeis' famous concurrence in Whitney v. California[14] for the proposition that public debate about matters of self-governance is uniquely valuable. On this view, the right is protected only so long as the activity is made public. Compare, for example, Hurley v. Irish-American Gay, Lesbian and Bisexual Group of Boston[15] (where the Court held unconstitutional the application of the Massachusetts antidiscrimination law insofar as it

---

*I note in passing that the verbs *keep* and *make* presuppose the sort of fixed baseline that unsettlement theory rejects.

†In Lovisi v. Slayton, 363 F. Supp. 620 (E.D.Va. 1973), for example, a district court rejected a constitutional attack on the sodomy conviction of a married couple because they had arranged to photograph their sexual activity. "The existence of seclusion in a sexual act . . . is a necessary prerequisite of that act's being protected from state regulation by the Constitution. Where that element has been relinquished by the parties in the performance of their sexual act, they have given up the Constitution's protection over the manner in which they choose to carry out tht act." Id. at 626. *See also* Bowers v. Hardwick, 478 U.S. 186, 212 (1986) (Blackmun, J., dissenting) (emphasizing the constitutionally significant distinction between "laws that protect public sensibilities and those that enforce private morality").

mandated the participation of a gay rights group in a St. Patrick's Day parade) with Bowers v. Hardwick[16] (where the Court rejected a claim that homosexual sodomy was constitutionally protected). *Hurley* held that the First Amendment trumped the antidiscrimination statute because the parade was a public event.[17] *Bowers* held that Hardwick's purely private conduct could not be "grounded in the First Amendment."*

The tension between these two parts of our rights tradition regularly causes confusion in constitutional doctrine. A rather obscure Supreme Court decision, Rankin v. McPherson,[18] provides a dramatic illustration. The Court held that the free-speech rights of a clerical employee in a county constable's office were violated when she was discharged because, shortly after the assassination attempt against President Ronald Reagan, she was overheard saying, "if they go for him again, I hope they get him."[19] Justice Thurgood Marshall's majority opinion held that the comment was constitutionally protected because it was public-regarding: "The inappropriate or controversial character of a statement is irrelevant to the question whether it deals with a matter of public concern. '[D]ebate on public issues should be uninhibited, robust, and wide-open, and . . . may well include vehement, caustic, and sometimes unpleasantly sharp attacks on government and public officials.' "[20] Justice Lewis Powell concurred in the result, but he thought the remark was protected because it was private-regarding: "There is no dispute that McPherson's comment was made during a private conversation with a co-worker who happened also to be her boyfriend. She had no intention or expectation it would be overheard or acted on by others. . . . [I]t will be an unusual case where the employer's legitimate interests will be so great as to justify punishing an employee for this

---

*Hardwick had relied in part on the Court's earlier decision in Stanley v. Georgia, 394 U.S. 557 (1969), where the Court had held that the First Amendment prevented conviction for possessing and reading obscene material in the privacy of the home. The *Bowers* Court distinguished *Stanley* as follows: "*Stanley* did protect conduct that would not have been protected outside the home, and it partially prevented the enforcement of state obscenity laws; but the decision was firmly grounded in the First Amendment. The right pressed upon us here has no similar support in the text of the Constitution, and it does not qualify for recognition under the prevailing principles for construing the Fourteenth Amendment." 478 U.S., at 195. As we shall see, *Stanley* is part of the tradition that treats First Amendment protection as private-regarding. If one is operating within that tradition, it is far from clear why Hardwick's right to communicate privately with his lover finds "no . . . support in the text of the Constitution." *Bowers* makes more sense when viewed from within the public-regarding tradition exemplified by *Hurley*. Given the fact that the *Bowers* Court is operating within a different, conflicting paradigm, it should come as no surprise that it must struggle to distinguish *Stanley*.

type of private speech that routinely takes place at all levels in the workplace."[21]

Remarkably, neither Marshall nor Powell evinced any awareness that these grounds for decision contradicted each other. This absence of conflict suggests that people somehow manage to hold both conceptions of rights simultaneously. At least Marshall and Powell were different Justices writing separate opinions, but on some occasions a single Justice will express both views in the same opinion. Consider, for example, Justice William Brennan's opinion for the Court in Roberts v. United States Jaycees.[22] In the course of upholding a prohibition on sexual discrimination as applied to the membership policy of the U.S. Jaycees, Brennan distinguished the case of truly private activity:

> The Court has long recognized that, because the Bill of Rights is designed to secure individual liberty, it must afford the formation and preservation of certain kinds of highly personal relationships a substantial measure of sanctuary from unjustified interference by the State. . . . [Such relationships] are distinguished by such attributes as relative smallness, a high degree of selectivity in decisions to begin and maintain the affiliation, and seclusion from others in critical aspects of the relationship. . . . [A]n association lacking these qualities . . . seems remote from the concerns giving rise to this constitutional protection.[23]

Yet Justice Brennan also felt called upon to claim that the statute did not interfere with the Jaycees' public activities: "[T]he Jaycees has failed to demonstrate that the Act imposes any serious burdens on the male members' freedom of expressive association. . . . The Act requires no change in the Jaycees' creed of promoting the interests of young men, and it imposes no restrictions on the organization's ability to exclude individuals with ideologies or philosophies different from those of its existing members."[24]

Sometimes this contradiction causes a Justice to denigrate the very activity he also wishes to celebrate. Consider, for example, Justice Oliver Wendell Holmes's dissent in Abrams v. United States.[25] The best-known passages in the dissent argue that speech is important because it accomplishes something in the public sphere. Speech must be protected because "the ultimate good desired is better reached by free trade in ideas" and "the best test of truth is the power of the thought to get itself accepted in the competition of the market."[26] There is a startling disjunction between this rationale for protection and Holmes's description of the actual speech being protected. It turns out that the pamphlets in question are "poor and puny anonymities."[27] They are entitled to First Amendment protection not because they contribute in a meaningful way to "the free trade in ideas" but because "nobody can suppose that the surreptitious publishing of a silly leaflet by an unknown man, without more, would present any immediate danger that its opinions would hinder the success of the government arms or have any appreciable tendency to do so."[28] This passage suggests that it is the fact that the pamphlets made no public contribution that justifies their protection.[29] In contrast, when Eugene Debs, a much more serious and popular war opponent, actually threatened to contribute to public debate about the war, Holmes wrote to affirm his conviction, precisely on the ground that if "one purpose of the speech . . . was to oppose [the] war, and [if] that opposition was so expressed that its natural and intended effect would be to obstruct recruiting" it would not be protected.[30]

For a more recent powerful example, consider the initial draft of Justice Douglas' opinion for the Court in Griswold v. Connecticut,[31] invalidating a Connecticut law prohibiting married couples from using contraceptive devices. We now know that the opinion as first drafted relied on a public-regarding, First Amendment rationale, arguing that the statute violated freedom of association by interfering with the marriage relationship, which "flourishes on the interchange of ideas."[32] This argument was apparently too much for Justice Hugo Black, a *Griswold* dissenter, who responded caustically that "[the right] of association is for me [a] right of assembly [and the right] of [a] husband [and] wife to assemble in bed is [a] new right of assembly to me."[33] Even Justice Brennan, a member of the *Griswold* majority, was unpersuaded by the First Amendment rationale. He wrote Douglas that the "association" of married couples had little to do with the public advocacy protected by the freedom of assembly clause.[34] Ultimately, Douglas was persuaded to abandon his "interchange of ideas" rationale. It did not follow that he changed his vote, however. Having failed to convince his colleagues that contraceptive use was protected because it contributed to public values, he ended up arguing for its protection because it did *not* make such a contribution. For the Douglas of the final opinion, marriage was protected because it was "an association that promotes a way of life, not causes; a harmony of living, not political faiths; a bilateral loyalty, not commercial or social projects."[35]

The Meanings of Privacy

If we had only the *Griswold* example before us, we might write off Justice Douglas' shift between rationales as mere opportunism. I hope that the other examples I have offered suggest that something more fundamental explains the Court's persistent waffling between public- and private-regarding theories of constitutional rights. In fact, the Justices are struggling with two conflicting intuitions, both so deeply held that neither can be abandoned. We have already explored this conflict at some length. Public and private theories of rights are simply another manifestation of the linked series of paired opposites that provide the raw material for liberal constitutional law.

At the core of the conflict is the struggle between universalism and particularism. One way to see this is by examining the connection between three different ways that the terms *private* and *public* are used in contemporary constitutional discourse.[36] Sometimes *private* means "autonomous," as when, for example, the Court holds that the right to choose an abortion is an aspect of privacy. The Anglo-American liberal tradition associates autonomy with particularism. On this view, we are free when we do not have to account to others for our actions. Thus, the woman's right to choose an abortion means that she cannot be forced to explain or justify her decision according to norms that are universally shared. As the plurality puts the point in Planned Parenthood of Southeastern Pennsylvania v. Casey, a pregnant woman's "suffering is too intimate and personal for the State to insist, without more, upon its own vision of the woman's role, however dominant that vision has been in the course of our history and our culture. The destiny of the woman must be shaped to a large extent on her own conception of her spiritual imperatives and her place in society."[37]

This conception of autonomy is opposed by a public-regarding view. For example, in the German idealist tradition, freedom does not mean doing whatever you want. To act on whim is to be a slave to passions. Freedom, on this view, is obedience to universal laws—the laws that a fully rational person would give to herself if freed from particularistic self-interest.[38] Similarly, for those attracted to the republican and communitarian perspectives, autonomy is associated with democratic self-governance. This conception also pushes us toward universalism. What self-governance means in these traditions is the transcendence of particularistic urges in favor of "civic virtue" and a public good that is independent of individual tastes and desires.[39]

It is easy to see the link between the particularist conception of autonomy and the second meaning of *privacy*. In contemporary constitutional discourse, *private* often means nongovernmental. Through this linguistic overlap, the nongovernmental sphere is associated with particularistic autonomy, while the governmental sphere is associated with universalistic, public autonomy. As discussed in Chapter 5, well-functioning political communities are defined by bounded universalism. For those within the community, the government must demonstrate equal concern and respect. The community puts flesh on this broad ideal through a process of deliberation and community self-definition which embodies the public idea of freedom. But precisely because the idea is public and universalist, liberals insist that the government's writ must be limited. There must also be a private sphere, walled off from government interference, within which particularistic autonomy can flourish.[40]

A third meaning of *privacy* helps explain how the two spheres can be kept separate. The Court sometimes uses *private* as a synonym for "secret" or "shielded from public view." For example, the Court has said that the Fourth Amendment search-and-seizure provision guarantees privacy in the sense that the Constitution permits people to keep certain things secret.[41]

Some legal theorists have wondered why we should value privacy conceived of as secrecy. Secrecy allows people to misrepresent important facts about themselves. Why, they have asked, should there be a fundamental right to mislead others?[42] Privacy as secrecy makes more sense when one understands that secrecy helps enforce a boundary between incompatible universalist and particularist conceptions of freedom. Secrecy is a necessary component of particularist autonomy because it shields conduct from public, universalist criticism.[43]

In Thornburgh v. American College of Obstetricians & Gynecologists,[44] the Court invalidated a record-keeping provision that risked making public the names of women who had had abortions. Because the abortion decision was "intensely private," it followed for the Court that it "must be protected in a way that assures anonymity." Were it not so protected, "[a] woman and her physician will necessarily be more reluctant to choose an abortion."[45]

On its face, this argument seems radically incomplete. Why does the fact that a decision-making context makes a woman "more reluctant to choose an abortion" discredit it? If it is really true that publicity discourages abortion, then one might also say that secrecy discourages live births. Apparently, there must also be choice at a second level—not just choice about the procedure itself but choice about who has knowledge of the choice. On other occasions, though, we do not require a decision-making context where the individual has control over such knowledge. Candidates for political office have a right to raise funds, but they have no general right to keep the source of the funds secret, even if public knowledge about the source will make them "reluctant" to accept the money.* The Constitution provides that "a regular Statement

---

*To be sure, the Court has invalidated disclosure requirements as applied to "a minor political party which historically has been the object of harassment by government officials and private parties." Brown v. Socialist Workers '74 Campaign Comm. (Ohio) 459 U.S. 87, 88 (1982). In the more usual context, however, it has recognized that the government has a legitimate interest in providing "the electorate with information 'as to where political campaign money comes from and how it is spent by the candidate' in order to aid the voters in evaluating those who seek federal office." Buckley v. Valeo, 424 U.S. 1, 66–67 (1976).

and Account of the Receipts and Expenditures of all public Money shall be published from time to time."[46] The framers were evidently unmoved by the argument that a public accounting might discourage Congress from certain expenditures of funds.

We can better understand *Thornburgh* if we interpret the Court as saying that there is something special about the abortion decision that makes secrecy the appropriate decision-making context. On this view, abortion decisions, unlike decisions about campaign contributions or the spending of public moneys, ought to be particularistic. Women deciding between abortion and live birth should not make the sort of disinterested, impartial judgments that universalism insists upon, any more than a parent should use these criteria when choosing between benefiting his own children and benefiting strangers in a foreign land. But particularistic judgments are fragile in the face of universalist criticism and must therefore be shielded from such criticism by keeping them secret.[47]

Secrecy also reenforces particularism in a second, more subtle fashion. As we have already seen, the notion of a private sphere is threatened by critical assaults on the paired opposites, especially the feasance-nonfeasance distinction. If government embodies a universalist conception of autonomy, and if government nonfeasance is equivalent to feasance, then how can we bound the realm of universalism? It would seem that merely permitting a private sphere to exist is itself a government decision that must be justified according to universalistic criteria.

In his work on precommitment and imperfect rationality, Jon Elster suggests a way out of this dilemma.[48] Elster explores Blaise Pascal's famous "wager argument" for belief in God.[49] If there is some possibility that God exists and if a person who believes in God will receive a large payoff if he is right, then a person intent on maximizing utility would so believe. Elster explores a problem with this position: the efficacy of a belief can never by itself provide reasons for adopting it.[50] I am certain that I would be happier if I could believe that I would never again suffer pain, but this fact standing alone cannot make me believe that the rest of my life will be pain-free.

A person wishing to pursue Pascal's strategy must therefore engage in some subtle intellectual game-playing. Since she cannot believe both that something is true and also that that belief stems solely from a decision to believe it is true regardless of whether it actually is, she must pursue a precommitment strategy that binds herself in a manner that induces forgetfulness about the source of the belief.

Something like this strategy is at work in the maintenance of separate government and nongovernment spheres. By manipulating the amount of information available—by creating in advance the correct mix of openness and secrecy—we can both precommit to separate particularist and universalist decision criteria and hide from ourselves the particularist or universalist motive for the precommitment.

Guido Calabresi and Philip Bobbitt have explored how governments make particularistic "tragic choices" through low-visibility mechanisms that maximize discretion and minimize the application of general standards.[51] Consider, for example, the secrecy that surrounds jury deliberations or end-of-life decisions about the withdrawal of medical intervention. Our precommitment to secrecy walls off these decisions from the need for universalist justification that would exist if they were public.

Conversely, when these decisions are publicized, we are sometimes unable to "forget" the consequences of government inaction, and the actor may be taken to have submitted herself to universalist jurisdiction. Thus, judges regularly tell jurors not to reveal the content of their deliberation.[52] When, despite this bar, judges do learn that jurors are behaving particularistically, they sometimes intervene to enforce universalist norms.[53] Similarly, in the abstract, we know that many doctors privately and secretly hasten the end of life with the approval of the patient and his relatives,* but when Dr. Jack Kevorkian insisted on televising his acts of euthanasia, he elicited a strongly negative public response and government intervention. The drama surrounding President Clinton's "private" life provides still another example. Throughout his presidency, many people in some sense "knew" about Clinton's history of sexual adventures, but they emphatically did not want to hear public discussion of it. A public discussion interfered with our ability to "forget" these uncomfortable facts. Such a discussion seemed to require a response justified by universalism, and most Americans did not want to be forced into such a response.

Just as a precommitment to secrecy protects particularism, so a precommitment to publicity protects universalism. A highly visible decision-making process is more likely to be criticized by all affected groups than a less visible process. The more visible decision maker is accordingly more likely to consider these criticisms. Visibility also promotes a public discussion in which people think as public citizens and so transcend, to some extent, particularist concerns. Theories of the First Amendment that emphasize the "checking" function of the press are based on some such notion.[54] So is the majority opinion in New York v. United States, emphasizing the lack of political ac-

---

*Although it is difficult to obtain reliable data, it has been estimated that between 3 and 37 percent of clinicians have actively assisted at least one patient to die. Timothy E. Quill, *Risk Taking by Physicians in Legally Gray Areas*, 57 Alb. L. Rev. 693, 698 (1994).

countability when the federal government "commandeers" state agencies to serve its purposes,[55] as well as the views of opponents of the vague delegation of lawmaking power to administrative agencies, who emphasize the role of delegation in avoiding political responsibility for difficult decisions.[56]

Styles of Judicial Activism

The next stage in the argument is to link these public- and private-regarding conceptions of rights to two competing styles of judicial review. I argue below that modern constitutional law vacillates between these styles and that both styles fail the test of political neutrality that settlement theory demands. Both founder on the dilemma for rights-specification strategies we have already discussed. However, when the two are considered together they promote a different sort of neutrality: the neutrality that comes with the permanent unsettlement of constitutional doctrine.

A casual observer might suppose that the chief dispute animating modern constitutional debate is the argument between advocates of judicial activism and advocates of judicial restraint. The two terms are imprecise, but for our purposes there is no need to get bogged down in complexity. Speaking loosely, we can define judicial activism as the relatively uninhibited utilization of judicial power to enforce the norms that judges "discover" in the Constitution. Judicial restraint, in contrast, is characterized by a reluctance to permit judicial interference with political outcomes.

Although popular constitutional rhetoric is dominated by the supposed disagreement between persons holding these two positions, there is something odd about the dispute: it has virtually nothing to do with the issues that actually divide Supreme Court Justices and other constitutional lawyers when they think about real cases. No Justice sitting on the Court within recent memory has been a consistent advocate of judicial restraint. The Court has recently invalidated political outcomes in areas as diverse as affirmative action,[57] federalism,[58] separation of powers,[59] free-speech rights,[60] reproductive autonomy,[61] sexual discrimination,[62] property rights,[63] and political districting.[64] Nor is there a significant difference between "liberal" and "conservative" Justices with regard to the frequency of their support for "activist" results or their willingness to depart from constitutional text or history when they reach these results. The stark fact is that both liberals and conservatives can regularly be found arguing for "loose construction" and for activism in a variety of contexts.

If we want to get to the nub of what actually divides us, we must end our obsession with the theoretical distinction between activism and restraint and focus instead on the real dispute, between libertarian and interventionist activists. Both libertarians and interventionists are prepared to substitute judicial for political judgments. But whereas libertarians favor an active judiciary to keep the political branches passive, interventionists favor an active judiciary to make the political branches more active. Put differently, whereas libertarians embrace the private conception of rights that associates freedom with government nonfeasance, interventionists embrace the public conception that links freedom to government intervention.

The Supreme Court's two encounters with gay rights provides a useful illustration of the distinction. In Bowers v. Hardwick,[65] the Court refused to invalidate a criminal prohibition against sodomy when the statute was applied to homosexual acts. Gay rights advocates unsuccessfully argued for libertarian activism and a private-regarding conception of rights. Their view was that the judiciary should restrain the political branches from intervening to control a decision best left to individual, particularist judgment.

A decade later, these advocates won their first major Supreme Court victory in Romer v. Evans.[66] Their victory, however, came in the form of an interventionist decision vindicating a public-regarding conception of rights. In *Romer*, the Court invalidated the results of a Colorado referendum that had prohibited localities from enacting ordinances protecting gay people from discrimination. The effect of the Court's decision was to extend government power into the private sphere (by reviving the ordinances, thereby prohibiting private acts of discrimination) rather than to protect the private sphere from government regulation.

It would be a mistake to suppose that there is a complete overlap between the libertarian-interventionist dispute on the one hand and the public-private divide on the other. Sometimes Justices have public-regarding motives for restraining government intervention. From James Madison[67] to Cass Sunstein,[68] constitutional theorists throughout our history have worried about the "corruption" that occurs when public institutions are captured by private power. One might justify a good deal of judicial activism to restrict government power on the theory that government intervention is not really public-regarding at all but is instead the assertion of private power through public means.

For example, some revisionist defenses of *Lochner* argue that much social and economic legislation is really the product of successful private rent-seeking activity.[69] We have already seen how judicial enforcement of limits on government power to regulate speech can serve public-regarding ends by making government more subject to universalist criticism. Akhil Amar has forcefully argued that the original Bill of Rights, although written in libertarian terms, was designed to promote public discussion.[70] And as Sunstein has demonstrated, much constitutional law can be conceptualized as protecting against the public enforcement of particularistic "naked preferences."[71]

Still, although our model oversimplifies somewhat, it nonetheless reveals important truths. There are two reasons why the model is useful despite the complications introduced in the last paragraph. First, no doubt some libertarians are motivated by public-regarding values. But this fact only serves to demonstrate the bias in favor of private power that is the hallmark of libertarian activism. Whereas libertarians are preoccupied by the risks to freedom posed by government (in part because government intervention is not always public-regarding), interventionists emphasize the risks to freedom posed by private conduct. With all its imperfections, interventionists say, government is at least somewhat responsive to the public will in a way that private decision making is not.

Interventionists are aware of the possibility of government capture by faction, but they are more likely to respond by attempting to make the government more public than by restricting its power. For example, the Warren Court's one person–one vote mandate was intended to make government institutions more responsive to the public interest. Reforms like the Freedom of Information Act[72] and campaign-finance regulation have similar objectives. These alternative strategies demonstrate that the difference between libertarians and interventionists is motivated, at least in part, by conflicting views of the relation between government and freedom. Whereas libertarians think that freedom can survive only in a private sphere, interventionists believe that government can be made sufficiently public-regarding to vindicate a public conception of freedom.

Second, to reduce libertarianism to a fear of government capture by private faction is to unfairly trivialize the libertarian argument. To see the point, imagine that somehow government could be made entirely public-regarding. Does anyone suppose that even this ideal, purified government should have free rein over the private sphere? Even a completely public government, in which all views are fully and equally expressed, can be totalitarian. Most of us would not want such a government making collective decisions about whom we could marry, whether we could have children, where we should live, or what occupations we should pursue. The hypothesized fully public character of such a government makes the problem worse. For libertarians, government intervention is problematic precisely *because* it is public.

The disagreement between libertarian and interventionist activists is thus real and important. Moreover, once we grasp the distinction between the two positions, much that is otherwise mysterious about the past century of constitutional argument becomes more comprehensible. Consider, for example, the relation between the activism of the *Lochner* and Warren Courts.* In the immediate wake of the Supreme Court's rejection of *Lochner* in 1937, the liberal Roosevelt Justices were strong advocates of judicial restraint. Within a short time, however, they began once again to invalidate legislation. Does this mean that *Lochner*'s liberal critics were hypocritical?

The charge of liberal hypocrisy has its roots in Justice Holmes's dissent in *Lochner* itself. Holmes accused the majority of reading the Fourteenth Amendment as if it "enact[ed] Mr. Herbert Spencer's Social Statics" and of "prevent[ing] the natural outcome of a dominant opinion."[73] In other words, Holmes argued for judicial restraint. If his criticisms are sound, then the Warren Court can, indeed, be accused of failing to learn the lessons of *Lochner*.

But the criticisms are not sound. Holmes confused the argument between activism and restraint with the argument between libertarianism and interventionism. To see this point, compare the *Lochner* majority's argument for freedom of contract with the argument against the establishment of an official state religion. Holmes would surely be right if he were to assert that the choice of a state religion should be made by democratic means. If we are to have a state religion at all, then the choice must be made by an institution representing all the people. But this observation misses the point. The crucial question is not who should choose the state religion but whether there should be one. In other words, the real issue is not between advocates of activism and advocates of restraint but between those who think that religious choice should be private and those who think it should be public. It follows that when a Court invalidates a religious establishment, it is not itself making a public religious choice, as it would be if, for example, it held that Methodism, rather than Presbyterianism, should the state religion. Instead, it is insisting that religious choice should be private and individual, rather than public and collective.

Similarly, the *Lochner* Court was not deciding for the country the appropriate hours that bakers should work. The *Lochner* majority might well have agreed that if this decision were to be made collectively, it should be made legislatively. But for the *Lochner* Court the issue was whether it *should* be made collectively. Justice Peckham and his colleagues thought that the statute

---

*I use these terms imprecisely not to denote a period defined by the actual decision in *Lochner* or the actual tenure of Chief Justice Warren. Instead, the terms identify judicial attitudes characterized on the one hand by opposition to redistributive legislation and on the other by moderate reformism. Speaking loosely, the first attitude predominated during the first third of the twentieth century. The second emerged with the creation of a Roosevelt-appointed majority on the Court in the late 1930s.

was invalid because New York had taken a question that should remain a matter of private, individual choice and inserted it into the public sphere.

Once we understand this point, it is easy to see why Holmes's attack on judicial activism misfires. The argument would have force if the Court were indeed choosing an employment policy for everyone in the country. Instead, the Court chose between a public and a private resolution of this question. It is unfair to accuse the Court of "activism" when it made this kind of choice because the choice was inevitable. Either employment policy will be decided by individual employees and employers negotiating over contract terms or it will be decided by legislators writing statutes. There is nothing more "activist" about placing the choice in one sphere than in the other. Nor is there some a priori reason why the choice between spheres should itself be relegated to public institutions. Public institutions, if they function properly, will make the choice according to public-regarding criteria. But the issue in dispute is whether these criteria are appropriate.

Of course, this argument does not demonstrate that *Lochner* was rightly decided. What it shows instead is that opposition to *Lochner* is consistent with much of the Warren Court's work. Whereas the "activism" of the *Lochner* Court was designed to protect a private sphere of freedom from public coercion, much of the Warren Court's "activism" was designed to force the public intervention necessary to regulate what it took to be unfree private decision making. Whereas *Lochner* was libertarian, the Warren Court was interventionist.

Viewed from this perspective, it is no coincidence that *Lochner* and Warren Court activism relied upon different constitutional texts. *Lochner* activism was most prominently associated with an expansive interpretation of the due-process clause. By its very structure, the clause associates liberty with restraint on government. Government conduct must be undertaken with due process of law because government conduct endangers life, liberty, and property. The much criticized "substantive" component to the due-process guarantee follows naturally from these assumptions. Process guarantees are meaningless unless one begins from a fixed, substantive, and prepolitical baseline. Consider, for example, the quintessential procedural right: the right to judicial process before property is seized. This right is useless if, as a substantive matter, the government can define property interests in any way it chooses. What good is a hearing if before the hearing begins, government has defined the property right out of existence? On the libertarian view, freedom can be protected only if there are enforceable, substantive limitations on the jurisdiction of public institutions.

It is more difficult to find a doctrinal rubric supporting the interventionism of the Warren Court. But although the Warren Court lacked the textual tools available to libertarians, it could rely on an analytic tradition, extending back to the legal realists, that justified intervention by destabilizing the baselines against which liberal constitutionalism's paired opposites were measured.

In the beginning the Court gained some traction through an attack on the "state action" requirement. Since there was always some government "action" in the background, the Court was able to treat this action as the baseline and to characterize private conduct as public, thereby subjecting it to constitutional constraint. Shelley v. Kraemer[74] provides the most famous example of this technique. The *Shelley* Court held that the judicial enforcement of racially discriminatory private covenants limiting the sale of real property was "state action" that had to satisfy the requirements of the Fourteenth Amendment's equal-protection clause. It followed that government intervention was required to regulate these covenants.

The trouble with this doctrinal approach was that the argument proved too much. Carried to the limit, it threatened to subsume the private sphere altogether. As the legal realists had demonstrated a generation earlier, every private action could be recharacterized as public. Background tort, contract, and property rules made the state complicit in even the most "private" of arrangements. For example, my "private" choice of whom to invite to a dinner party is backed up by the willingness of state officials to enforce trespass laws against those who crash the party. The Warren Court was populated by liberals, but not by radicals. It was interested in ameliorating particular injustices in the private sphere, not in doing away with privacy altogether.

The solution to this problem was to shift doctrinal focus from state action to substantive analysis of equal-protection and First Amendment law. Consider, first, the equal-protection clause. Through the development of "two-tiered" review, the Court was able to compel public intervention in some areas while leaving private decision making protected in others.[75] Occupying the top tier and eliciting "strict scrutiny" were statutes that impinged upon "fundamental rights" or that discriminated on the basis of a "suspect classification."[76] These statutes were said to be "strictly scrutinized" and were almost always invalidated. The bottom tier consisted of "ordinary social and economic legislation," subject only to rational-basis review, that was almost always upheld.[77]

How did this categorization promote interventionism? The answer is most obvious in the context of the "fundamental rights" strand of strict scrutiny. At first it might seem that equal-protection analysis of these cases is superfluous. If a "fundamental" right is constitutionally protected, then, it would seem, impingement on the right would be unconstitutional because of the right itself. Reference to equal protection adds nothing to the analysis. If the right is not constitutionally protected, then why should it receive "back-door" protection through heightened equal-protection scrutiny?

Fundamental-rights analysis is more understandable when seen as a means of implementing an interventionist agenda. For both textual and historical reasons, substantive rights commonly follow the libertarian, due-process model. They serve to protect a private sphere, associated with freedom, from government encroachment. For example, speech is said to be "free" when the government makes "no laws." It is difficult to generate a positive right to government subvention of speech, or to government control of private actors limiting speech, from this command. In contrast, the equal-protection clause can shift the baseline to a norm of public intervention, thereby bringing into question government passivity. The structure of an equal-protection case often involves discretionary government action that benefits one class but not another. To be sure, if a court holds that this differential treatment violates equal protection, the government can satisfy its constitutional obligations by withdrawing the benefit from the favored class. But often this course will be politically impractical, and the result will be an extension of a government benefit to a broader group of people. Thus, by manipulating the definition of "fundamental rights," the Court was able to force government intervention in some cases without the wholesale abandonment of the public-private distinction threatened by the assault on the "state action" requirement.

Shapiro v. Thompson,[78] a landmark Warren-era case, illustrates how this process worked. The Court's analysis began with the observation that New York's policy of withholding welfare benefits to newly arrived residents was subject to heightened scrutiny because it impinged on the constitutional right to travel between the states. Because none of the proffered reasons for the differential treatment satisfied this scrutiny, the Court went on to hold that the discrimination between old residents, who were entitled to benefits, and new residents, who were not, violated the equal-protection clause.[79]

If the right to travel is indeed constitutionally protected, as the *Shapiro* Court asserted, one might wonder why the Court did not rely directly on this right. The problem was that this, like most rights, is libertarian. The right protects against government intervention; it does not require government subsidies. A New Jersey resident who was too poor to move to New York could hardly claim that his right to interstate travel was denied by New York's refusal to purchase a bus ticket for him. Because New York has "merely" refused to act, the poor person's disability is relegated to the sphere of private freedom.

The *Shapiro* Court's equal-protection analysis converts this libertarian, negative right into an interventionist, positive one. Our libertarian constitutional tradition means that New York need not provide welfare at all, but the equal-protection clause mandates that so long as it provides welfare for one class, it must also do so for other classes unless there is sufficient reason to distinguish between the two groups. By subjecting the distinction to heightened scrutiny, the Court made it impossible for New York to meet this requirement. To be sure, theoretically the state might have responded to *Shapiro* by ending welfare benefits for its long-time residents. The Court's bet, upon which interventionist activism rested, was that it would instead respond by extending government economic protection to the broader class.*

The association between the "suspect-class" strand of the strict scrutiny doctrine and interventionism is less obvious. Suspect-class analysis can be mobilized in the service of libertarian as well as interventionist activism. Consider, for example, the first Justice John Harlan's dissent in Plessy v. Ferguson.[80] The *Plessy* majority upheld the constitutionality of a state law requiring private companies to segregate their black and white passengers. Justice Harlan's dissent, which famously asserted that the Constitution was "colorblind," would have invalidated the legislation.[81] Significantly, though, Harlan did not claim that it was unconstitutional for the private companies themselves to discriminate on the basis of race. Instead, his objection was to government regulation. For him the Constitution was satisfied as long as choice was left to the private sphere.†

There is a superficial resemblance between Harlan's *Plessy* dissent and the Court's holding sixty years later in Brown v. Board of Education.[82] In fact, though, the two approaches are fundamentally different. At issue in *Plessy* was public control of private entities. Justice Harlan would have granted these entities immunity from public intervention in the form of compelled segregation. There is therefore a sense in which the Harlan dissent is in the same tradition as *Lochner*. In contrast, *Brown* posed an issue about *public* schools. The Warren Court required a restructuring of *public* education to ameliorate African American subjugation. *Brown* and its progeny therefore made clear that at least in some contexts, the government had positive obligations with respect to race.

There are only hints of this position in *Brown* itself. The Court's focus on

---

*The extent to which the bet paid off is debatable. Arguably, the long-term effect of *Shapiro* was to depress the level of welfare benefits. Unable to wall themselves off from an influx of out-of-staters if they were too generous, states may have lowered benefits so as not to become "welfare magnets."

†Harlan's dissenting opinion in The Civil Rights Cases, 109 U.S. 3, 33–62 (1883), leaves this point more ambiguous. He was prepared to subject private entities to non-discrimination requirements, at least when a federal statute mandated this result.

the importance of public education at least suggests an affirmative government obligation. A thoroughgoing libertarian might argue that the government has no obligation to subsidize education through a public school system. It might follow that if the government chooses to provide this benefit, it can do so on any terms it sees fit.[83] *Brown* emphatically rejects this sort of reasoning.

Moreover, in the most famous passage in the opinion, the Court warned that segregation may "affect [the] hearts and minds [of children] in a way unlikely ever to be undone."[84] This passage might be read as prohibiting no more than government conduct that harmed African Americans. On the other hand, the emphasis on effect can also be read to suggest that the government has an affirmative obligation to arrange public education so as to help rectify prior deprivations. After all, even a "neutral" policy might adversely affect a group when it intersects with background, "private" social facts. By making the government responsible for these effects, the Court can be read as imposing a positive obligation to depart from "neutrality" when such intervention is necessary to ensure real, not just formal, equality.

Whatever the original intent of the *Brown* Court, its opinion took on this meaning over the next two decades as the Court molded doctrine to overcome southern intransigence. It is no accident that this interventionist stance ended up reversing Justice Harlan's insistence on color blindness. The Court's opinions on this subject are complicated by the distinction it insisted on drawing between right and remedy. Still, however one categorizes the Court's actions, the fact is that for a period it insisted on race-conscious school assignments affirmatively designed to overcome centuries of racism and oppression.[85]

A logical extension of this position would have been the constitutional mandating of affirmative action more generally. An interventionist view of racial discrimination would have insisted upon government action to counter discrimination in the private sphere. However, Warren Court activism ran out of steam long before it reached this destination, replaced by a libertarian stance that first marginalized[86] and then retreated from[87] *Brown*-era race-conscious desegregation requirements and ended up treating affirmative action as a presumptively invalid interference with the private sphere.[88]

Before examining the decline of Warren Court activism in more detail, it is worth briefly examining a third doctrinal locus for the development of interventionism: the free-speech clause of the First Amendment. On its face, this guarantee provides an unlikely basis for justifying government regulation. As we have already seen, the clause is a limitation on, rather than an authorization of, government intervention. Indeed, an interventionist reading of the clause seems to turn it on its head. It might, for example, justify (or, indeed, require) government review of the editorial policies of private newspapers at the behest of potential authors whose speech was "silenced" by newspaper editors.

In the pre-Warren period, the clause was almost universally understood as embodying libertarian constitutional principles. For example, in an opinion written while he was on the Massachusetts Supreme Judicial Court, Justice Holmes rejected the idea that free speech protected a police officer who solicited money to aid a political purpose. "The petitioner may have a constitutional right to talk politics," he wrote, "but he has no constitutional right to be a policeman."[89] Because the petitioner was claiming a right to "feasance" — government employment — rather than "nonfeasance" — remaining free from government interference when he spoke — his claim amounted to a reversal of the First Amendment guarantee.[90]

Beginning in the 1930s, the Roosevelt Justices eroded this understanding. They did so through the familiar critical device of attacking the baseline that established the distinction between feasance and nonfeasance. The most significant of these cases involved the articulation and development of a right to a "public forum." Instead of a baseline formed by private arrangements, the Court resorted to an alternative baseline grounded in tradition. In Justice Owen Roberts' words, "Wherever the title of streets and parks may rest, they have immemorially been held in trust for the use of the public and time out of mind, have been used for purposes of assembly, communicating thoughts between citizens, and discussing public questions."[91] Use of this baseline reversed the valence of First Amendment law. Whereas a prior generation conceptualized the denial of government subsidies as a protection of freedom in the private sphere, the Warren Court saw these denials as active departures from the baseline formed by the traditional right to use streets and parks for the purpose of speech. The upshot was a constitutional right to a kind of free-speech subsidy through the required use of public property to facilitate First Amendment activity.[92]

The Warren Court's encounter with libel law can be understood in the same way. In order for private markets to function efficiently, participants must bear their own costs. When participants are not made to do so, they are said to be "subsidized." On the traditional view, the First Amendment requires no more than government noninterference and therefore does not mandate subsidies for the press. This is so because the idea of freedom is linked to private, market outcomes. Thus, newspapers have no First Amendment right to free use of the mails or to special immunities from labor or antitrust restrictions. These "special" rights can all easily be conceptualized as subsidies that allow externalization of costs.

Traditional libel law can be thought of as no more than an extension of this principle. When a newspaper pays damages to a public figure who has been libeled, the paper is made to bear the costs of its activity. The newspaper may nonetheless choose to publish the libelous information, but it will do so only if the choice is cost-justified — that is, if it is worth it to the paper after it has captured all the benefits and borne all the costs of its decision. On a libertarian view, the free-speech guarantee requires no more than this.

New York Times Co. v. Sullivan[93] radically alters this framework. The decision, which exempted newspapers from paying damages for libeling public figures in the absence of a showing of deliberate or reckless disregard for the truth of the statements, in effect shifted some of the costs of publication from the papers to the public officials. The Court's justification for the shift was the supposed overdeterrence that occurred when newspapers were forced to guess at their peril whether they had crossed the legal line. This argument destabilizes the distinction between the failure to subsidize and the imposition of a burden. By recharacterizing the one as the other, the Court, in effect, mandated government intervention to transfer resources from public officials to newspapers. The decision is roughly equivalent to a judicial order to the legislature requiring it to impose a tax on public officials with the proceeds going to newspapers.

At the same time that the Court was recharacterizing what had formally been thought permissible failures to subsidize as invasions of a right, it also supported government intervention by recharacterizing what might otherwise have been thought a "right" as a mere "subsidy." In Red Lion Broadcasting Co. v. FCC,[94] the Court relied upon the supposed scarcity of broadcast frequencies to treat the grant of broadcast licenses as a discretionary government subsidy rather than mandatory government noninterference. It followed that this subsidy could be linked to extensive regulation of broadcaster speech that would not otherwise be permitted. Strikingly, the Court held that it was government intervention, rather than noninterference, that protected First Amendment freedoms. Writing for the majority, Justice Byron White argued that "if there is to be any effective communication by radio, only a few can be licensed and the rest must be barred from the airwaves. It would be strange if the First Amendment, aimed at protecting and furthering communications, prevented the Government from making radio communication possible by requiring licenses to broadcast and by limiting the number of licenses so as not to overcrowd the spectrum."[95]

A contemporary reader of the Warren Court decisions summarized above can be forgiven for feeling like a traveler who has somehow wandered into a foreign country. We have come a long way from the interventionism that marked the Warren Court period. An important turning point came in the

1972 term, when the Court decided San Antonio Independent School District v. Rodriguez[96] and Roe v. Wade.[97]

Rodriguez sharply limited the substantive equal-protection doctrine by proclaiming the Court's refusal to heighten the level of scrutiny to protect nontextual rights. Like Justice Holmes, the Court used the rhetoric of judicial restraint to justify this refusal. Writing for the majority, Justice Powell argued that the judiciary lacked legitimate authority to protect rights not specified in the text of the Constitution.[98] But this explanation was no more convincing than it had been several generations earlier when Holmes advanced it in his *Lochner* dissent. In the same term that Justice Powell wrote *Rodriguez,* he joined the Court's majority in Roe v. Wade, one of the most important activist decisions of the century, which plainly gave protection to nontextual rights.

Instead of shifting the Court from activism to restraint, *Rodriguez* and *Roe* announced the movement from interventionism to libertarianism. Significantly, the *Roe* Court relied upon substantive due process, rather than equal protection, to invalidate abortion laws. Its decision narrowed, rather than broadened, the public sphere.

This shift from equality to liberty was linked to a return to a private-regarding conception of rights. Justice Marshall's *Rodriguez* dissent was grounded in the *Brown* tradition. He argued for a constitutional requirement to make free-speech rights truly meaningful by affirmative government intervention through the provision of adequate education.[99] In contrast, the majority held that the government had no obligation to make the exercise of rights effective.[100] The Constitution was satisfied so long as the government did not formally obstruct that exercise. This point was driven home a few years after *Roe* when the Court rejected a substantive equal-protection challenge to the failure to fund abortions for poor women.[101] *Roe* required a withdrawal of government coercion, not the provision of a government subsidy.

Four years after *Rodriguez,* the Court effectively extended this analysis to the suspect-class strand of equal-protection doctrine. In Washington v. Davis,[102] it held that the Fourteenth Amendment required no more than the formal equality espoused in Justice Harlan's *Plessy* dissent. As long as the government did not intervene to make things worse for African Americans, it had no constitutional responsibility to make things better. Their actual status in society was determined in the private sphere, which was not the product of government action.

Standing alone, Washington v. Davis might be read as a manifestation of judicial restraint. It goes no further than to say that the Constitution did not mandate government action to improve the status of African Americans. However, the Court's more recent affirmative-action holdings[103] make clear that it has now adopted a libertarian activist stance with regard to race. Now federal courts stand ready to intervene to prevent government action that goes beyond the guarantee of formal equality. In effect, the Court has read the Constitution as protecting the integrity of a private sphere within which the fate of African Americans will be decided.

During the same period, the Court also began the process of limiting the reach of the public forum doctrine, New York Times v. Sullivan, and *Red Lion*. There is no need to rehearse the painfully complex and tendentious doctrinal moves that accomplished these objectives. It is sufficient to say that contemporary free-speech law has at least partially recaptured the traditional libertarian understanding that it creates immunities from government intervention rather than guarantees of government subsidies.[104]

And yet for all the efforts to bury interventionism, it is not quite dead. Its tenuous but tenacious grip on our legal imagination is manifested by the Court's continuing refusal to declare affirmative action constitutionally invalid under all circumstances[105] or to hold flatly unconstitutional legislative districting deliberately drawn so as to enhance African American voting strength.[106]

More surprising, in recent years there have been signs that interventionism may be on the verge of a renaissance. As already noted, the most dramatic recent example is the Court's *Romer* decision. In some ways, the issue of gay rights provided an ideal setting for the reinvigoration of interventionism. In this country it is obvious that even if the government were entirely passive — indeed, especially when it remains entirely passive — gay people do not lead lives that are free. Government coercion plays only a secondary role in the subjugation of gay people, and the direct impact of criminal statutes such as the one validated in *Bowers* is trivial. Instead, the subjugation is accomplished through a system of private violence, social ostracism, and ostentatious indifference — attitudes that the government tolerates even when it does not promote them.

To the surprise of many, the *Romer* Court built its opinion on these interventionist insights. The Court refused to accept a laissez-faire baseline against which constitutional rights should be measured. Instead, it acknowledged that the web of antidiscrimination laws defines the supposedly "private" space within which individual choices about sexual relations are made.[107] Because the state had excepted gay people from this general norm of government intervention in the private sphere, the Court was able to use equal-protection analysis to force government action. In the course of doing so, the Court pointedly refused to equate government nonintervention with freedom. On the contrary, it recognized that it is antidiscrimination law, rather than government passivity, that makes possible "an almost limitless number of transactions and endeavors that constitute ordinary civic life in a free society."[108]

Two terms later, the Court rendered another important interventionist decision. In Saenz v. Roe,[109] it not only reaffirmed Shapiro v. Thompson but actually extended its holding. The California statute challenged in *Saenz* did not interfere with the right to travel in any obvious way, since it guaranteed new arrivals the same welfare benefits they would have received in their old states. Yet the Court nonetheless forced California to extend its benefits to newly arrived residents, holding that equality of treatment was a privilege or immunity of U.S. citizenship.

Romer and *Saenz* provoked dissents from some of the Court's most conservative Justices, but even these Justices have been unable wholly to resist the temptations of interventionism. Conservatives on the court have led the way in utilizing interventionist arguments to compel public subsidies for religious speech and activity.[110] These opinions might be dismissed as merely instrumental, providing support for groups for whom the conservatives have special sympathy. Chief Justice William Rehnquist's remarkable concurring opinion in United States v. Virginia[111] cannot be so dismissed.

At stake was the Virginia Military Institute's refusal to admit women students. The majority opinion, written by Justice Ruth Bader Ginsburg, invalidated the policy on grounds analogous to Justice Harlan's color-blind stance in *Plessy*. The Court was ready to accept VMI's system of "adversative training" as a baseline. It went out of its way to make clear that the academy was under no obligation to make major changes in its educational philosophy and methods, even if adherence to its previous practices meant that the number of women choosing to attend would remain small.[112] Essentially all that was required was an end to facial discrimination. If a facially neutral policy led to a virtually all-male school, then the disadvantage suffered by women could be attributed to private choice.

Chief Justice Rehnquist would have taken a radically different approach. For him the difficulty was not VMI's facial discrimination between men and women, but the failure of Virginia to offer comparable single-sex education to women. To satisfy the equal-protection clause, the state must demonstrate "that its interest in educating men in a single-sex environment is matched by its interest in educating women in a single-sex institution."[113] Although these two institutions need not be identical, they must offer "the same quality of education and [be of] the same overall caliber."[114] To be sure, Virginia claimed to have such an institution — the Virginia Women's Institute of Leadership, created in response to the state's earlier defeat in a lower court. In Rehnquist's view, though, this response was plainly inadequate because the new women's college was "distinctly inferior to the existing men's institution and will continue to be for the foreseeable future."[115] In effect, then, Rehnquist would have used equal-protection doctrine to shift the baseline so as to require a kind of "affirmative action" for women in the form of large additional subsidies to an educational program that met their needs.

Activism and Political Neutrality

The failure to put interventionism to rest poses something of an embarrassment for settlement theory. It leaves in place two radically incompatible ways of understanding our rights tradition. How can a constitutional specification of rights possibly resolve our political disagreements, as settlement theory requires, if the rights can be and are conceptualized in these two conflicting ways?

Moreover, even if one of the two approaches were ultimately to prevail, the difficulties run deeper. Recall that settlement theories require agreement on a metalevel in order to settle our disagreements on the political level. Such agreement is obviously impossible if our metaprinciples reflect the political disagreements they are meant to settle. For this reason, settlement theory insists that the metaprinciples must be politically neutral. Unfortunately, however, neither libertarianism nor interventionism can satisfy the neutrality requirement. Both approaches bump up against the fundamental problem with the rights specification approach discussed at the beginning of this chapter.

Consider first the difficulty with libertarianism. Justice Harlan's dissenting opinion in *Lochner* illustrates the problem. Harlan pointed out that even the majority was unprepared to carry its libertarian premises to their ultimate conclusion. For example, an earlier decision, specifically reaffirmed by the *Lochner* majority, had upheld the constitutionality of maximum-hours legislation for miners.[116] Harlan argued that the distinction between miners and bakers could not be maintained; scientific study showed that baking, like mining, was a dangerous profession.[117]

Standing alone, the fact that some activity is subject to public regulation does not defeat libertarianism. Libertarians, after all, need not be anarchists. Hence, most libertarians are ready to concede that there is a residual category of "police power" cases where government regulation is necessary to protect public health, safety, welfare, and morals.[118] What libertarianism does require, however, is a clear and uncontroversial boundary that prevents this residual category from subsuming the dominant category of private freedom. In the absence of such a boundary, judges themselves would be exercising government power when they shielded a "private" activity from regulation but subjected other activity to government control.

This requirement poses two difficulties. First, it is simply not possible to generate such a boundary without making politically contestable judgments. Speaking for the majority, Justice Peckham responded to Harlan's argument by pointing out that virtually all occupations are dangerous to some degree. If government regulation could be justified by demonstrating any risk at all, there would be nothing left of the dominant category.[119] Of course, Peckham was right about this, but he failed to see how his argument undermined his own position. If danger is, indeed, a matter of degree, then the line that divides the categories will inevitably be controversial. Judges will make choices about how much danger justifies intervention, and these choices will inevitably reflect politically contestable value judgments.

Second, suppose we assume (implausibly) that this difficulty were somehow resolved. If it were, then the line-drawing would be neutral, objective, and lawlike. But the very insistence on these qualities undermines the particularist values the Court wishes to protect. Libertarians insist that when a court decides which private activity will be subject to government control, it must justify its conclusions in terms of public, universalist criteria that guard against idiosyncratic, personal exercises of power. Yet the private sphere has value in the first place just because it provides refuge from such public-regarding judgments. We can hardly demonstrate respect for particularism by holding it hostage to universalist criteria.

As a result of these difficulties, libertarianism constantly teeters on the edge of self-contradiction. Consider Moore v. City of East Cleveland.[120] An East Cleveland ordinance had the effect of prohibiting a grandmother from living with two grandchildren who were first cousins. The plurality struck down the law because it was an intrusive regulation of the family — the primary locus for particularist autonomy. According to the plurality, people have a constitutionally protected liberty interest in deciding for themselves what family groupings to choose.[121]

The problem with this argument is that it begs the question at issue in the case. The city took the position that this particular grouping was *not* a "family." Plainly the Court was not prepared to say that any group of people who happened to live together was a family. Indeed, it squarely rejected this position in Village of Belle Terre v. Boraas,[122] where it upheld a limitation on family-living arrangements not defined by "blood," adoption, or marriage. Thus *Moore* and *Belle Terre* together articulate an official definition of family for constitutional purposes even as the Court insists that such official definitions are unconstitutional.

The effort to bound the domain of religious freedom provides a second illustration. Libertarians defend the free-exercise clause as protecting autonomy and particularism with regard to religious belief. No person should have to justify religious commitment by demonstrating that it satisfies public criteria. But in order to make this freedom operational, we must differentiate between protected religion and unprotected nonreligion. Unfortunately, whatever test we use to define the categories will deny the particularistic judgments of some people who assert beliefs that do not meet the official definition.* The clause thus mandates an official government position on religion in the name of disabling government from adopting an official position on religion.

Interventionist critics of libertarianism delight in pointing out these contradictions, but interventionism, too, fails to satisfy the neutrality requirement. As discussed above, interventionism typically exploits critical insights to destabilize the baseline against which neutrality is measured. But once this deconstruction is accomplished, it is difficult to see how neutrality can ever be reestablished. If there is indeed no "natural" state of affairs, departures from

---

*As Laurence Tribe points out, "At least through the nineteenth century, courts defined 'religion' narrowly in terms of theistic notions respecting divinity, morality, and worship. In order to be considered legitimate, religions had to be viewed as 'civilized' by Western standards." Laurence H. Tribe, American Constitutional Law 1179 (2d ed., 1988). The exclusionary nature of this definition is obvious, and the modern Court has moved away from it. See, e.g., Thomas v. Review Board, 450 U.S. 707, 714 (1981) (holding that beliefs are religious even if not "acceptable, logical, consistent, or comprehensible"); and United States v. Ballard, 322 U.S. 78 (1944) (holding that courts may not inquire into the accuracy or truthfulness of religious belief). Cf. United States v. Seeger, 380 U.S. 163, 166 (1965) (construing a statutory right to conscientious objection to include beliefs that occupy "a place in the life of its possessor parallel to that filled by the orthodox belief in God").

Yet for all the attraction of this more expansive approach, it remains true that the protection of religious freedom must be exclusionary to some extent. The point of the First Amendment is to make religion special, and it would lose this status if it could not be distinguished from nonreligion. Cf. John H. Mansfield, The Religion Clauses of the First Amendment and the Philosophy of the Constitution, 72 Cal. L. Rev. 847, 851 (1984) ("If [the definition of religion] excludes some philosophies, that, it may be said, is exactly what the Constitution intended"). It therefore comes as no surprise that "[a]lthough the Court has abandoned its narrow, theistic view of religion in free exercise analysis, it has not escaped the necessity of drawing some boundary around religion. Indeed, avoiding the task would violate the principles underlying the Clause." Tribe, supra, at 1180. See, e.g., Wisconsin v. Yoder, 406 U.S. 205, 216 (1972) ("[I]f the Amish asserted their claims because of their subjective evaluation and rejection of the contemporary secular values accepted by the majority, much as Thoreau rejected the social values of his time and isolated himself at Walden Pond, their claims would not rest on a religious basis").

which (associated with government changes in the "private" status quo) are nonneutral, then legal neutrality is a chimera.

Romer, once again, provides a powerful illustration. Because government nonintervention is not a natural state of affairs, the Court, in good interventionist fashion, takes the general regime of government-mandated antidiscrimination as a baseline. It claims that it is enforcing the neutrality requirement by insisting that gay people receive the same benefits from antidiscrimination policy accorded to other groups.

There is a sense in which this stance does indeed require neutrality. But there is an obvious sense in which it does not. The failure to protect gay people from discrimination is nonneutral only to the extent that homosexuality is an irrelevant characteristic that does not justify different treatment. Moral conservatives who oppose gay rights deny precisely this point, and by dismissing their objection, the Court plainly allies itself with the enemies of moral conservatism — a fact that it cannot obscure by rhetorically equating moral disapproval with irrational animus.

The Court acknowledges the state's argument that the amendment is designed to protect "other citizens' freedom of association, and in particular the liberties of landlords or employers who have personal or religious objections to homosexuality"[123] but asserts that "[t]he breadth of the Amendment is so far removed from these particular justifications that we find it impossible to credit them."[124] The Court's position ignores the possibility that the amendment is based upon broader respect for, and agreement with, persons who have generalized "personal or religious objections to homosexuality" and, therefore, object to the recognition or encouragement of the practice in any context. The breadth of the amendment is completely consistent with the government objective of favoring this view.

Similarly, although the Court asserts that the statute involves "a classification of persons undertaken for its own sake,"[125] this claim will not withstand analysis. The classification is not undertaken "for its own sake" but rather to express disapproval of homosexuality. Imagine, for example, a statute that precluded municipalities from enacting measures recognizing claims of discrimination against spouse abusers. This statute would not discriminate "for its own sake." Rather, it would "discriminate" for the purpose of discouraging spouse abuse. An advocate of the measure could rightly claim that spouse abusers are different from, say, African Americans, the physically handicapped, or other groups protected by antidiscrimination law because spouse abusers have done something "wrong." Of course, this is precisely the claim made by moral conservatives with respect to homosexuality. By treating the amendment as if it were no more than "a classification of persons undertaken for its own sake," the Court implicitly rejects that claim and therefore acts nonneutrally with respect to the moral conservatives who advance it.

Justice Scalia has no trouble exploiting these difficulties to accuse the Court of blatant inconsistency. The majority has no real answer when he points out that although its analysis would apply to polygamy as well as homosexuality, it is plainly unwilling to follow the uncomfortable logic of its own argument.[126] And Scalia hits pay dirt when he accuses the majority of elitism by siding with "the views and values of the lawyer class from which the Court's Members are drawn."[127] Although Scalia himself does not emphasize the fact, his argument highlights an important symmetry: just as libertarianism ends in contradiction because the private, particularist realm libertarians wish to defend must be bounded and justified by public, universalist decisions, so too, interventionists end up relying on idiosyncratic, particularist value choices — for example, the values of "the lawyer class" — to justify public, universalist intervention.

A great virtue of unsettlement theory is that it avoids these difficulties. Unsettlement theory begins by forthrightly conceding the point that is so troublesome for settlement theories: judicial decisions that recognize, or fail to recognize, rights are not — and cannot be — politically neutral. It follows that when one focuses on individual decisions, there is no method independent of our political commitments by which we can evaluate rightness or wrongness of these decisions. People who disagree about redistribution ought to disagree about *Lochner,* and people who disagree about abortion ought to disagree about *Roe.* To the extent that they don't, it is because they have been fooled into believing that a settlement which is properly contestable is somehow necessary and inevitable. We need to face up to this fact and let go of the comforting myth that there is a neutral, apolitical, and uncontroversial method for permanently resolving the arguments that divide us.

To this extent, then, the federalists' initial objection to the Bill of Rights was correct: the specification strategy necessarily requires a grant of power to a government enforcement institution that will make politically contestable choices — choices that, from some political perspectives, will seem like invasions rather than protections of rights. But whereas this concession is fatal for settlement theories, it does not doom unsettlement theory. The unsettlement approach can accommodate a link between political commitments and judicial judgments because it establishes a different sort of neutrality. Unsettlement theory emphasizes the contradictions inherent in constitutional law that keep matters unresolved. Because both sides of the argument can go on using constitutional rhetoric that appeals to our core commitments, both sides have a reason not to sever their ties with the community.

At first it might seem that a rights-specification strategy is poorly suited to keeping matters unsettled. The whole point of the strategy, after all, is to take certain options permanently off the table. In fact, though, there are two ways in which the rights strategy promotes unsettlement. First, as discussed above, we are stuck with an unresolvable conflict between our libertarian and interventionist traditions. It is no accident that we have been unable to reconcile these two approaches. We have already seen the ways in which they are linked to the deep conflict between universalism and particularism — a conflict that is built into the way most of us perceive the world. Each of us struggles with this conflict on a daily basis when we decide how to do our jobs, behave toward our friends and relatives, respond to our civic obligations, and otherwise live our lives. Because constitutional law replicates this fundamental antimony at the root of human experience, it provides a uniquely powerful set of arguments that are always available to destabilize any political outcome.

Standing alone, this argument says nothing about the association between constitutional law and judicial review. If I am right about the power that it has over us, constitutional rhetoric should be effective in a variety of institutional settings. In fact, I believe that it is, or at least has the potential to be. There is nonetheless a second method, uniquely tied to courts, by which rights specification unsettles. As we have seen, the fundamental incompatibility of the libertarian and interventionist positions leads to a problem whenever we try to settle the argument between advocates of the two approaches. If our political institutions are indeed public-regarding, then they will inevitably utilize public-regarding criteria when they establish the boundary of private freedom. But holding the exercise of this freedom hostage to universalist judgments undercuts the value of particularism. To be sure, our political institutions sometimes utilize particularist criteria, but this is only because they have been captured by special interests who are able to use public power for private purposes.

Legal realist insights about the pervasiveness of public power make it more difficult for us to imagine a parallel system where the boundaries of public power are subject to a private check. These insights have become so much a part of our world that it may seem that boundary decisions are inevitably public. Still, an adherent to natural-rights theory might believe that the private precedes the public. It is possible to conceptualize the public sphere as carved out of the preexisting realm of private rights. But to the extent that we conceptualize the boundary in this fashion, we run up against the converse of the difficulty described in the previous paragraph. Now the size and shape of the public, universalist sphere is determined by private, particularist values.

So long as we think of constitutional law as embodying a permanent working out of the public-private boundary, there is no escape from this dilemma. Suppose instead that we think of constitutional law as preventing such a settlement — as keeping the boundary permanently contested and uncertain. On this view, judges who pursue the rights-specification strategy can have a uniquely valuable role to play. The judiciary sits astride the public-private divide. The legal and customary structure of judicial review encapsulates the ambivalence that we ought to nurture when choosing between particularism and universalism. It is not as though judges can avoid this choice when they decide individual cases. Like everyone else, they must do one thing or another. But because judges are public actors who are nonetheless shielded from certain universalist pressures, and because they work with analytical tools that regularly force the antinomy to the forefront, they are less likely to entrench a permanent solution.

It follows that if judges properly understand their role, there is good reason to privilege the results they reach. It bears emphasis that the reason is not grounded in the substantive rightness of these decisions. Views about substantive rightness require criteria for judgment, and these criteria must be grounded in either universalism or particularism. We can escape this problem only if we think of judicial decisions as worthy of respect not because they are substantively right but because they are (or at least can be) grounded in a method and a culture that encourages uncertainty, ambivalence, and contradiction.

How might courts nurture this unsettlement when they enforce rights? Two examples — one drawn from contemporary doctrine, the other from a contemporary controversy that the Court might someday utilize to produce doctrine — provide concrete illustrations.

Consider first the religion clauses of the First Amendment. The amendment protects against laws "respecting an establishment of religion" and against laws "prohibiting the free exercise thereof." There is a sense in which these two rights are compatible. Both protect religious liberty, the first by preventing religious dominance over government, the second by preventing government dominance over religion. There is another sense, however, in which the two clauses are at war. It is not hard to see how the clauses taken together embody the conflict between public- and private-regarding theories of rights that we have already discussed. The establishment clause is public-regarding. It protects universalism by preventing the capture of government either by a particular religious sect or by religion in general. Because we are divided over religious belief, and because there is no metadiscourse through which our divisions can be resolved, religious capture would make public institutions the property of only some, thereby violating the requirement of bounded universalism. But precisely because the establishment clause helps make the government public-regarding, government jurisdiction must be limited. The free-exercise clause accomplishes this goal. It is private-regarding in the sense that it walls off particularistic religious belief from government interference.

If the public- and private-regarding theories of rights are indeed incompatible, then there are bound to be difficulties in reconciling the requirements of the two clauses. The case law provides ample evidence that the difficulties are real. Consider, for example, Rosenberger v. Rectors and Visitors of the University of Virginia.[128] The university, a public institution, authorized payments from a Student Activities Fund for the printing costs of various student publications but prohibited payment for any publication that "primarily promotes or manifests a particular belief in or about a deity or an ultimate reality." The university justified its policy as required by the establishment clause, and when the case reached the Supreme Court, four Justices agreed. Without the exception, these Justices argued, there would be direct public funding of sectarian activities, thereby allowing the private to subsume the public.[129] However, five other Justices thought that such funding was not only constitutionally permissible; it was constitutionally mandatory. According to these Justices, university discrimination against religious groups solely because they were expressing religious views amounted to impermissible public control over the private.*

Which side is right? There are four possible ways in which the two clauses might interact, illustrated by the following matrix:[130]

	Weak free-exercise clause	Strong free-exercise clause
Weak establishment clause	Scalia's position Legislative reconciliation Private justified in terms of public or public justified in terms of private	McConnell's position No reconciliation necessary Private predominates over public
Strong establishment clause	Stevens' position No reconciliation necessary Public predominates over private	Brennan's position Judicial reconciliation Public and private in tension

The possibilities represented by the upper right and lower left quadrants avoid the necessity of reconciliation by the simple expedient of suppressing

---

*515 U.S. 819, 830 (1995). As a doctrinal matter, the Court held that the discrimination violated free-speech, rather than free-exercise, guarantees. For purposes of this discussion, locating the right in one clause rather than another makes no difference.

one of the conflicting values. Michael McConnell is the most eloquent and sophisticated proponent of the weak establishment clause–strong free-exercise clause combination.[131] This reading of the First Amendment powerfully protects the private sphere from government intervention but does little to impede private capture of public institutions. In contrast, Justice Stevens' opinions articulate the strong establishment clause–weak free-exercise clause position.[132] His stance privileges public-regarding rights. A strong reading of the establishment clause prevents religious groups from capturing the political branches, but the weakness of free-exercise rights means that there is little protection against public invasions of the private sphere of religious particularism.

For obvious reasons, neither of these alternatives will be attractive to advocates of unsettlement theory. Each achieves the goal of harmonizing the two clauses but only at the expense of ignoring one set of values embodied in them. In other words, each alternative reflects a final resolution of a conflict that should remain unsettled.

In contrast, each of the other two possibilities preserves the possibility of conflict. The weak establishment clause–weak free-exercise clause position locates the conflict in the political branches. This stance is most prominently associated with Justice Scalia.[133] It maximizes political discretion and minimizes judicial interference with that discretion. On this view, the legislature may, but need not, adjust its policies so as to support or accommodate particularistic religious belief and it may, but need not, shield such belief from public interference.

Advocates of unsettlement theory will find this approach attractive insofar as it avoids the constitutional entrenchment of any particular reconciliation between the values. However, it runs afoul of the boundary difficulty discussed in the previous section. If our political institutions remain public and universalist, then adherents to particularist religions will have to justify their activity with a public-regarding vocabulary. The controversy over state aid to faith-based drug and alcohol treatment programs illustrates the difficulty. Because the aid comes from public sources, it is typically justified with public-regarding reasons. It follows that entitlement to funds turns on whether the religious activity in question is effective in achieving public ends. Advocates of particularism should be disturbed by the degradation of their belief systems that such funding entails. Suppose it turns out that Protestant but not Catholic doctrine is correlated with success in conquering addiction? Does this mean that one religious group but not the other is entitled to public subvention? Surely, Catholics are justified in responding that their belief system is justified on its own terms. Catholics believe in Catholic doctrine because (by their lights) it is true, not because it accomplishes public, instrumental purposes.*

Alternatively, the absence of establishment-clause protections might lead to the capture of political institutions by religious groups. If there were such capture, public subvention of private religious belief would no longer have to be justified by public-regarding reasons that are incompatible with that belief. But the price of this victory for particularism would be the sacrifice of universalism. Under such a regime, public institutions that should belong to us all would, instead, be dominated by particular groups.

This leaves us with the final possibility, represented by the lower-right-hand quadrant and most closely associated with the opinions of Justice Brennan.[134] Like the Scalia position, Brennan's approach leaves the status of the religion clauses unsettled. But whereas the weak free-exercise–weak establishment clause possibility locates unresolved conflict in the political branches, the strong free-exercise–strong establishment clause alternative locates the conflict in the judicial branch.[135] Whereas the Scalia view deconstitutionalizes the religion question, the Brennan view means that every statute touching on religion raises a constitutional issue.[136]

It is important to understand that a judicial locus does not mean that judges will effectively replace legislators. Free-exercise clause and establishment clause values conflict, so there is a sense in which the legislature simply cannot "get it right." Whatever choice the legislature makes will be subject to constitutional criticism because the choice will privilege one value or the other.

This is what it means to say that the Constitution leaves the matter unsettled. Obviously, though, no sensible court would invalidate every choice the legislature makes. As discussed in Chapter 3, unsettlement theory must allow settlement on the level of the individual case. Judges will inevitably vote to uphold some legislative reconciliations and to strike down others. But although unsettlement does not mean that courts will invalidate all laws touching on religion, it does mean that all these laws pose constitutional issues, and that these issues cannot be resolved by reference to a grand theory that finally works out the conflict. This, too, is what unsettlement means. Moreover, precisely because the resolution of these issues is unconstrained by theory,

---

*This objection does not arise as long as funding is limited to nonsectarian programs that happen to be administered by religious institutions. To the extent that the program is "faith-based" however, the funding is not so limited. People of faith have grounds to object when the government funds some religions but not others because some religions serve the government's secular objectives.

judicial decisions will reflect the individual commitments, belief systems, and prejudices of the Justices making them. Whether we approve or disapprove of the decisions themselves will turn on our own commitments, belief systems, and prejudices. Regardless of our views on the merits, though, the decisions gain legitimacy from the fact that they are rendered by actors who themselves straddle the public and private spheres and can therefore police an uncertain, shifting, and contested boundary between them.

After more than a hundred years of litigation, the Supreme Court's First Amendment doctrine is richly textured and well developed. In contrast, there is virtually no Second Amendment doctrine. The Second Amendment states, "A well regulated Militia, being necessary to the security of a free State, the right of the people to keep and bear Arms, shall not be infringed." There are only a handful of Supreme Court decisions interpreting this language, the last rendered in 1939.[137] This paucity of judicial precedent has not prevented a lively controversy in the literature, however. Commentators have disagreed about how the qualifying clause ("A well regulated Militia being necessary . . .") should be reconciled with the substantive clause ("the right of the people . . ."). Opponents of gun control have emphasized the substantive clause and argued that this clause creates an individual, personal right to "keep and bear" firearms.[138] In contrast, gun control advocates have emphasized the qualifying clause and argued that the right protected is not personal at all, but adheres only in "well regulated Militia[s]," which, at the time of the framing, were under the control of state governments.[139]

Most of the scholarship addressing this issue has focused on originalist methodology. Scholars have tried to determine what the framers intended to accomplish and how that intent might be implemented in the radically different world in which we live.[140] Unfortunately, these efforts run into the difficulties already discussed at length in the first two chapters. Even if we could definitively uncover the framers' intent and uncontroversially "translate" it in light of modern conditions, we would be left wondering why this settlement, as opposed to numerous other possible settlements, should prevail. Why should someone who favors a different result accede to the wishes of the small group of men who thought about the issue more than two hundred years ago?

Unsettlement theory suggests a different approach that better deals with these difficulties. The language of the two clauses is relevant not because it instantiates a particular settlement which we are bound to respect but because it captures an ambivalence that can help build political community among people who disagree about what the settlement should be. Like their companions in the First Amendment, the two clauses can be understood as reflecting conflicting public and private values. The substantive clause is libertarian. It protects a private sphere from government interference. This is true in a double sense. First, the clause itself seems to prohibit collective, governmental choice about the bearing of arms. Second, this prohibition, by preserving a means of coercion in private hands, helps deter government overreaching. A government that extends its writ too far into the private sphere will have an armed citizenry to deal with.

But this libertarian right is qualified by an inconsistent interventionist caveat. "Militias" that bear arms are not left in a state of private freedom to do what they will. Rather, such militias must be "well regulated." The regulation requirement, which, surprisingly, courts and scholars have mostly ignored, seems to mandate government intervention to control or limit the private freedom that the substantive clause creates. Instead of walling off private choice from public power, it requires some sort of public control presumably intended to vindicate public values.

How might these two clauses be read together? There is no need to re-create our religion clause matrix in this different setting. Mutatis mutandis, the same possibilities present themselves. For the reasons we have already explored, unsettlement theory once again argues for a strong reading of both clauses. This approach exploits the contradiction between the two clauses instead of avoiding it. It helps erect a constitution that destabilizes any resolution, instead of a constitution that purports finally to end the conflict.

It is not the job of unsettlement theory to resolve the gun control controversy. Only settlement theories dictate outcomes. Still, we can suggest how judges devoted to unsettlement theory might think about the problem. They might decide, for instance, that legislatures are not free to outlaw all guns under all circumstances in order to achieve public-regarding purposes, yet they are required to couple a respect for private freedom with some degree of public-regarding regulation.

How much freedom, and how much regulation? These are political questions, which unsettlement theory does not purport to resolve. Depending on their political views, judges will disagree about whether a given statutory scheme provides enough protection for, and regulation of, the individual right. Unsettlement theory deliberately leaves these issues unresolved by subjecting any purported resolution to constitutional criticism.

The hope is that this possibility of criticism will draw losers into a continuing conversation by giving them a constitutional vocabulary to achieve their goals, instead of entrenching their loss in a foundational settlement. For it is only this sort of contradictory, inclusionary, and open-textured constitution that holds out promise that the very guns receiving uncertain Second Amendment protection will never be used to settle our political disputes.

Conclusion
Unsettling Unsettlement

Finally, we come to the challenge of reflexivity. If the constitution is indeed successful in unsettling, must it not entrench settled structures (like expansive judicial review) that assure its continued capacity to unsettle? After all, if the unsettling structures were themselves unsettled, they might be abandoned and so produce settlement.

The problem runs deeper. I have argued that any constitutional settlement obstructs just community by excluding people who disagree with the settlement. But what of people who disagree with unsettlement? Aren't *they* excluded by a constitution that entrenches a condition — unsettlement — that they detest? It would seem that authentic unsettlement requires that unsettlement must itself be unsettled, which, of course, introduces the possibility of settlement.

These are hard problems, and I do not pretend to have a wholly satisfactory solution to them.[1] The logical and philosophical difficulties posed by self-reference of this sort are well known and extend far beyond constitutional theory. I do not have the expertise to attack these problems in a general way, and any effort to do so would take us far afield. Still, I take some solace from the knowledge that the reflexivity problem is shared by all comprehensive theories. Marxists, too, must explain why Marxism itself is not a product of the relation between intellectual workers and the means of production;[2]

Freudians have a hard time accounting for the fact that their theory alone stands outside the unconscious urges that dominate all other important activity;[3] law and economics advocates might be challenged to explain why their approach cannot itself be understood as a rational adaptation to the market forces that favored its development;[4] deconstructionists must deal with the temptation to deconstruct deconstruction.[5] In short, if theorizing is indeed unavoidable, then perhaps paradoxes of this sort are unavoidable as well.*

Still, there is a sense in which the problem for unsettlement theory is more acute. Some other comprehensive theories make claims to foundational validity. Their adherents can use the foundational status of the theories to resist reflexivity. To be sure, critics of the theories can score points by turning the theories on themselves, but as long as the theorists believe their own foundational claims, they can resist this move on the ground that their theory stands apart from and explains everything else.

In contrast, the theory I propound is antifoundational. It is attractive precisely because it rejects the authoritarian insistence that someone must accept a view that cannot be explained to her in ways that make sense within her own frameworks. My strategy has been to problematize foundational claims by pointing to disagreement. My central argument is that we have not one settlement but many competing settlements, with no mediating discourse between them. For example, even if textualism produced determinate results, I argue that these results lack normative force for those who are outside the practice of textualism. Because textualists have no argument external to textualism itself for why antitextualists should be bound by the rules of the practice, textualism fails to provide a just basis for community cooperation.

I have presented my theory as one that textualists, antitextualists, and proponents of all other foundational theories can agree upon. In this sense, the theory is political, rather than comprehensive, to borrow from the terminology made famous by John Rawls.[6] Such a claim is peculiarly vulnerable to its own argumentative strategy. Just as there are antitextualists, so too there are people who believe in settlement. Unsettlement theory has nothing to offer

---

*Which is to say no more than that even critical theories are subject to critique. Two decades ago, Alvin Gouldner made the point as well as anyone: "To critique a theory . . . is to think about it not as a culturally privileged object but as another object of culture. . . . Such a view of theory, it must be admitted, is somewhat at variance with theory's own exalted self-conception, which tends to present itself as if it were altogether transparent to itself and knowledgeable to what it is up to. The first commandment of the theorist's guild is, after all, know what you are doing. Critique takes note of this special requirement, sees theorists as bound by such a pledge, but yet is no more capable of living life without shadows than anyone else." Alvin W. Gouldner, The Two Marxisms 9 (1980).

these people outside the practice itself for why they should accept unsettlement. Because the theory is antifoundational, it cannot gain the footing that foundational theories have when they resist this self-application.

There are only two strategies for dealing with this difficulty. First, one might give up on the antifoundational status of unsettlement theory. Foundational unsettlement insists that the theory is something more than one among many possible stances. It claims that unsettlement stands above other contending approaches and serves as a master theory that reasonable adherents to all other theories must accept. Second, one might admit the political contestability of unsettlement. Pursuing this alternative means following unsettlement all the way to the bottom, acknowledging the possibility that unsettlement itself might be unsettled, and thereby giving up on the claim that constitutional law should never be settled. There is something to be said for both of these alternatives, but neither of them is entirely satisfactory.

Consider first foundational unsettlement. Must all reasonable people accept unsettlement theory? It is important to understand that constitutional unsettlement does not require adherents to substantive theories to give up on their commitments. Political actors remain free to act according to these commitments and to attempt to vindicate them within the political sphere. Indeed, they need not even give up on their commitments in the constitutional sphere. Part of my argument is that the contradictions in liberal constitutionalism will produce unsettlement more or less automatically, even when individual actors are attempting to entrench their preferences on the constitutional level.

My approach is thus fundamentally different from other theories that are less inclusive. Theorists like Ronald Dworkin and Richard Epstein claim that their theories generate particular and controversial policy conclusions that should be entrenched against political challenge on contested matters like abortion and property rights.[7] It is no wonder that people who reject these substantive conclusions also reject the theories that generate them. In this respect, my approach is closer to that of John Rawls, who advances a theory that purports to rest on an "overlapping consensus" between different comprehensive theories.[8] But even Rawls's conception of political liberalism would place limits on the ability of some individuals to make certain sorts of arguments grounded in their comprehensive theories.[9] In contrast, unsettlement theory requires no such self-restraint. On the contrary, it provides reasons that would not otherwise exist for why it is legitimate for individuals to attempt to secure political implementation of their controversial, comprehensive views. Precisely because constitutional law unsettles any political resolution, dissenters have reason to remain part of the political community even when they suffer grievous political losses through the enactment of laws that implement comprehensive views that they oppose.

It might therefore be argued that the unsettled constitution embodies a metatheory that operates on a different level from the contending settlements that other constitutional theorists have defended. It presents itself as an inclusive, all-encompassing theory in the sense that advocates of all these settlements can accept it without in any way sacrificing their particularistic commitments.

Yet for all its pretensions to universality, unsettlement theory cannot fully suppress dissent. Even if the theory operates at a different, and higher, level than substantive settlements, dissenters can always locate themselves outside the practice on this higher level, and if they do so, there will again be no mediating discourse between those within and those without.

Why might one locate oneself outside the practice of unsettlement? Unsettlement theory purports to provide just reasons why people should maintain their commitment to the community. But we must come to grips with the raw, empirical fact that these reasons will not be persuasive to everyone. As I acknowledged in the introductory chapter, no theory can ever be wholly successful in universally justifying a course of conduct. No matter how forceful the argument, there are bound to be some who remain unconvinced.

We might try to soften the stringency of the requirement of universal acceptance by insisting only that a theory offer reasons that will be persuasive to everyone who is reasonable. But this move is already exclusionary. Reasoned argument itself is a practice that is not universally accepted, and, in any event, what counts as reasoned argument is sharply contested. A theory of unsettlement that rests on any particular version of reasoned argument therefore labels some people unreasonable and exiles them from the community of reason that it creates.

Worse still, it is simply not plausible to insist that all reasonable people will accept unsettlement. For example, there are people who would rather see things settled — even unjustly — than live with the knowledge that everything might yet be turned upside-down. Moreover, the unsettled constitution puts great weight on community. It provides a strategy that should be attractive to people who wish to maintain a community built on reasons that make sense to people with different views. But this objective can reasonably be attacked by those who place little or no value on political community. Perhaps these individuals would prefer to live in a smaller, less heterogeneous environment where a sectarian, prevailing settlement remains unchallenged from the outside. Alternatively, some may place less value on giving just reasons for maintaining community. Perhaps these individuals believe in their substantive commitments with such fervor that they are unwilling to risk displacing them. If these individuals have sufficient power to implement their views — and are willing to use that power — then they will see no point to an unsettled constitution.

A possible response to these objections is to retreat to a partially descriptive stance. An advocate of unsettlement might say that this is simply the way constitutional law is. On this argument, constitutionalism's unsettling properties are not chosen attributes. For reasons I have already explored at length, they are inherent in the enterprise and largely independent of the behavior of individual actors. Given this fact, there is no point in a normative discussion about whether constitutional law should unsettle. Its unsettling qualities are built into the vocabulary of liberal constitutionalism, and it will therefore have unsettling effects whether we like it or not. To the extent that the argument for unsettlement is normative at all, it merely asserts that constitutionalism's defenders and critics have each tended to misunderstand what it is all about, and that a better understanding may turn some of its critics into defenders.

I must confess an attraction to this more modest approach, but it has difficulties as well. In particular, it is subject to the same criticisms I advanced against the limits on Ronald Dworkin's constructivism in Chapter 2. The practice of constitutional law does not simply exist, any more than our community's history and boundaries do. Rather, it is constructed and defined through ongoing struggle. This point, central to unsettlement theory, also serves to unravel its descriptive claims. Perhaps a certain version of constitutional law has unsettling effects, but this is not the only version we can imagine. Unsettlement theory's descriptive version seems to use definitional fiat to rule out of bounds a competing version of constitutionalism that would, in fact, settle. Yet it is the refusal to tolerate this move that distinguishes the unsettled constitution from its rivals.

Suppose, then, that we pursue the alternative strategy and embrace unsettlement all the way to the bottom. On the structural level, it is possible to accept a version of this deep unsettlement without generating paradox. For example, I have argued at some length that judicial review serves the purposes of unsettlement, but I have also conceded that the practice has features that serve to entrench rather than unsettle. Reasonable people can disagree about which effect outweighs the other, and there is nothing to prevent this balance from changing over time. Even if it remains static, surely we should hold ourselves open to new data that might change our beliefs about its net effect. In this sense, it is right for our commitment to supposedly unsettling institutions to be, itself, unsettled. And the same point applies more broadly to the practice of constitutionalism as a whole. I have argued that liberal constitutionalism's paired opposites generate unsettlement, but their continuing power to do so is contingent and contextual. Adherents to unsettlement theory should remain open to the possibility that constitutionalism might no longer serve their goals.

We run into more serious difficulties when we try to apply deep unsettlement to the goals themselves. If we are to be truly nonexclusionary, then unsettlement must acknowledge the fact that some people prefer settlement. It must, in other words, unsettle itself—a move that seems to invite settlement and thereby create contradiction.

One response to this difficulty is simply to acknowledge it. In other words, we might concede that an embrace of the unsettled constitution is itself properly contestable. The day may come when even its defenders will be persuaded that a final settlement is better. On this view, a just constitution should and must bring into question its own justness. If this result is paradoxical, then it is paradox inevitably generated by the skepticism that makes just community possible.

There is a second response. Perhaps we cannot follow unsettlement all the way to the bottom because there is no bottom: the struggle between settlement and unsettlement is itself unsettling and unresolvable. Any settlement that purports to be at the bottom can itself be destabilized and therefore lead to unsettlement.

We have already seen how this unsettlement comes about. First, any settlement is subject to the reflexivity problem. It can always be applied to itself and thereby yield contradiction. Second, any settlement necessarily requires a bounding of the community. Oddly, the settlement's claim to universalism depends upon a commitment to particularist boundaries. The settlement is always defined and formed against a backdrop of others who do not accept it and who therefore must be treated as outsiders. But as we have already seen, boundaries of this sort are fiercely defended precisely because they are so porous. Universalist impulses push against community borders and make them appear arbitrary. As hard as we try to wall ourselves off from these outsiders, we can never do so completely. Their presence stands as a constant reproach to our claims to certainty. This effect is intensified by the unsuppressible knowledge that our views are culturally and historically located. Historicism inevitably unsettles because it focuses our attention on the fact that we may hold our beliefs not because of their truth but because of our location.

It does not follow, however, that we find unsettlement at the bottom. As the previous paragraphs demonstrate, unsettlement, too, can be turned upon itself and thereby unsettled. Even if it is true that people press against community boundaries, they also need boundaries to press against. Even as we recognize the historic and cultural contingency of our beliefs, we continue to hold and defend them.

In this way, our ambivalence about unsettlement produces unsettlement at a yet deeper level. Of course, the impulse toward settlement will lead us to attempt to resolve this contradiction. But the effort to do so merely regenerates it. It is no accident that this recursive battle between commitment and doubt reproduces the contradictions of liberal constitutionalism itself. The reason we cannot decide between settlement and unsettlement is that our indecision is grounded in the fundamental and unresolvable struggle between particularism and universalism that drives the unsettled constitution in the first place.

There is an ironic sense, then, in which unsettlement theory is foundational after all. This is so not because no reasonable person can reject it but because its rejection serves only to generate unsettlement at a deeper level. So long as people remain unable to suppress reflection on their own actions, our unsettled constitution is also unavoidable. To give up on it would require us to crush our own wonder at the contradictory ways we experience the world. We can be thankful that this is a goal which, so far at least, remains beyond our grasp.

Notes

Introduction

1. *See* Richard A. Posner, *Against Constitutional Theory,* 73 N.Y.U. L. Rev. 1 (1998); *and* Richard Rorty, Contingency, Irony, and Solidarity 44, 52 (1989) (arguing against the possibility that liberal society can have "philosophical foundations"); Richard Rorty, Achieving Our Country: Leftist Thought in Twentieth-Century America 36 (1998) (criticizing contemporary leftists as "eager to theorize [and] to become spectators rather than agents"); Rebecca L. Brown, *Accountability, Liberty, and the Constitution,* 98 Colum. L. Rev. 531, 531 (1998).

2. *See* Alexander M. Bickel, The Least Dangerous Branch: The Supreme Court at the Bar of Politics 16–23 (2d ed., 1986); *and* Learned Hand, The Bill of Rights 10 (1958). For a more explicit statement of the notion that the disarmament would be mutual, *see* Learned Hand, The Spirit of Liberty 204–07 (2d ed., 1953).

3. For an account of Judge Hand's proposal and of its reception, *see* Morton J. Horwitz, The Transformation of American Law, 1870–1960: The Crisis of Legal Orthodoxy 258–65 (1992).

4. For some distinguished examples, see Gerald N. Rosenberg, The Hollow Hope: Can Courts Bring about Social Change? (1991); Mark Tushnet, Taking the Constitution away from the Courts (1999); *and* Michael Klarman, *Rethinking the Civil Rights and Civil Liberties Revolutions,* 82 Va. L. Rev. 1 (1996).

5. 121 S. Ct. 525 (2001).

6. *Compare* Judge Bork's proposal to allow Congress to override Supreme Court decisions in Robert H. Bork, Slouching toward Gomorah: Modern Liberalism and Amer-

ican Decline 117 (1996), *with* Professor Tushnet's argument against judicial supremacy in Mark Tushnet, Taking the Constitution away from the Courts 6–32 (1999); *compare* Lino A. Graglia, Disaster by Decree: The Supreme Court Decisions on Race and the Schools (1976) *with* Girardeau A. Spann, Race against the Court: The Supreme Court and Race in Contemporary America (1993); Cass R. Sunstein, *Foreword: Leaving Things Undecided,* 110 Harv. L. Rev. 4 (1996); Cass R. Sunstein, One Case at a Time: Judicial Minimalism on the Supreme Court (1999).

7. *See, e.g.,* Harry T. Edwards, *The Growing Disjunction between Legal Education and the Legal Profession,* 91 Mich. L. Rev. 34 (1992).

8. In the immediate wake of Bush v. Gore, a Gallup poll found that a plurality of the respondents thought that the U.S. Supreme Court Justices were influenced by their personal political views when deciding the case. Yet the same poll found that 49 percent of the respondents accepted and agreed with the Court's decision, while another 32 percent accepted but did not agree with it. Despite the widespread belief that the decision was "political," 49 percent of those polled had a "high level of confidence in the Supreme Court" — a percentage considerably higher than that enjoyed by other major institutions, and an improvement of two percentage points over the Court's approval rating six months earlier. The poll, taken between December 15 and December 17, 2000, is reported at www.cnn.com/2000/ALLPOLITICS/stories/12/18/cnn.poll/index (site visited December 19, 2000).

9. Robert Nozick, Philosophical Explanations 13 (1981).

10. Constitutional theorists need not feel that Judge Posner is picking on them. He has also launched a more general attack on any sort of moral theorizing. *See* Richard A. Posner, The Problematics of Moral and Legal Theory (1999).

11. Richard A. Posner, *Against Constitutional Theory,* 73 N.Y.U. L. Rev. 1, 3, 8, 11 (1998).

12. Id., at 21–22.

13. Id., at 5. In an essay devoted to castigating others for their inattention to empirical detail, it is surprising that Posner offers no empirical data on this or other questions discussed in the essay.

14. *See* Steven D. Smith, The Constitution and the Pride of Reason (1998).

15. *See* Frank Michelman, *Foreword: On Protecting the Poor through the Fourteenth Amendment,* 83 Harv. L. Rev. 7 (1969) (right to subsistence); Ronald Dworkin, *Euthanasia, Morality and the Law,* 31 Loy. L. Rev. 1147 (1998) (euthanasia); Michael Perry, *Abortion, the Public Morals, and Police Power: The Ethical Function of Substantive Due Process,* 23 UCLA L. Rev. 689 (1976) (abortion); John Hart Ely, War and Responsibility: Constitutional Lessons of Vietnam and Its Aftermath (1993) (Vietnam War); Michael J. Sandel, Democracy's Discontent: America in Search of a Public Philosophy 103–08 (1996) (homosexuality); *and* Richard Epstein, Takings: Private Property and the Power of Eminent Domain (1985) (redistribution).

16. *See* note 8, *supra.*

17. This is the starting point for critics as diverse as Alexander Bickel, John Ely, Robert Bork, and Mark Tushnet. *See* Alexander M. Bickel, The Least Dangerous Branch: The Supreme Court at the Bar of Politics (2d ed., 1986); John Hart Ely, Democracy and Distrust: A Theory of Judicial Review (1980); Robert Bork, *Neutral Principles and Some*

First Amendment Problems, 47 Ind. L. J. 1 (1971); *and* Mark V. Tushnet, Taking the Constitution away from the Courts (1999).

18. *See, e.g.,* Gerald N. Rosenberg, The Hollow Hope: Can Courts Bring about Social Change? (1991); *and* Michael Klarman, *An Interpretive History of Modern Equal Protection,* 90 Mich. L. Rev. 213 (1991).

19. For representative examples, see Mark Tushnet, *Following the Rules Laid Down: A Critique of Interpretivism and Neutral Principles,* 96 Harv. L. Rev. 781 (1983); *and* Duncan Kennedy, *The Stages of the Decline of the Public/Private Distinction,* 130 U. Pa. L. Rev. 1349 (1989).

Chapter 1: The Impossible Constitution

1. *See, e.g.,* Washington v. Glucksberg, 521 U.S. 702 (1997); Vacco v. Quill, 521 U.S. 793 (1997); Cruzan v. Director, Missouri Department of Health, 495 U.S. 261 (1990) (right to die); Clinton v. City of New York, 524 U.S. 417 (1998) (veto power); United Bldg. and Construction Trades Council of Camden v. Mayor and Council of Camden, 465 U.S. 208 (1984); White v. Massachusetts Council of Construction Employers, 460 U.S. 204 (1983); McCarthy v. Philadelphia Civil Service Commn., 424 U.S. 645 (1976) (state employees); *compare, e.g.,* Paul Brest, *The Misconceived Quest for the Original Understanding,* 60 B.U. L. Rev. 204 (1980) (arguing against originalism) *with* Richard S. Kay, *Adherence to the Original Intentions in Constitutional Adjudication: Three Objections and Responses,* 82 Nw. L. Rev. 226 (1988) (arguing for it); *see, e.g.,* Washington v. Glucksberg, 521 U.S. 702, 720 (1997) (plurality opinion) (holding that "the Due Process Clause specially protects those fundamental rights and liberties which are, objectively, 'deeply rooted in this Nation's history and tradition'" (quoting Moore v. City of East Cleveland, 431 U.S. 494, 503 [1977]). *Cf.* Michael H. v. Gerald D., 491 U.S. 110, 127 n. 6 (1989) (plurality opinion) (arguing that court should "refer to the most specific level at which a relevant tradition protecting, or denying protection to, the asserted right can be identified"); Ronald Dworkin, Freedom's Law: The Moral Reading of the American Constitution 7–12 (1996) (arguing that judges should decide cases on the basis of abstract moral principles that are incorporated in the Constitution); Hadley Arkes, Beyond the Constitution 40–57 (1990) (arguing that the Constitution is a means for translating the "character of the American republic" into a legal structure that reflects natural law understandings in existence before the creation of the Constitution itself); *compare, e.g.,* Katz v. United States, 389 U.S. 347, 364 (1967) (Black, J., dissenting) (arguing that the "language of the [Fourth] Amendment is the crucial place to look in constructing a written document such as our Constitution") *with* Boyd v. United States, 116 U.S. 616, 635 (1886) (arguing that "constitutional provisions for the security of person and property should be liberally construed [because a] close and literal construction deprives them of half their efficacy, and leads to gradual depreciation of the right, as if it consisted more in sound than in substance").

2. *See, e.g.,* Gerald N. Rosenberg, The Hollow Hope 336–338 (1991) (arguing that courts are ineffective in producing change when faced with serious political opposition); Girardeau A. Spann, Race against the Court 27–31 (1993) (arguing that the Supreme Court's decisions have always been consistent with majority preferences); Barry Fried-

man, *When Rights Encounter Reality: Enforcing Federal Remedies,* 65 Cal. L. Rev. 735, 738 (1992) (arguing that courts take popular will into account); Michael J. Klarman, *Rethinking the Civil Rights and Civil Liberties Revolutions,* 82 Va. L. Rev. 1, 6–7 (1996) (maintaining that courts have neither the inclination nor the power to play the "counter-majoritarian hero"); *compare, e.g.,* Learned Hand, The Bill of Rights 27–29 (1958) (criticizing judicial review), *with* Alexander M. Bickel, The Least Dangerous Branch 23–29 (2d ed., 1986) (offering a qualified defense of judicial review).

3. 529 U.S. 598 (2000).

4. *See, e.g.,* Nixon v. United States, 506 U.S. 224 (1993) (holding that Senate impeachment procedures posed a nonjusticiable political question); Allen v. Wright, 468 U.S. 737 (1984) (relying upon concerns about scope of judicial power over the executive to find that plaintiffs lacked standing); Quackenbush v. Allstate Ins. Co., 517 U.S. 706, 716 (1996) (abstention); *and* Younger v. Harris, 401 U.S. 37 (1971) (interference with pending state criminal proceeding).

5. 505 U.S. 833 (1992) (Casey); 410 U.S. 113 (1973) (Roe). *See* 505 U.S., at 865–868.

6. 469 U.S. 528 (1985).

7. *See, e.g.,* Vacco v. Quill, 521 U.S. 793 (1997) (applying the "rational basis" test to uphold a statute banning physician-assisted suicide); Heller v. Doe, 509 U.S. 312 (1993) (holding that there was a "rational basis" for a statutory distinction between mental illness and mental retardation in the context of involuntary civil commitment); Hazelwood School Dist. v. Kuhlmeier, 484 U.S. 260 (1988) (holding that educators can regulate student speech in school-sponsored activities so long as regulation is reasonably related to legitimate pedagogical concern); Jones v. North Carolina Prisoners' Union, 433 U.S. 119 (1977) (according "wide-ranging deference" to prison officials in regulating prisoner speech); County of Sacramento v. Lewis, 523 U.S. 833 (1998) (deferring to police judgment in context of due process challenge to dangerous, high-speed chases); Katzenbach v. McClung, 379 U.S. 294 (1964) (upholding Congress' commerce-clause power to enact public accommodations provisions as applied to a restaurant that received a substantial portion of its food from out of state); Wickard v. Filburn, 317 U.S. 111 (1942) (upholding the Agricultural Adjustment Act as applied to regulate the production of wheat for home use); Morrison v. Olson, 487 U.S. 654 (1988) (upholding the special prosecutor law); *and* Mistretta v. United States, 488 U.S. 361 (1989) (upholding a sentencing commission).

8. *See, e.g.,* Mark V. Tushnet, Taking the Constitution away from the Courts (1999) (arguing for popular control over constitutional issues); *and* Robert H. Bork, Slouching towards Gomorrah: Modern Liberalism and American Decline 318 (1996) (maintaining that modern liberalism has allowed the Supreme Court to govern the country "in the name of the Constitution in ways not remotely contemplated by the framers and ratifiers of the Constitution").

9. The view that it does not has a long and distinguished pedigree. *See* Richard Hofstadter, The Progressive Historians 167–345 (1968). For a powerful modern work in this tradition, *see* Robin West, *Constitutional Scepticism,* 72 B.U. L. Rev. 765 (1992).

10. *See, e.g.,* Ronald Dworkin, Freedom's Law: The Moral Reading of the American Constitution 7–11 (1996) (arguing that judges "treat the Constitution as expressing

abstract moral requirements that can only be applied to concrete cases through fresh moral judgments").

11. For a cogent effort to provide such an explanation, see Mark V. Tushnet, Taking the Constitution away from the Courts (1999).

12. 5 U.S. (1 Cranch.) 137, 176, 177 (1803).

13. Id., at 178.

14. Id., at 177.

15. As Larry Alexander writes, "[I]f we *now* accept the metaconstitutional norm that makes what we judged *then* to trump what we judge *now,* then *we,* not some third party, are holding ourselves to our earlier commitment." Larry Alexander, *Introduction,* in Constitutionalism: Philosophical Foundations 13 (1998; Larry Alexander, ed.).

16. For a famous article that falls into this trap, see Robert Bork, *Neutral Principles and Some First Amendment Problems,* 47 Ind. L. J. 1 (1971).

17. There is an obvious link between this specification of function and contractarian political theories. Both Locke and Hobbes thought of the social contract as a means by which destabilizing political disagreement might be settled. *See* John Locke, Political Writings 304 (David Wootton, ed., 1993) ("And thus all private judgment of every particular member being excluded, the community comes to be umpire, by settled standing rules, indifferent and the same to all parties; and, by men having authority from the community for the execution of those rules, decides all differences that may happen between any members of that society concerning any matter of right; and punishes those offenses which any member hath commited against the society with such penalties as the law established."); Thomas Hobbes, Leviathan 117 (Richard Tuck, ed., 1991) ("The final Cause, End, or Designe of men . . . in the introduction of that restraining upon themselves, [in which wee see them live in Commonwealths,] is the foresight of their own preservation, and of a more contented life thereby; that is to say, of getting themselves out from that miserable condition of Warre, which is necessarily consequent . . . to the naturall Passions of men, when there is no visible Power to keep them in awe."). One need not posit an actual or hypothetical social contract to embrace this function, however. *See* David Hume, A Treatise of Human Nature 542–49 (2d ed., L. A. Selby-Rigge, ed., 1978) (arguing that although government is necessary to avoid human conflict, its legitimacy need not rest upon consent).

18. I draw intentionally here on terminology made famous by Henry Hart and Albert Sacks. *See* Henry M. Hart, Jr., and Albert Sacks, The Legal Process: Basic Problems in the Making and Application of Law 4–5 (William N. Eskridge, Jr., and Philip P. Frickey, eds., 1994).

19. *See* U.S. Const. art. 1 sec. 9, cl. 5.

20. *See* Robin West, *Constitutional Scepticism,* 72 B.U. L. Rev. 765, 766 (1992) (arguing that the current debate over indeterminacy has overshadowed the more basic question of whether the Constitution is "desirable").

21. *See* John Rawls, A Theory of Justice 17–22 (1971) (describing the "original position"); John Locke, Political Writings 309–324 (David Wootton, ed., 1993) (defending contractarian theory); Aristotle, Politics, in Richard M. Keon, Introduction to Aristotle 631 (1947) (arguing that the nature of a constitution derives from the "chief end" of

individuals and the state); *and* John Stewart Mill, Utilitarianism 17–30 (Samuel Gorovitz, ed., 1971) (defining and defending utilitarian principle). *See* Henry M. Hart, Jr., and Albert Sacks, The Legal Process: Basic Problems in the Making and Application of Law (William N. Eskridge, Jr., and Philip P. Frickey, eds., 1994) (defending pragmatic and functional views about institutions likely to make the wisest decisions).

22. The best-known defense of this position in the constitutional context is Mark V. Tushnet, *Following the Rules Laid Down: A Critique of Interpretivism and Neutral Principles,* 96 Harv. L. Rev. 781 (1983). *See generally* Mark V. Tushnet, Red, White and Blue: A Critical Analysis of Constitutional Law (1988).

23. For a detailed description of this psychological reality, see Duncan Kennedy, *Freedom and Constraint in Adjudication: A Critical Phenomenology,* 36 J. Leg. Ed. 518 (1986).

24. This point has been made powerfully by Owen Fiss. *See* Owen Fiss, *Conventionalism,* 58 Cal. L. Rev. 177 (1985).

25. As Mark Sagoff has written in a somewhat different context: "Conceptions of rationality, neutrality, freedom, equality, truth, and progress abound in our society, and we are the richer for them. An advocate of any of these conceptions of the common good or the common will might argue that we would surely agree with him, if only our heads were screwed on right. The difficulty with hypothetical consent arguments of this sort is that there are so many of them. To judge politically, in principle, is to judge from an impersonal point of view. One might then expect others who take an impersonal point of view to make the same judgment. The problem is that they do not. People advocate different conceptions of the good society just as they pursue different conceptions of the good life." Mark Sagoff, *Values and Preferences,* 96 Ethics 301, 307 (1986).

26. This seems to be the position Judge Bork espouses. *See* Robert Bork, *Neutral Principles and Some First Amendment Problems,* 47 Ind. L. J. 1 (1971).

27. Michael McConnell espouses something close to this view with regard to the desegregation decisions. He argues in favor of originalism on the ground that, properly deployed, originalist methodology supports the result in Brown v. Board of Education. *See* Michael W. McConnell, *Originalism and the Desegregation Decisions,* 81 Va. L. Rev. 947 (1995).

28. *See* J. M. Balkin, *Agreements with Hell and Other Objects of Our Faith,* 65 Fordham L. Rev. 1703, 1706 (1997).

29. *See, e.g.,* Larry Stammer, *Amid Questions, Priests, Nuns Back Key Doctrine,* Los Angeles Times, Feb. 21, 1994, at part A, p. 1 col. 1 (noting opposition of conservative Catholics to "cafeteria Catholicism" in the context of, inter alia, the controversy over women in the priesthood).

30. The examples in this text are illustrations of a deeper problem about whether rule following is ever a coherent practice. For insightful discussions in the legal context, *see* Frederick Schauer, Playing by the Rules 1–16, 207–228 (1991); Larry Alexander and Emily Sherwin, *The Deceptive Nature of Rules,* 142 U. Pa. L. Rev. 1191, 1197 (1994); *and* Larry Alexander, *The Gap,* 14 Harv. J. L. & Pub. Pol'y 695 (1995).

31. Or at least almost no one. *Cf.* Mark V. Tushnet, *Clarence Thomas: The Constitutional Problems,* 63 Geo. Wash. L. Rev. 466, 476 (1995) (suggesting that citizens should not regard Supreme Court cases in which Justice Thomas cast the deciding vote as law).

32. If it were, Thomas' nomination would have been defeated. *See* William N. Eskridge, Jr., *The One Senator, One Vote Clauses,* in Constitutional Stupidities, Constitutional Tragedies 35–39 (William N. Eskridge and Sanford Levinson, eds., 1998).

33. As Richard Kay has written, "Mere coincidence of a result reached by a judge and a result indicated by the rule does not demonstrate a case of rule compliance if the judge reaches that result for reasons other than the force of the rule as a rule of the legal system. So a judge may, for reasons of personal taste or political principle, believe the state ought never to confiscate private property without compensation. When such a judge declares an uncompensated taking invalid, we cannot be sure that the constitutional rule is the effective cause of that decision. This quality of genuine law-following has been summed up by describing the obligation of the judge to apply the law as *content-independent.* The practical test of action pursuant to such a commitment is the decision made by a judge who would, but for this obligation, decide a given case the opposite way." Richard Kay, *American Constitutionalism,* in Constitutionalism: Philosophical Foundations 43–44 (Larry Alexander, ed., 1998).

34. This is a version of the problem discussed in Frank I. Michelman, *Always under Law?* 12 Const. Comm. 227 (1995).

35. For classic discussions, see Thomas Shelling, Choice and Consequence 98 (1984); Jon Elster, Ulysses and the Sirens: Studies in Rationality and Irrationality (1979).

36. For an excellent discussion, see Michael J. Klarman, *What's So Great about Constitutionalism?* 93 Nw. L. Rev. 145 (1998).

37. *See, e.g.,* John Locke, Two Treatises of Government 322–23, in John Locke: Political Writings (David Wootton, ed., 1993); *and* John Rawls, A Theory of Justice 115–16 (1971).

38. For a well-known exploration of these problems, see Michael J. Sandel, Liberalism and the Limits of Justice 105–31 (1982).

39. *See* John Rawls, A Theory of Justice 152–58 (1971).

40. For the classic exposition of this view, see H. L. A. Hart, The Concept of Law 97–114, 245–47 (1961).

41. I understand Philip Bobbitt to defend something like this view. *See* Philip Bobbitt, Constitutional Fate: Theory of the Constitution (1982); *and* Philip Bobbitt, Constitutional Interpretation (1991). *See also* Dennis M. Patterson, Law and Truth (1992).

42. *See* Philip Soper, A Theory of Law 46–51 (1984) (arguing that theories of academic "outsiders" are irrelevant to "insiders," who must make legal decisions).

43. *See* Frederick Schauer, *Amending the Presuppositions of the Constitution,* in Responding to Imperfections: The Theory and Practice of Constitutional Amendment (Sanford Levinson, ed., 1995) ("The Constitution . . . is law not because the Framers and Ratifiers said so, but because we today accept it as such"). Frank Michelman has tied this observation to the definition of the political community bound by constitutional obligation. *See* Frank Michelman, *Always under Law,* 12 Const. Comm. 227, 240 (1995) (arguing that people can know themselves as a political entity "only by knowing themselves as a group of sharers, joint participants in some already present, contentful idea, or proto idea, of political reason or right").

44. As Frank Michelman has argued: "Constitutional-democratic thought is always taking for granted that whoever is engaged in higher lawmaking for a country . . . is, in

that engagement, answering to some still higher law that is already there, in place." Id., at 229.

45. See John Rawls, Political Liberalism 135–72 (1996).

46. See Cass R. Sunstein, One Case at a Time: Judicial Minimalism in the Supreme Court (1999).

47. Although this position has enjoyed a modern revival among academic lawyers, it is associated with historians who wrote almost a half-century ago. See, e.g., Louis Hartz, The Liberal Tradition in America 35–66 (1955); Daniel J. Boorstin, The Genius of American Politics 1–10, 31–35 (1953); Arthur Schlesinger, Jr., The Vital Center 11–34 (1949); Richard Hofstadter, The American Tradition and the Men Who Made It 3–17 (10th ed., 1996).

48. See Cass R. Sunstein, Incompletely Theorized Agreements, 108 Harv. L. Rev. 1733, 1739–42 (1995).

49. See Cass R. Sunstein, Foreword: Leaving Things Undecided, 110 Harv. L. Rev. 4, 21 (1996) ("a crucial goal of a liberal political system [is] to make it possible for people to agree when agreement is necessary, and to make it unnecessary for people to agree when agreement is impossible").

50. This possibility is discussed at greater length in Chapter 2.

51. See John Rawls, Political Liberalism xxxix (1996) (arguing against modus vivendi).

52. For an example of a failed effort to bridge the gap, see Stephen Macedo, Homosexuality and the Conservative Mind, 84 Geo. L. J. 261 (1995); Robert P. George and Gerald V. Bradley, Marriage and the Liberal Imagination, 84 Geo. L. J. 301 (1995); Hadley Arkes, Questions of Principle, not Prediction: A Reply to Macedo, 84 Geo. L. J. 321 (1995); and Stephen Macedo, A Reply to Critics, 84 Geo. L. J. 329 (1995).

53. See Cruzan v. Director, Missouri Dept. of Health, 497 U.S. 261, 293 (1990) (Scalia, J., concurring); Romer v. Evans, 517 U.S. 620, 636 (1996) (Scalia, J., dissenting).

Chapter 2: Strategies for a Just Peace

1. See Thomas Hobbes, Leviathan 117–121 (Richard Tuck, ed., 1991).

2. The original model for such a community was Rousseau's Geneva. See Jean-Jacques Rousseau, Discourse on the Origin and Foundations of Inequality among Men, in The First and Second Discourses 78–90 (R. Masters, ed.; R. Masters and J. Masters, trans., 1964).

3. The anti-federalist argument against a strong central government was premised on this view. See 2 The Complete Antifederalist 369 (Herbert Storing, ed., 1980) (quoting "Brutus" as arguing that "[i]n a republic, the manners, sentiments, and interests of the people should be similar").

4. For example, Frank Michelman has argued that republican thought can be reconciled with the nurturing of a "social plurality." See Frank Michelman, Law's Republic, 97 Yale L. J. 1493, 1533 (1988). Kathleen Sullivan refers to this view as "rainbow republicanism." See Kathleen M. Sullivan, Rainbow Republicanism, 97 Yale L. J. 1713 (1988).

5. For some proposals along these lines, see Michael Sandel, Introduction, in Liberalism and Its Critics 6 (Michael Sandel, ed., 1984).

6. *See, e.g.,* Cass R. Sunstein, *Interest Groups in American Public Law,* 38 Stan. L. Rev. 29, 32 (1985) (arguing that republican theory conceives of education as critical to the process of instilling civic virtue that will, in turn, prevent the "spirit of faction" from developing).

7. *See* Montesquieu, The Spirit of the Laws, bk. 5, chs. iii–iv (D. Carrithers, ed.; T. Nugent, trans., 1977). Significantly, others have argued that constitutional *prohibitions* on redistribution are required to eliminate the temptation to engage in factional politics. *See, e.g.,* James. M. Buchanan and Gordon Tullock, The Calculus of Consent: Logical Foundations of Constitutional Democracy 220–48 (1965) (justifying bicameralism and separation of powers doctrines as raising the costs of redistributive legislation); *and* Lynn A. Stout, *Strict Scrutiny and Social Choice: An Economic Inquiry into Fundamental Rights and Suspect Classifications,* 80 Geo. L. Rev. 1787, 1814–22 (1992) (justifying strict scrutiny for "suspect" classifications on similar grounds).

8. *See* Gordon Wood, The Creation of the American Republic, 1776–1787, 427–28 (1969) (describing the use of religion by eighteenth-century republicans to inculcate public values).

9. *See* Richard H. Fallon, *What Is Republicanism and Is It Worth Reviving?* 102 Harv. L. Rev. 1695, 1723 (1989) (criticizing republicanism on these grounds).

10. *See, e.g.,* Jerome Frank, Law and the Modern Mind 21 (1930) (arguing that people naturally seek the "authoritativeness, certainty and predictability" of settled law just as a child seeks the controlled world created by its parents in order to avoid uncertainty and confusion); Thurman Arnold, The Symbols of Government 34–35 (1935) ("It is part of the function of 'Law' to give recognition to ideals representing the exact opposite of established conduct. . . . It develops the structure of an elaborate dream world where logic creates justice").

11. *See* Leo Strauss, Persecution and the Art of Writing (1952).

12. *See, e.g.,* Bruce Ackerman, Social Justice in the Liberal State 10–12, 349–69 (1980); Ronald Dworkin, A Matter of Principle 191 (1985).

13. *See* Santa Fe Ind. School Dist. v. Doe, 530 U.S. 290 (2000) (holding that selection of particular prayer " 'substitutes majority determinations for viewpoint neutrality' " [quoting from Board of Regents of University of Wisconsin System v. Southworth, 529 U.S. 217, 235 (2000)]).

14. *See* School Dist. of Abington Township v. Schempp, 374 U.S. 203, 312 (1963) (Stewart, J., dissenting) (arguing that there is "a substantial free exercise claim on the part of those who affirmatively desire to have their children's school day open with the reading of passages from the Bible").

15. *See, e.g.,* Buckley v. Valeo, 424 U.S. 1 (1976) (invalidating spending limitations for political campaigns).

16. *See, e.g.,* Arizona v. Hicks, 480 U.S. 321, 329 (1986) (acknowledging that the Fourth Amendment "sometimes insulates the criminality of a few in order to protect the privacy of us all").

17. The Constitution grants both houses of Congress the power to declare war. *See* art. I, sec. 8, cl. 11. In contrast, the president is granted the authority to make treaties with the advice and consent of two-thirds of the Senate. *See* art. II, sec. 2, cl. 2.

18. This is, of course, the premise that animates John Rawls, A Theory of Justice (1971).

19. *Cf.* Steven D. Smith, The Constitution and the Pride of Reason 31 (1998) (pointing out that readers of the Constitution are "almost immediately . . . inundated by a flood of petty detail").

20. As Steven Smith points out, the framers doubted the ability of other people to make political decisions on the basis of reason; yet their skepticism somehow did not extend to their own decisions when drafting the Constitution. Id., at 37.

21. *See* Larry Alexander, *The Constitution as Law,* 6 Con Comm. 103, 107–09 (1989) ("[N]o one may believe that the Constitution is an ideal set of authoritative rules in terms of his or her own political/moral principles. But everyone may believe that the Constitution is, in terms of those same principles, the best set of authoritative rules that it is possible to get everyone, or enough others, to accept as authoritative."). *Cf.* David A. Strauss, *Common Law Constitutional Interpretation,* 63 U. Chi. L. Rev. 877, 910–11 (1996) (arguing that "our culture has given [the Constitution] salience that makes it the natural choice when cooperation is valuable").

22. Michael Klarman and Lawrence Lessig agree on this point, although they disagree as to the relevance it has for constitutional interpretation. *Compare* Lawrence Lessig, *Fidelity in Translation,* 72 Tex. L. Rev. 1165, 1179 (1993) (arguing that judges can take into account changes in context when interpreting the Constitution) *with* Michael J. Klarman, *What's So Great about Constitutionalism?* 93 Nw. U. L. Rev. 145, 155 (1998) (arguing that the instability of context makes constitutional interpretation fundamentally illegitimate).

23. *See, e.g.,* Mark A. Graber, *Desperately Ducking Slavery: Dred Scott and Contemporary Constitutional Theory,* 14 Con. Comm. 271, 294 (1997) (concluding that "on the whole, Taney, Daniel, Catron, and Campbell presented a reasonable interpretation of the original Constitution and subsequent legal developments").

For our purposes, there is no need to resolve the dispute about whether Taney accurately interpreted the Constitution. Does anyone suppose that Dred Scott is a bad decision solely because Taney made a technical legal or historical mistake about the framers' words and purposes? Surely the moral failures of the opinion lie elsewhere.

24. *See* Eric L. McKitrick, Andrew Johnson and Reconstruction 108–09 (1960).

25. *See, e.g.,* Carter v. Carter Coal Co., 298 U.S. 238 (1936); United States v. Butler, 297 U.S. 1 (1936); Home Building & Loan Assn. v. Blaisdell, 290 U.S. 398, 448 (1934) (Southerland, J., dissenting).

26. *See* Ronald Dworkin, Taking Rights Seriously 132–37 (1977) (arguing that the open texture of constitutional provisions invites readings that would develop and change over time); *and* Lawrence Lessig, *Fidelity in Translation,* 71 Tex. L. Rev. 1165, 1166 (1993) (arguing that new interpretations of the original text based on changed circumstances may be a valid interpretation of the text).

27. Not quite everyone agrees with this conclusion. *See* Akhil Reed Amar, *The Consent of the Governed: Constitutional Amendment outside Article V,* 94 Colum. L. Rev. 457 (1994); *and* Akhil Reed Amar, *Philadelphia Revisited: Amending the Constitution outside Article V,* 55 U. Chi. L. Rev. 1043 (1988).

28. *See* Bruce Ackerman, We the People: Transformations (1998) (hereinafter cited as

"Transformations"), *and* Bruce Ackerman, We the People: Foundations (1991) (herein-after cited as "Foundations").

29. *See* Foundations 62.

30. *See* id., at 58–67.

31. *See* Transformations 92.

32. *See* Foundations 10–16.

33. *See* Transformations 81–95.

34. *See* Michael J. Klarman, *Constitutional Fact/Constitutional Fiction: A Critique of Bruce Ackerman's Theory of Constitutional Moments,* 44 Stan. L. Rev. 759 (1992).

35. *See* Frank I. Michelman, *Thirteen Easy Pieces,* 93 Mich. L. Rev. 1297, 1301–04 (1995).

36. *See* Foundations 266–69.

37. *See* Mark Tushnet, *Living in a Constitutional Moment? Lopez and Constitutional Theory,* 46 Case W. Res. L. Rev. 845, 854–856 (1996).

38. Tushnet cites Bruce Ackerman, *Rooted Cosmopolitanism,* 104 Ethics 516, 517 (1994) in support of this reading of Ackerman's project. *See* id. at 854 n. 46.

39. Id., at 855.

40. For the relevant statistics, see The World Almanac and Book of Facts — 1999 at 209.

41. *See* Gary Lawson, *The Constitutional Case against Precedent,* 17 Harv. J. L. & Pub. Pol'y 23 (1994).

42. *See, e.g.,* Planned Parenthood of Southeastern Pennsylvania v. Casey, 505 U.S. 833, 855 (1992) (application of stare decisis depends in part on "whether the rule's limitation on state power could be removed without serious inequity to those who have relied upon it or significant damage to the stability of the society governed by the rule in question").

43. For another example, *see* Michael Klarman, *Constitutional Fact/Constitutional Fiction: A Critique of Bruce Ackerman's Theory of Constitutional Moments,* 44 Stan. L. Rev. 759, 791 (1992) (arguing that "gradual accretion of power in the presidency" did not result from a "single dramatic transformation").

44. *See* Ronald Dworkin, Law's Empire (1986) [hereinafter cited as "Law's Empire"].

45. *See* Law's Empire, at 52; *and* Ronald Dworkin, Taking Rights Seriously 159–68 (1977).

46. *See* Ronald Dworkin, Taking Rights Seriously 131–49 (1977).

47. *See* Ronald Dworkin, Freedom's Law: The Moral Reading of the American Consti-tution 10 (1996) [hereinafter cited as "Freedom's Law"].

48. *See* Freedom's Law, at 21–26

49. Id., at 11.

50. Law's Empire, at 93 (emphasis added).

51. Id., at at 22.

52. Id., at 211.

53. Id.

54. Id., at 22.

55. Duncan Kennedy has criticized Dworkin on somewhat similar grounds. *See* Dun-can Kennedy, *Strategizing Strategic Behavior in Legal Interpretation,* 1996 Utah L. Rev. 785, 817–18 (1996).

56. *See* Kevin Sack, *Blacks Strip Slaveholders' Names off School,* N.Y. Times, Nov. 12, 1997 at A1.

57. *See, e.g.,* Dick Feagler, *It's a Very Short Step from Diversity to Division,* Cleveland Plain Dealer, Nov. 14, 1997, at 2A.

58. *See* Mark V. Tushnet, *Following the Rules Laid Down: A Critique of Interpretivism and Neutral Principles,* 96 Harv. L. Rev. 781 (1983).

59. *See* Akhil Reed Amar, *Remember the Thirteenth,* 10 Const. Comm. 403, 403–06 (1993) (child abuse); Akhil Reed Amar, The Constitution and Criminal Procedure 119 (1997) (exclusionary rule); Akhil Reed Amar, *The Fifteenth Amendment and "Political Rights,"* 17 Cardozo L. Rev. 2225, 2226–29 (1996) (jury rights).

60. *See* David Ray Papke, Heretics in the Temple: Americans Who Reject the Nation's Legal Faith 152 (1998).

61. Id., at 140.

62. *See* Ronald Dworkin, *The Arduous Virtue of Fidelity: Originalism, Scalia, Tribe, and Nerve,* 65 Fordham L. Rev. 1249, 1254–55 (1997).

63. *See, e.g.,* Frank I. Michelman, *Welfare Rights in a Constitutional Democracy,* Wash. U. L. Qu. 659, 678–85 (1979); Charles L. Black, Jr., *Further Reflections on the Constitutional Justice of Livelihood,* 86 Colum. L. Rev. 1103 (1986); Peter B. Edelman, *The Next Century of Our Constitution: Rethinking Our Duty to the Poor,* 39 Hast. L.J. 1 (1987).

64. Indeed, Dworkin shares the political views of advocates of welfare rights. *See* Ronald Dworkin, *The Arduous Virtue of Fidelity: Originalism, Scalia, Tribe, and Nerve,* 65 Fordham L. Rev. 1249, 1254–55 (1997).

65. *See, e.g.,* Louis Hartz, The Liberal Tradition in America 35–66 (1955); Daniel J. Boorstin, The Genius of American Politics 1–7, 8–10, 31–35 (1953).

66. Annie Hall (United Artists, 1977).

67. It was for just this reason that Thomas Jefferson thought that "it may be proved that no society can make a perpetual constitution, or even a perpetual law." In a letter to James Madison, he argued that constitutions should become invalid after each genera- tion. *See* Letter from Thomas Jefferson to James Madison (Sept. 6, 1789), in 1 The Republic of Letters 631–36 (James Morton Smith ed., 1995). See also Letter to Samuel Kercheval, July 12, 1816 in The Portable Thomas Jefferson 553–58 (M. Peterson ed., 1975). For Madison's response, see 16 The Papers of Thomas Jefferson 151–54 (J. Boyd ed., 1961).

68. Roberto Mangabeira Unger, False Necessity: Anti-Necessitarian Social Theory in the Service of Radical Democracy 452 (1987).

69. Id., at 530.

70. Id., at 437.

71. Id., at 465–67.

72. *See* John Dewey, Freedom and Culture (1939).

73. *See, e.g.,* Michael C. Dorf and Charles F. Sabel, *A Constitution of Democratic Experimentalism,* 98 Colum. L. Rev. 267, 276 (1998); *and* James Gray Pope, *Republican Moments: The Role of Direct Popular Power in the American Constitutional Order,* 139 U. Pa. L. Rev. 287, 290 (1990).

74. *See* The Federalist No. 51, at 322 (James Madison) (Clinton Rossiter ed., 1961)

(criticizing "parchment barriers"); The Federalist No. 48, at 308 (James Madison) (Clinton Rossiter ed., 1961) (arguing against utility of a bill of rights).

Chapter 3: Constitutional Boundaries

1. For this reason some might think that constitutional law, like jurisprudence more generally, is characteristically male. *See* Robin West, *Jurisprudence and Gender,* in Feminist Jurisprudence 493–530 (Patricia Smith, ed., 1993).

2. For similar efforts to organize law around these and related dichotomies, see Morton J. Horwitz, The Transformation of American Law, 1870–1960, 255–56 (1977); Duncan Kennedy, *Form and Substance in Private Law Adjudication,* 89 Harv. L. Rev. 1685, 1745–55 (1976); *and* Duncan Kennedy, *Towards an Understanding of Legal Consciousness: The Case of Classical Legal Thought in America, 1850–1940,* 3 Research in Law & Sociology 3, 8–9 (1980).

3. This conceptualization has an obvious link to the idea of the "dangerous supplement" central to some versions of deconstructive theory. For a discussion in a legal context, see Jack Balkin, *Deconstructive Practice and Legal Theory,* 96 Yale L. J. 743, 770 (1986).

4. This mode of thinking is connected to what Duncan Kennedy has called classical legal thought. *See* Duncan Kennedy, *Towards an Understanding of Legal Consciousness: The Case of Classical Legal Thought in American, 1850–1940,* 3 Research in Law & Sociology 3 (1980).

5. 198 U.S. 45 (1905).

6. *See* Laurence H. Tribe, American Constitutional Law 1344 (3d ed. 2000); Benjamin Wright, The Growth of American Constitutional Law 154, 176 (1942).

7. *See* Holden v. Hardy, 169 U.S. 366 (1898), *distinguished in* Lochner v. New York, 198 U.S. 45, 54 (1905).

8. 198 U.S. 45, at 56–57.

9. For early criticisms along these lines, see Roscoe Pound, *Liberty of Contract,* 18 Yale L. J. 454 (1909); Morris Cohen, *Property and Sovereignty,* 13 Cornell L. Q. 8 (1927).

10. 198 U.S. 45, at 70 (Harlan, J., dissenting).

11. Id., at 58.

12. As Justice Peckham put it, "We think that there can be no fair doubt that the trade of a baker, in and of itself, is not an unhealthy one to that degree that would authorize the legislature to interfere with the right to labor. . . . In looking through statistics regarding all trades and occupations, it may be true that the trade of a baker does not appear to be as healthy as some other trades, and is also vastly more healthy than still others. To the common understanding the trade of a baker has never been regarded as an unhealthy one." Id.

13. As Walter Wheeler Cook complained, "Nearly every discussion seems to proceed on the tacit assumption that the supposed 'line' between the two categories has some kind of objective existence . . . and that the object is to find out . . . 'on which side of the line a set of facts falls.' . . . This way of stating the problem . . . [diverts] our attention from the fact that we are thinking about the case precisely because there is no 'line' already in

'existence' which can be 'discovered' by analysis alone." Walter Wheeler Cook, *Substance and Procedure in the Conflict of Laws*, 42 Yale L. J. 333, 335 (1933).

14. For the classic argument to this effect, see Robert L. Hale, *Coercion and Distribution in the Supposedly Non-Coercive State*, 38 Pol. Sci. Q. 470 (1923).

15. *See* Morris Cohen, *Property and Sovereignty*, 13 Cornell L. Q. 8 (1927).

16. Richard A. Epstein, Takings: Private Property and the Power of Eminent Domain (1985).

17. Robert Nozick, Anarchy, State, and Utopia (1974).

18. *See, e.g.*, Day-Brite Lighting, Inc., v. Missouri, 342 U.S. 421 (1952) (workplace); Cruzan v. Director, Missouri Dept. of Health, 457 U.S. 261 (1990) (right to die).

19. *See, e.g.*, City of Richmond v. J. A. Croson Co., 488 U.S. 469, 523 (1989) (Scalia, J., concurring) ("An acute awareness of the heightened danger of oppression from political factions in small, rather than large, political units dates from the beginning of our national history"). *See generally* Sheryll Cashin, *Federalism, Welfare Reform, and the Minority Poor: Accounting for the Tyranny of State Majorities*, 99 Colum. L. Rev. 552 (1999).

20. For an early recognition of the "race to the bottom" problem, see Stewart Machine Co. v. Davis, 301 U.S. 548 (1937).

21. In *Cruzan*, Chief Justice Rehnquist's majority opinion conceded that "the principle that a competent person has a constitutionally protected liberty interest in refusing unwanted medical treatment may be inferred from our prior decisions." 457 U.S., at 278. Moreover, Justice O'Connor, whose vote was necessary for the majority, made clear that in her view, this interest extended to the refusal to accept artificial feeding. Id., at 287. In Washington v. Glucksburg, 521 U.S. 702 (1997), a unanimous Court rejected a facial challenge to a state ban on assisted suicide. However, Justices O'Connor, Stevens, Souter, Ginsburg, and Breyer each wrote separately to indicate, with varying degrees of clarity, their belief that there might be a constitutional right in some circumstances to medication that hastened death. See id., at 702, 738, 751, 752, 752.

22. *See* Cruzan v. Director, Missouri Dept. of Health, 457 U.S., at 292 (Scalia, J., concurring).

23. *See, e.g.*, Yale Kamisar, *Against Assisted Suicide — Even in Very Limited Form*, 72 Det. Mercy L. Rev. 735, 738 (1995).

24. For representative examples, see Bernard H. Sagan, Economic Liberties and the Constitution 110–25 (1980); *and* David E. Bernstein, *Lochner, Parity, and the Chinese Laundry Cases*, 41 Wm. & Mary L. Rev. 211, 292 (1999).

25. *See* Quill v. Vacco, 80 3d 716, 732 (2d Cir. 1996) (Calabresi, J., concurring).

26. According to one estimate, physicians may help hasten the death of 6,000 terminally ill patients per day. *See* Timothy E. Quill et al., *Care of the Hopelessly Ill: Proposed Clinical Criteria for Physicians — Assisted Suicide*, 327 New Eng. J. Med, 1380, 1381 (1992), cited in Compassion in Dying v. Washington, 79 F.3d 790, 811 n. 56 (9th Cir. 1996).

27. *See, e.g.*, Griswold v. Connecticut, 381 U.S. 479, 523 (1965) (Black, J., dissenting).

28. *See, e.g.*, Cass R. Sunstein, *Lochner's Legacy*, 87 Colum. L. Rev. 873 (1987).

29. *See, e.g.*, Richard Posner, *Against Constitutional Theory*, 73 N.Y.U. L. Rev. 1

(1998); Daniel A. Farber, *Legal Pragmatism and the Constitution,* 72 Minn. L. Rev. 1331 (1988).

30. For some examples, see Arthur A. Leff, *Memorandum,* 29 Stan. L. Rev. 879 (1977); Arthur A. Leff, *Unspeakable Ethics, Unnatural Law,* 1979 Duke L. J. 1229; Arthur A. Leff, *Law and Technology: On Shoring up a Void,* 8 Ottawa L. Rev. 536 (1976); Arthur A. Leff, *Economic Analysis of Law: Some Realism about Nominalism,* 60 Cal. L. Rev. 451 (1974); *and* Arthur A. Leff, *Law And,* 87 Yale L. J. 573 (1977).

31. The recent work of Pierre Schlag is in the same genre and is similarly powerful. *See, e.g.,* Pierre Schlag, *Values,* 6 Yale J. L. & Hum. 219 (1994); *and* Pierre Schlag, *Normative and Nowhere to Go,* 43 Stan. L. Rev. 167 (1990).

32. *See* Arthur A. Leff, *The Leff Dictionary of Law: A Fragment,* 94 Yale L. J. 1855 (1985).

33. For a discussion, see Martha C. Nussbaum, *Sophistry about Conventions,* in Love's Knowledge (1990).

34. *See* Philip Bobbitt, Constitutional Interpretation (1991); *and* Philip Bobbitt, Constitutional Fate: Theory of the Constitution (1982).

35. Philip Bobbitt, Constitutional Interpretation 186 (1991).

36. *See, e.g.,* Mari J. Matsuda, *Looking to the Bottom: Critical Legal Studies and Reparations,* 22 Harv. C.R.-C.L. L. Rev. 323 (1987).

37. *See* Patricia Williams, The Alchemy of Race and Rights (1991).

38. *See, e.g.,* Richard Delgado, *The Imperial Scholar: Reflections on a Review of Civil Rights Literature,* 132 U. Pa. L. Rev. 561 (1989).

39. *See* id., at 569–71.

40. *See* Terrance Sandalow, *Racial Preferences in Higher Education: Political Responsibility and the Judicial Role,* 42 U. Chi. L. Rev. 653, 686 (1975).

41. *See, e.g.,* William Van Alsytne, *Rites of Passage: Race, the Supreme Court, and the Constitution,* 46 U. Chi. L. Rev. 775, 809 (1979).

42. *See, e.g.,* City of Richmond v. J. A. Croson Co., 488 U.S. 469, 493 (1989).

43. *See, e.g.,* Duncan Kennedy, *A Cultural Pluralist Case for Affirmative Action in Legal Academia,* 1990 Duke L. J. 705, 707–12; *and* Gary Peller, *The Discourse of Constitutional Degradation,* 81 Geo. L. J. 313, 340 (1992).

44. For a discussion of the empirical literature on how these background assumptions are formed, see Linda Hamilton Krieger, *Civil Rights Perestroika: Intergroup Relations after Affirmative Action,* 86 Cal. L. Rev. 1251, 1293–99 (1998).

45. For an example of how perspectivist criticism can generate controversy without moving the contending forces closer to resolution, *compare* Daniel A. Farber and Suzanna Sherry, *Is the Radical Critique of Merit Anti-Semitic?* 83 Cal. L. Rev. 853 (1995), *with* Daria Roithmayr, *Guerrillas in Our Midst: The Assault on Radicals in American Law,* 96 Mich. L. Rev. 1658 (1999).

46. *See* Louis Michael Seidman and Mark V. Tushnet, Remnants of Belief (1996).

47. As I use these terms here, they overlap with, but are not identical to, the philosophical concepts of "justice" and "virtue." For a discussion, see Onora O'Neill, *Toward Justice and Virtue: A Constructive Account of Practical Reasoning* 9–37 (1998).

48. *See, e.g.,* Peter Singer, Animal Liberation (2d ed., 1990).

49. *Cf.* Christopher D. Stone, *Should Trees Have Standing? Toward Legal Rights for Natural Objects,* 45 Cal. L. Rev. 1393 (1991).

50. For a sophisticated attempt to reconcile the conflict, see Onora O'Neill, Towards Justice and Virtue: A Constructive Account of Practical Reasoning (1996).

51. *Cf.* Peter Gabel and Duncan Kennedy, *Roll Over Beethoven,* 36 Stan. L. Rev. 1, 15 (1984).

52. For a discussion of the problem, see Thomas Nagel, The Possibility of Altruism (1970).

53. *See* William Raspberry, "Mrs. Luce: An Awful Interview," Washington Post, Sept 15, 1982.

54. Although even here our intuitions are unstable. Consider, for example, whether parents should be permitted to specify the race of children they adopt. For an argument that they should not, see Richard Banks, *The Color of Desire: Fulfilling Adoptive Parents' Racial Preferences through Discriminatory State Action,* 107 Yale L. J. 875 (1998).

55. *See, e.g.,* Daphna Lewinsohn-Zamir, *Consumer Preferences, Citizen Preferences, and the Provision of Public Goods,* 108 Yale L. J. 377, 382 n. 11 (1998); Amartya K. Sen, *Rational Fools: A Critique of the Behavioral Foundations of Economic Theory,* 6 J. Phil. & Pub. Aff. 317, 332–33 (1977).

56. This point is spelled out in more detail in Chapter 5.

57. For discussion, see Laurence H. Tribe, God Save This Honorable Court: How the Choice of Supreme Court Justices Shapes Our History (1985); *and* Stephen L. Carter, The Confirmation Mess: Cleaning up the Federal Appointments Process (1994). Of course, many state judges are elected. Typically, however, they are chosen for lengthy terms. Moreover, there are norms that limit the kind of campaigning that judges engage in.

58. *See, e.g.,* Martin Shapiro, Law and Politics in the Supreme Court (1964); Barry Friedman, *When Rights Encounter Reality: Enforcing Federal Remedies,* 65 S. Cal. L. Rev. 735, 738 (1992); *and* Michael J. Klarman, *Rethinking the Civil Rights and Civil Liberties Revolutions,* 82 Va. L. Rev. 1, 7–18 (1996).

59. *See* Ann Devroy, *Clinton's Holiday from Polls: This Post Election Summer, He Doesn't Need to Head for the Hills,* Washington Post, July 5, 1997, at C1 (describing how President Clinton selected his vacation sites during election years based on polls designed to establish "what 'married people with kids' approved of for vacation activities").

60. *See* Melinda Henneberger, *The 1998 Campaign: The Message; Political Wives Cast as Leads in TV Testimonials for Votes,* N.Y. Times, Oct. 31, 1998, at A1 (describing how the wives of candidates are being asked to speak out about their personal lives with respect to their husbands as part of campaign advertising strategy, including commercials that depict their "happy home").

61. *See* David A. Strauss, *Common Law Constitutional Interpretation,* 63 U. Chi. L. Rev. 877 (1996).

62. *See* Mark V. Tushnet, *Following the Rules Laid Down: A Critique of Interpretivism and Neutral Principles,* 96 Harv. L. Rev. 781 (1983); *and* Jan G. Deutsch, *Neutrality, Legitimacy, and the Supreme Court: Some Intersections between Law and Political Science,* 20 Stan. L. Rev. 169 (1968).

Chapter 4: The Elusive Goal of Unsettlement

1. *Cf.* Michael J. Klarman, *Rethinking the Civil Rights and Civil Liberties Revolutions,* 82 Va. L. Rev. 1, 16 n. 72 (1996) (noting that Justices, being part of popular culture "[stray] relatively little from majoritarian impulses"); *and* Robert G. McCloskey, The American Supreme Court 208–09 (Sanford Levinson, ed., 1994) (noting that the Court's decisions have generally been in line with "public sentiment").

2. The most widely cited work on this point is Gerald N. Rosenberg, The Hollow Hope: Can Courts Bring about Social Change? (1991). *See also* Barry Friedman, *Dialogue and Judicial Review,* 91 Mich. L. Rev. 577, 581 (1993); Girardeau A. Spann, Race against the Court 27–31 (1993); *and* Michael J. Klarman, *Rethinking the Civil Rights and Civil Liberties Revolution,* 82 Va. L. Rev. 1, 6–7 (1996).

3. *See* Barry Cushman, Rethinking the New Deal Court: The Structure of a Constitutional Revolution 33–44 (1998).

4. *See* Lucas A. Powe, Jr., The Warren Court and American Politics (2000); *and* Gerald N. Rosenberg, The Hollow Hope: Can Courts Bring about Social Change? (1991).

5. *See* Michael J. Klarman, *Rethinking the Civil Rights and Civil Liberties Revolution,* 82 Va. L. Rev. 1, 6 (1996).

6. *Cf.* Barry Friedman, *"Things Forgotten" in the Debate over Judicial Independence,* 14 Ga. St. U. L. Rev. 737, 762–65 (1998) (arguing that although it may have been the framers' intent to establish an independent judiciary, political appointments and attrition are likely to produce outcomes that do not depart much from popular opinion).

7. For example, Harry T. Edwards, the chief judge of the U.S. Court of Appeals for the D.C. Circuit, has argued that in the majority of cases, Court of Appeals judges are in agreement as to the appropriate outcome. Yet even Judge Edwards concedes that in a minority of "very hard" cases, "judges often find themselves in basic disagreement" and the outcome "may be influenced by . . . ideology." Harry T. Edwards, *Public Misperceptions Concerning the "Politics" of Judging: Dispelling Some Myths about the D.C. Circuit,* 56 U. Colo. L. Rev. 619, 632, 626 (1985). Others have argued that ideology plays an important role more frequently than Judge Edwards acknowledges. *See* Richard L. Revesz, *Environmental Regulation Ideology and the D.C. Circuit,* 83 Va. L. Rev., 1717 (1997); *and* Frank B. Cross and Emerson H. Tiller, *Judicial Partisanship and Obedience to Legal Doctrine: Whistleblowing on the Federal Courts of Appeals,* 107 Yale L. J. 2155 (1998). For Judge Edwards' response, see Harry T. Edwards, *Collegiality and Decision Making on the D.C. Circuit,* 84 Va. L. Rev. 1355 (1998).

8. Indeed, some constitutional scholars have argued that judicial review is legitimate precisely because it legitimates the exercise of governmental power. *See, e.g.,* Charles L. Black, Jr., The People and the Court 47–53 (1960) (arguing that the "Court, through its history, has acted as the legitimator of the government").

9. Justice Scalia has made such predictions his rhetorical specialty. *See, e.g.,* Planned Parenthood of Southeastern Pennsylvania v. Casey, 505 U.S. 833, 1000–01 (1992) (Scalia, J., dissenting) ("As long as this Court thought [and the people thought] that we Justices were doing essentially lawyers' work up here — reading text and discerning our society's traditional understanding of that text — the public pretty much left us alone. . . .

But if in reality our process of constitutional adjudication consists primarily of making value judgments . . . then a free and intelligent people's attitude towards us can be expected to be [ought to be] quite different"); Cruzan v. Director, Missouri Dept. of Health, 497 U.S. 261, 300–01 (1990) (Scalia, J., concurring) ("This Court need not, and has no authority to, inject itself into every field of human activity where irrationality and oppression may theoretically occur, and if it tries to do so it will destroy itself"); Mistretta v. United States, 488 U.S. 361, 427 (1989) (Scalia, J., dissenting) ("[I]n the long run the improvisation of a constitutional structure on the basis of currently perceived utility will be disastrous").

10. Bush v. Gore, 121 S. Ct. 525, 542, 557 (2001) (Stevens and Breyer, JJ., dissenting).

11. 505 U.S. 833 (1992).

12. 410 U.S. 113 (1973).

13. 505 U.S., at 844.

14. Id., at 865.

15. Id., at 866.

16. Id., at 867.

17. Id.

18. Bush v. Gore, 121 S. Ct. 525, 533 (2001).

19. *See* Barry Friedman, *Dialogue and Judicial Review,* 91 Mich. L. Rev. 577, 580 (1993).

20. *See* Robert A Burt, The Constitution in Conflict (1992).

21. Dred Scott v. Sandford, 60 U.S. (19 How.) 393 (1857).

22. Brown v. Board of Education, 394 U.S. 294, 301 (1955).

23. *See* Robert A. Burt, The Constitution in Conflict (1992).

24. *See* Robert M. Cover, *Violence and the Word,* 95 Yale L. J. 1601 (1986).

25. *See* Robert M. Cover, Justice Accused: Antislavery and the Judicial Process 233 (1975) (explaining how antislavery judges dealt with their moral discomfort when issuing proslavery decisions by purporting to apply "the law and the law alone").

26. 478 U.S. 186 (1986).

27. 319 U.S. 624 (1943).

28. Id., at 642.

29. United States v. Carolene Products, 304 U.S. 144, 152–53 n.4 (1938).

30. *See* Richard Davies Parker, *The Past of Constitutional Theory — and Its Future,* 42 Ohio St. L. J. 223 (1981).

31. 268 U.S. 510 (1925).

32. Bruce Ackerman has made a closely related point. *See* Bruce Ackerman, *Beyond Carolene Products,* 98 Harv. L. Rev. 713, 730 (1985). Ackerman relies on seminal work by Albert Hirschman. *See* Albert Hirschman, Exit, Voice, and Loyalty: Responses to Decline in Firms, Organizations, and States (1970).

33. 60 U.S. (19 How.) 393 (1857).

34. Republican editors had a field day attacking the decision. *See* Don E. Fehrenbacher, The Dred Scott Case: Its Significance in American Law and Politics 417 (1978). Although reaction to the decision failed to produce a significant number of new party members, Republicans successfully mobilized their adherents by playing on the fear that the decision presaged a legalization of slavery throughout the country. *See* id., at 437–38.

35. For a good account, see David J. Garrow, Liberty and Sexuality: The Right to Privacy and the Making of Roe v. Wade 609–19 (1998).

36. 478 U.S. 186 (1986).

37. 384 U.S. 436 (1966).

38. *See, e.g.,* Brown v. Mississippi, 297 U.S. 278 (1936); Chambers v. Florida, 309 U.S. 227 (1940); *and* Ashcraft v. Tennessee, 322 U.S. 143 (1944). *See generally* Yale Kamisar, *A Dissent from the Miranda Dissents: Some Comments on the "New" Fifth Amendment and the Old "Voluntariness" Test,* in Police Interrogation and Confession: Essays in Law and Policy 41, 75 (1980).

39. For some forceful examples, see Robert L. Hale, *Bargaining, Duress, and Economic Liberty,* 43 Colum. L. Rev. 603 (1943); *and* Morris R. Cohen, *The Basis of Contract,* 46 Harv. L. Rev. 553 (1933).

40. Columbe v. Connecticut, 367 U.S. 568, 601 (1961).

41. For a discussion of the Court's limited ability to enforce the voluntariness standard, see Yale Kamisar, *A Dissent from the Miranda Dissents: Some Comments on the "New" Fifth Amendment and the Old "Voluntariness" Test,* in Police Interrogation and Confession: Essays in Law and Policy 75 (1980).

42. 384 U.S., at 467–72.

43. 120 S. Ct. 2326 (2000).

44. Id., at 2336.

45. Id. (quoting from Berkemer v. McCarty, 468 U.S. 420, 433 n. 20 [1984]).

46. Id.

47. 305 U.S. 337 (1938).

48. Id., at 349.

49. For an eloquent elaboration of this point, see Gary Peller, *Race Consciousness,* 1990 Duke L. J. 758, 775.

50. 369 U.S. 186 (1962).

51. 377 U.S. 533 (1964).

52. Colegrove v. Green, 328 U.S. 547, 556 (1946).

53. *See, e.g.,* Martin Shapiro, Law and Politics in the Supreme Court 230–49 (1964) (arguing that the effects of blanket enforcement of electoral equality will be "largely random").

54. *See* John Hart Ely, Democracy and Distrust 124 (1980).

55. Lucas v. Forty-Fourth General Assembly of Colorado, 377 U.S. 713, 748 (1964) (Stewart, J., dissenting).

56. Id., at 751.

57. *See* id.

58. Within four years of the *Reynolds* decision, congressional and state legislative district lines had been redrawn in almost every state. *See* Robert B. McKay, *Reapportionment: Success Story of the Warren Court,* 67 Mich. L. Rev. 223, 226–29 (1968).

59. In Kirkpatrick v. Preisler, 394 U.S. 526 (1969), the Court held that no variance from absolute equality in congressional districts could be dismissed as de minimis, and in Karcher v. Daggett, 462 U.S. 725 (1983), it held that such districts must come as nearly as practicable to population equality. Although the Court has been somewhat more lenient in assessing population deviations in state and local districting, it has nonetheless con-

tinued to insist that mathematical equality is the touchstone. *See* Mahan v. Howell, 410 U.S. 315 (1973); *and* Gaffney v. Cummings, 412 U.S. 735 (1973). In contrast, the Court has held that only a consistent pattern of electoral defeat will justify review of gerrymandering. *See* Davis v. Bandemer, 478 U.S. 109 (1986).

60. *See, e.g.,* Bush v. Vera, 517 U.S. 952 (1996); *and* Shaw v. Hunt, 517 U.S. 899 (1996).

61. *See, e.g.,* Dennis v. United States, 341 U.S. 494, 517–56 (1951) (Frankfurter, J., concurring) (arguing that the legislature, rather than a court, should establish the balance between free speech and the interest in national security); *and* Washington v. Glucksburg, 521 U.S. 702 (1997) (noting that the "morality, legality, and practicality" of physician-assisted suicide should be determined by democratic debate, rather than constitutional doctrine). *See generally* Cass R. Sunstein, *The Supreme Court 1995 Term: Forward: Leaving Things Undecided,* 110 Harv. L. Rev. 4 (1996).

62. *See* Alan Hyde, *The Concept of Legitimation in the Sociology of Law,* 1983 Wisc. L. Rev. 379, 400–07 (1983).

63. *See, e.g.,* Edwards v. Arizona, 451 U.S. 477 (1981) (holding that a defendant who requested counsel could not waive her rights unless she initiated the subsequent conversation); Arizona v. Roberson, 486 U.S. 675 (1988) (applying *Edwards* rule to assertion of counsel in unrelated offense).

64. *See, e.g.,* Green v. County School Board, 391 U.S. 430 (1968); Swann v. Charlotte-Mecklenburg Board of Education, 402 U.S. 1 (1971).

65. As John Rawls has written, "[I]t is [only] by accepting that politics in a democratic society can never be guided by what we see as the whole truth, that we can realize the ideal expressed by the principle of legitimacy: to live politically with others in the light of reasons all might reasonably be expected to endorse." John Rawls, Political Liberalism 243 (1993).

Chapter 5: The Constitution of Political Community

1. *See* Saenz v. Roe, 526 U.S. 489 (1999).

2. *See* Plyler v. Doe, 457 U.S. 202 (1982).

3. *See* Shaw v. Reno, 509 U.S. 630 (1993).

4. *See* United States v. Verdugo-Urquidez, 494 U.S. 259 (1990).

5. *See* Oregon Waste Systems v. Department of Environmental Quality, 511 U.S. 93 (1994).

6. *See* United States v. Lopez, 514 U.S. 549 (1995).

7. *See, e.g.,* Neumeier v. Kuehner, 31 N.Y. 2d 121, 335 N.Y.S. 2d 64, 286 N.E. 2d 454 (1972) (applying Canadian law to a suit brought by a Canadian plaintiff against New York and Canadian defendants arising out of an accident in Canada).

8. U.S. Const. art. VI, cl. 2.

9. 21 U.S. (8 Wheat.) 543 (1823).

10. Id., at 572.

11. Id., at 588–89.

12. 17 U.S. (4 Wheat.) 316 (1819).

13. Id., at 405.

14. Id., at 435–36.

15. 630 F.2d 876 (2d Cir. 1980).

16. *See* Curtis A. Bradley and Jack L. Goldsmith, *Customary International Law as Federal Common Law: A Critique of the Modern Position,* 110 Harv. L. Rev. 815 (1997). For some criticisms of this position, *see* Harold Hongju Koh, *Is International Law Really State Law?* 111 Harv. L. Rev. 1824 (1998); *and* Gerald L. Neuman, *Sense and Nonsense about Customary International Law: A Response to Professors Bradley and Goldsmith,* 66 Ford. L. Rev. 371 (1997).

17. *See, e.g.,* Ian Brownlie, Principles of Public International Law 32–35 (4th ed., 1990); *and* Louis Henkin, International Law: Politics and Values 64–67 (1995).

18. *See, e.g.,* Curtis A. Bradley, *Breard, Our Dualist Constitution, and the Internationalist Conception,* 51 Stan. L. Rev. 529 (1999) (defending dualist argument).

19. *See* Curtis A. Bradley and Jack L. Goldsmith, *Customary International Law as Federal Common Law: A Critique of the Modern Position,* 110 Harv. L. Rev. 815, 819 n. 21 (1997).

20. 7 Constitutions of the Countries of the World 117 (Albert P. Blaustein and Gisbert H. Flanz, eds., 1994).

21. *See* John C. Calhoun, *Address at Fort Hill on the Relations of the States and Federal Government (June 26, 1831),* in Union and Liberty: The Political Philosophy of John C. Calhoun 371 (Ross M. Lence, ed., 1992); John C. Calhoun, *Letter to General Hamilton on the Subject of State Interposition* in 6 Works of John C. Calhoun 144, 146 (D. Appleton, ed., 1855).

22. For example, Virginia enacted legislation purporting to "interpose" itself between the state and the Supreme Court's decision in *Brown. See Virginia Rejects Order of U.S. Supreme Court,* Richmond News Leader, 1 Jan. 18, 1956.

23. *See, e.g.,* Cooper v. Aaron, 358 U.S. 1, 18 (1958).

24. *See, e.g.,* John Austin, *The Province of Jurisprudence Determined,* in Readings in the Philosophy of Law (John Arthur and William H. Shaw, eds., 1993).

25. *See* Hans Kelsen, General Theory of Law and State 110–24, 131–34, 369–73, 395–96 (1961); *and* H. L. A. Hart, The Concept of Law 97–120 (1961).

26. *See* Philip Soper, A Theory of Law 46–51 (1984) (distinguishing between "outsiders" who develop academic theories of law and "insiders" who must choose how to act within a legal system).

27. For example, Richard Posner justifies federal jurisdiction over interstate disputes on the ground that without such jurisdiction, states would be tempted to externalize costs on sister states. *See* Richard A. Posner, The Federal Courts: Challenge and Reform 280–83 (1996).

28. *Compare* Kramer v. Union Free Sch. Dist., 395 U.S. 621 (1969) (holding that a state may not disfranchise residents who have direct interest in the subject matter of election) *with* Salyer Land Co. v. Tulare Lake Basin Water Storage Dist., 410 U.S. 719 (1973) (holding that a state may disfranchise residents who lack the required special interest in the subject of election). *But see* Holt Civic Club v. City of Tuscaloosa, 439 U.S. 60 (1978) (holding that extraterritorial application of a municipality's laws does not create a constitutional right to vote in the municipality's elections).

29. *Compare* Sierra Club v. Morton, 405 U.S. 727 (1972) (denying standing to sue on

ground that plaintiff did not suffer an "injury in fact") *with* Perry v. Sindermann, 408 U.S. 593 (1972) (holding that the due process clause guarantees a right to a hearing when the government is alleged to interfere with the plaintiff's constitutionally protected property interest).

30. *See, e.g.,* Graham v. Richardson, 403 U.S. 365, 372 (1971); United States v. Carolene Products, 304 U.S. 144, 152–53 n. 4 (1938).

See generally John Hart Ely, Democracy and Distrust 145–57 (1980).

31. As Lea Brilmayer has pointed out, the Court's remedy for the "discrete and insular minority" problem on the one hand and the extraterritorial effect problem on the other has not been completely consistent. When dealing with "insider-outsiders" — discrete and insular minorities — the Court generally requires no more than nondiscrimination. In contrast, when dealing with outsider-outsiders — individuals who belong to a separate community — the Court sometimes rejects even nondiscriminatory regulation. *See* Lea Brilmayer, Carolene *Conflicts, and the Fate of the "Inside-Outsider,"* 134 U. Pa. L. Rev. 1291, 1311–12 (1986).

32. *See, e.g.,* Holt Civic Club v. City of Tuscaloosa, 439 U.S. 60, 69–70 (1978).

33. This problem of "externalities run wild" has become part of the standard set of criticisms directed against law and economics more generally. *See, e.g.,* Duncan Kennedy, *Cost-Benefit Analysis of Entitlement Problems: A Critique,* 33 Stan. L. Rev. 387, 398–400 (1981).

34. The hypothetical, and some of the discussion that follows, is drawn from Brian Barry, Political Argument 63–65 (1990), *and* Charles R. Beitz, *Procedural Equality in Democratic Theory: A Preliminary Examination,* in Nomos: Liberal Democracy 80–81 (J. Roland Pinnock and John W. Chapman, eds., 1983).

35. This thought experiment and some of the argument derived from it are drawn from Jules L. Coleman and Sarah K. Harding, *Citizenship, the Demands of Justice, and the Moral Relevance of Political Borders,* in Justice in Immigration, at 18 (Warren F. Schwartz, ed., 1995).

36. *See* id.

37. *See* Michael J. Sandel, Democracy's Discontent: America in Search of a Public Philosophy 5–6 (1996).

38. For some social science studies supporting this hypothesis, see Samuel L. Gaertner et al., *Reducing Intergroup Bias: The Benefits of Recategorization* 57 J. Personality & Soc. Psychol. 239, 246 (1989); Marilynn B. Brewer and Norman Miller, *Beyond the Contact Hypothesis: Theoretical Perspectives on Desegregation,* in Groups in Contact 281, 290 (Norman Miller and Marilynn B. Brewer, eds., 1984).

39. 509 U.S. 630 (1993).

40. Id., at 647–48.

41. Miller v. Johnson, 515 U.S. 900, 916 (1995).

42. For some examples, *see* T. Alexander Aleinikoff and Samuel Issacharoff, *Race and Redistricting: Drawing Constitutional Lines after Shaw v. Reno,* 92 Mich. L. Rev. 588 (1993); Anthony Q. Fletcher, *White Lines, Black Districts: Shaw v. Reno and the Dilution of the Anti-Dilution Principle,* 29 Harv. C.R.-C.L. L. Rev. 231 (1994); *and* Shavar Jeffries, *Colorblind Faith: Process Theory, Ely and Standing for White Voters in Shaw v. Reno,* 16 Nat. Black L J. 169 (1999–2000).

43. There is some social science research supporting the view that the mixing of different ethnic groups within the same neighborhoods or institutions produces cross-cutting identities which compete with one another and render each less significant. *See, e.g.,* Samuel L. Gaertner et al., *Reducing Intergroup Bias: The Benefits of Recategorization* 57 J. Personality & Soc. Psychol. 239, 246 (1989); *and* Marilynn B. Brewer and Norman Miller, *Beyond the Contact Hypothesis: Theoretical Perspectives on Desegregation,* in Groups in Contact 281, 290 (Norman Miller and Marilynn B. Brewer, eds., 1984).

44. A large body of psychological research demonstrates more generally that when people are divided into groups, even on a random basis, they tend to favor intragroup members. For a summary of the literature, see Samuel L. Gaertner et al., *Reducing Intergroup Bias: Elements of Intergoup Cooperation,* 76 J. Personality & Soc. Psychol. 388, 398 (1999); Marilynn B. Brewer, *In-Group Bias in the Minimal Intergroup Situation: A Cognitive-Motivational Analysis,* 86 Psychol. Bull. 307 (1989).

45. Although she is certainly no fan of *Shaw,* Lani Guinier has advanced arguments that bear some resemblance to those suggested in text. Guinier is a strong critic of what she calls the "electoral" success theory, which reconfigures districts to ensure black representation. She argues that "[r]epresenting a geographically and socially isolated constituency in a racially polarized environment, blacks elected from single-member districts have little control over policy choices made by their white counterparts. Thus, although it ensures more representatives, district-based black electoral success may not necessarily result in more responsive government." Lani Guinier, *The Triumph of Tokenism: The Voting Rights Act and the Theory of Black Electoral Success,* 89 Mich. L. Rev. 1077, 1079 (1991). Instead Guinier proposes "proportionate interest representation." Through a system of cumulative voting in integrated districts, Guinier argues, cross-racial coalitions, which "disaggregate the majority" might be achieved. *See* id., at 1138–39.

46. *See* Lani Guinier, *Group Representation and Race-Conscious Districting: A Case of the Emperor's Clothes,* 71 Tex. L. Rev. 1589, 1617 (1993) ("Race in this country has defined individual identities, opportunities, frames of reference, and relationships. Where race has been of historical importance and continues to play a significant role, racial-group membership often serves as a political proxy for shared experience and common interests.").

47. As Pamela Karlan has pointed out, the districts questioned by the Court in *Shaw* and other cases were "among the most racially diverse districts in the country." Pamela S. Karlan, *Still Hazy after All These Years: Voting Rights in the Post-Shaw Era,* 26 Cumb. L. Rev. 287, 293 (1995–96).

48. *See* Lani Guinier, *The Triumph of Tokenism: The Voting Rights Act and the Theory of Black Electoral Success,* 89 Mich. L. Rev. 1077, 1079 (1991). *See also* Anthony Q. Fletcher, *White Lines, Black Districts: Shaw v. Reno and the Dilution of the Anti-Dilution Principle,* 29 Harv. C.R.-C.L. L. Rev. 231, 251 (1994) (noting that "during the Reagan-Bush administrations, the Republican National Committee purposely advocated the creation of majority black districts in an effort to enhance the competitiveness of Republican candidates in neighboring districts, not to promote the interests of minority voters who continue to overwhelmingly support the Democratic Party").

49. Miller v. Johnson, 515 U.S. 900, 930 (1995) (Stevens, J., dissenting).

50. *See Judge Dismisses Jewish Students' Lawsuit on Yale Housing Policy,* Washington Post, Aug. 9, 1998, at A5.

51. *See* Hunt v. Cromartie, 2001 W.L. 387421 (U.S. Sup. Ct. 2001); Miller v. Johnson, 515 U.S. 900, 915–917 (1993).

52. *See* Hunt v. Cromartie, 2001 W. L. 387421 (U.S. Sup. Ct. 2001); Hunt v. Cromartie, 526 U.S. 541,551 (1999) ("Our prior decisions have made clear that a jurisdiction may engage in constitutional political gerrymandering, even if it so happens that the most loyal Democrats happen to be black Democrats and even if the State were conscious of that fact").

53. 526 U.S. 489 (1999).

54. *See, e.g.,* Shapiro v. Thompson, 396 U.S. 618 (1969); Zobel v. Williams, 457 U.S. 55 (1982); *and* Hooper v. Bernalillo County Assessor, 472 U.S. 612 (1985).

55. 526 U.S. 489, at 502–03.

56. The opinion speaks throughout of the rights of California *citizens. See, e.g.,* 526 U.S. 489, at 502 ("What is at issue in this case, then, is . . . the right of the newly arrived citizen to the same privileges and immunities enjoyed by other citizens of the same State"). The Court has uniformly upheld "bona fide" residency requirements that restrict state benefits to legitimate residents of a state. *See, e.g.,* McCarthy v. Philadelphia Civil Service Comm'n, 424 U.S. 645 (1976); *and* Martinez v. Bynum, 461 U.S. 321 (1983).

57. 419 U.S. 393 (1975).

58. 526 U.S. 489, at 504.

59. As the *Sosna* Court noted, a state has an interest "in avoiding officious intermeddling in matters in which another State has a paramount interest." 419 U.S., at 407. The problem arises because states almost uniformly apply the law of the forum to determine whether a divorce should be granted. *See, e.g.,* Restatement, Second, Conflict of Laws 285. Jurisdictional limits therefore must do the work more typically done by choice of law rules.

60. 511 U.S. 93 (1994).

61. Id., at 107 n. 9.

62. *See* Personal Responsibility and Work Opportunity Reconciliation Act of 1996, 110 Stat. 2105, codified at 42 U.S.C. 604(c) (1994 ed., Supp II).

63. 526 U.S. 489, at 507.

64. 514 U.S. 549 (1995).

65. Id., at 564.

66. The Court points out that the statute "contains no jurisdictional element" but does not say that the addition of one would change the result. *See* id., at 561–62.

67. The Court suggests that a legislative finding of an effect on interstate commerce might assist in detecting such an effect even though it "was not visible to the naked eye," but nowhere holds that such a finding would change the result in this case. *See* id., at 562–63.

68. The Court notes that the statute does not regulate commercial activity but does not say what the outcome would be if it did. *See* id., at 565–66.

69. Id., at 566.

70. *See* In re Rahrer, 140 U.S. 545 (1891) (upholding the power of Congress to grant

permission to states to enact statutes previously held to violate the dormant commerce clause).

71. *Cf.* Duckworth v. Arkansas, 314 U.S. 390, 400 (1941) (Jackson, J., concurring) (arguing that state restraints on commerce "are individually too petty, too diversified, and too local to get the attention of a Congress hard pressed with more urgent matters").

72. *See, e.g.,* Martinez v. Bynum, 461 U.S. 321 (1983) (upholding "bona fide" residency requirement for public school education). *Cf.* Vlandis v. Kline, 412 U.S. 441 (1973) (invalidating "irrebuttable presumption" concerning residency).

73. *See, e.g.,* White v. Massachusetts Council of Constr. Employers, Inc., 460 U.S. 204 (1983); Reeves, Inc., v. Stake, 447 U.S. 429 (1980); *and* Hughes v. Alexandria Scrap Corp., 426 U.S. 794 (1976). *Cf.* South-Central Timber Dev. v. Wunnicke, 467 U.S. 82 (1984) (limiting scope of market participant doctrine).

74. 512 U.S. 186 (1994).

75. *See, e.g.,* Landon v. Plasencia, 459 U.S. 21, 32 (1982); *and* Kleindienst v. Mandel, 408 U.S. 753, 769–70 (1972).

76. For an interesting discussion, see Peter J. Spiro, *New Players on the International Stage,* 2 Hofstra L. & Pol'y Symp. 19 (1997).

77. *See, e.g.,* Lucian Arye Bebchuck, *Federalism and the Corporation: The Desirable Limits on State Competition in Corporate Law,* 105 Harv. L. Rev. 1435, 1437–42 (1992). For an argument grounded in public choice theory that states are unlikely to pursue redistributive ends, *see* Sheryll D. Cashin, *Federalism, Welfare Reform, and the Minority Poor: Accounting for the Tyranny of State Majorities,* 99 Colum. L. Rev. 552 (1999).

78. 457 U.S. 202 (1982).

79. 494 U.S. 259 (1990).

80. Id., at 265.

81. 457 U.S., at 210.

82. 313 U.S. 69 (1941).

83. *See* id., at 76–77 (distinguishing Manchester v. Massachusetts, 139 U.S. 240 [1891]).

84. *Cf.* World Wide Volkswagen v. Woodson, 444 U.S. 286 (1980) (upholding state jurisdiction when action in one state causes foreseeable consequences in another state).

85. 494 U.S., at 279.

86. The Court argued that "[a]t the least, those who elect to enter our territory by stealth and in violation of our law should be prepared to bear the consequences, including, but not limited to, deportation. But the children of those illegal entrants are not comparably situated. Their 'parents have the ability to conform their conduct to societal norms,' and presumably the ability to remove themselves from the State's jurisdiction; but the children who are plaintiffs in these cases 'can affect neither their parents' conduct nor their own status.'" 457 U.S., at 220 (quoting Trimble v. Gordon, 430 U.S. 762, 770 ([1977]).

87. *Cf.* Vlandis v. Kline, 412 U.S. 441 (1973) (invalidating durational residency requirement for access to public education).

Chapter 6: The Structure of Unsettlement

1. *See, e.g.,* U.S. Const., art. I, sec. 2, cl. 1 (setting House terms at two years); id., at art. I, sec. 3, cl. 1 (setting Senate terms at six years); id., at art. II, sec. 1, cl. 1 (setting presidential term at four years).

2. *See, e.g.,* id, at art. I, sec. 1 (legislative power); id., at art. II, sec. 1, cl. 1 (executive power); id., at art. II, sec. 1 (judicial power).

3. *See* id., at art. I, sec. 7, cl. 2.

4. *See* id., at art. II, sec. 1, cl. 6; id, at amend. XX, secs. 3–4; id, at amend. XXV, secs. 1, 3–4.

5. In the famous Federalist Paper No. 10, Madison argued that in a large republic particular factions would find it more difficult to achieve individual permanent control over the machinery of government. *See* The Federalist No. 10 in The Federalist 63–64 (Jacob E. Cooke, ed., 1961). In Federalist No. 51, he argued that a system of checks and balances between branches of government would cause "ambition to counteract ambition," thereby preventing any branch from achieving dominance. *See* The Federalist No. 51, in id., at 349.

6. *See, e.g.,* John Dewey, Freedom and Culture (1939).

7. Thus, Madison favored a large republic because a "rage for paper money, for abolition of debt, for an equal division of property, or for any other improper and wicked project, will be less apt to pervade the whole body of the Union than a particular member of it." The Federalist No. 10, in The Federalist 65 (Jacob E. Cooke, ed., 1961).

8. In a speech before the convention, Alexander Hamilton praised the British monarchy, arguing, "An Executive for life has not [the] motive for forgetting his fidelity, and will therefore be a safer depository of power." James Madison, Debate in the Federal Convention of 1787, 117 (Gillard Hunt and James Scott, eds., 1920). Hamilton later claimed that his speech amounted to no more than speculation and that he had in fact favored a three- or four-year term at the convention. *See* Thomas E. Cronin, *Presidential Term, Tenure and Reeligibility,* in Inventing the American Presidency 67 (1989).

9. In his classic study, Robert Axelrod demonstrated that in repeat games, the best strategy is "tit for tat." It is in the self-interest of individuals to continue to cooperate until others defect. They should then continue to defect until cooperation resumes. *See* Robert Axelrod, The Evolution of Cooperation (1984).

10. This is why Justice Scalia characterizes his originalism as "faint-hearted." *See* Antonin Scalia, *Originalism: The Lesser Evil,* 57 U. Cin. L. Rev. 849, 864 (1989).

11. 121 S. Ct. 525 (2001).

12. 357 U.S. 449 (1958).

13. 378 U.S. 347 (1964).

14. 121 S. Ct. 525, at 548 (Ginsburg, J., dissenting).

15. Lucas A. Powe, Jr., The Warren Court and American Politics (2000).

16. 323 U.S. 214 (1944).

17. 343 U.S. 579 (1952).

18. 323 U.S. 214, at 244 (Jackson, J., dissenting).

19. Id. He went on to point out that "[n]o court can require such a commander in such circumstances to act as a reasonable man; he may be unreasonably cautious and exacting.

Perhaps he should be. But a commander in temporarily focusing the life of a community on defense is carrying out a military program; he is not making law in the sense the courts know the term. He issues orders, and they may have a certain authority as military commands, although they may be very bad as constitutional law." Id.

20. Id., at 245.

21. Id., at 247–48.

22. Jackson argued that "[t]he actual art of governing under our Constitution does not and cannot conform to judicial definitions of the power of any of its branches based on isolated clauses or even single Articles torn from context. . . . Presidential powers are not fixed but fluctuate, depending upon their disjunction or conjunction with those of Congress." 343 U.S., at 635 (Jackson, J., concurring).

23. See id., at 654: "I have no illusion that any decision by this Court can keep power in the hands of Congress if it is not wise and timely in meeting its problems. . . . If not good law, there was worldly wisdom in the maxim attributed to Napoleon that 'The tools belong to the man who can use them.' We may say that power to legislate for emergencies belongs in the hands of Congress, but only Congress itself can prevent power from slipping through its fingers."

24. See Larry Alexander, *The Gap*, 14 Harv. J. L. & Pub. Pol'y 695 (1991).

25. See Meir Dan-Cohen, *Decision Rules and Conduct Rules: On Acoustic Separation in Criminal Law*, 97 Harv. L. Rev. 625 (1984).

26. 299 U.S. 304 (1936).

27. Id., at 320.

28. 487 U.S. 654 (1988).

29. Id., at 727–34.

30. Id., at 734.

31. See, e.g., William Eskridge, *Relationships between Formalism and Functionalism in Separation of Powers Cases*, 22 Harv. J. L. & Pub. Pol'y 21 (1998); and Peter L. Strauss, *Formal and Functional Approaches to Separation-of-Powers Questions—A Foolish Inconsistency?* 72 Cornell L. Rev. 488 (1987).

32. 462 U.S. 919 (1983).

33. See, e.g., Harold H. Bruff and Ernest Gellhorn, *Congressional Control of Administrative Regulation: A Study of Legislative Vetoes*, 90 Harv. L. Rev. 1369 (1977); Antonin Scalia, *The Legislative Veto: A False Remedy for System Overload*, 3 Reg. 19 (1979); and Jacob K. Javits and Gary J. Klein, *Congressional Oversight and the Legislative Veto: A Constitutional Analysis*, 52 N.Y.U. L. Rev. 455 (1977).

34. 462 U.S. 919, at 945.

35. Id., at 959.

36. Id.

37. Id., at 945.

38. Id.

39. 343 U.S. 579, at 587–88.

40. Id., at 634–35 (Jackson, J., concurring).

41. Id., at 635.

42. Id., at 637.

43. Id.

44. Id.

45. Id.

46. Id., at 639.

47. Id., at 640.

48. Id., at 654.

49. Id., at 637.

50. Id., at 634.

51. *See, e.g.,* Whitman v. American Trucking Assn., 121 S. Ct. 903 (2001).

52. *See, e.g.,* Future Trading Comm'n v. Schor, 478 U.S. 833 (1986); *and* Thomas v. Union Carbide Agricultural Products Co., 473 U.S. 568 (1985).

53. *See* Mistretta v. United States, 488 U.S. 361 (1989).

54. *See* Morrison v. Olson, 487 U.S. 654 (1988).

55. 462 U.S. 919, at 945.

56. Id., at 948–49.

57. Id., at 948.

58. U.S. Const., art. I, sec. 1.

59. Id., at art. I, sec. 7, cl. 2.

60. 462 U.S. 919, at 945. Oddly, Article I also contains a second presentment requirement. Art. I, sec. 7, cl. 2 provides, "Every Order, Resolution, or Vote to which the Concurrence of the Senate and the House of Representatives may be necessary (except on a question of Adjournment) shall be presented to the President of the United States; and before the Same shall take Effect, shall be approved by him, or being disapproved by him, shall be repassed by two thirds of the Senate and the House of Representatives, according to the Rules and Limitations prescribed in the Case of a Bill." By its unambiguous terms, this provision is inapplicable to one-house vetoes, since these measures do not require "the Concurrence of the Senate and the House of Representatives."

61. 462 U.S. 919, at 955 n. 19.

62. *See* Hollingsworth v. Virginia, 3 U.S. (3 Dall.) 378 (1798). Chief Justice Burger's *Chadha* opinion acknowledges as much. *See* 462 U.S. 919, at 955 n. 20.

63. 462 U.S. 919, at 959.

64. 524 U.S. 417 (1998).

65. Line Item Veto Act, Pub. L. No. 104–30, 110 Stat. 1200 (1996) (codified at 2 U.S.C. secs. 691–92 [Supp. II 1997]). The act provided some guidelines limiting the president's discretion. In identifying items for cancellation, the president was directed to consider the legislative history, purposes, and other relevant information about the canceled items. Cancellations were permitted upon a presidential finding that the cancellation would reduce the federal budget deficit, would not impair an essential government function, and would not harm the national interest. Id., at sec. 691(a)(A).

66. 524 U.S. 417, at 438–39.

67. Id., at 419.

68. Id., at 448.

69. As noted above, the act provides some standards to limit the president's discretion. These standards are probably sufficient to satisfy the loose requirements of the modern antidelegation doctrine. *See* Loving v. United States, 517 U.S. 748 (1996); *and* Amalgamated Meat Cutters v. Connelly, 337 F. Supp. 737 (D.D.C. 1971).

70. 524 U.S. 417, at 469.

71. *See* 462 U.S. 919, at 967.

72. *See, e.g.,* Bordenkircher v. Hayes, 434 U.S. 357, 366 (1978) (Blackmun, J., dissenting).

73. This is how the Court characterized plea-bargaining in upholding the practice. *See id.,* at 362 ("In the 'give-and-take' of plea bargaining, there is no . . . element of punishment or retaliation so long as the accused is free to accept or reject the prosecution's offer").

Chapter 7: The Right to Unsettlement

1. *See, e.g.,* Roderick M. Hills, Jr., *Back to the Future? How the Bill of Rights Might Be about Structure after All,* 93 Nw. U. L. Rev. 977, 996 (1999) (arguing that "rights depend on a set of complex institutions for their defense and definition and that without these institutions rights [become] mere 'parchment barriers'").

2. Alexander Hamilton put the point succinctly when he argued that "the Constitution is itself, in every rational sense, and to every useful purpose A BILL OF RIGHTS." The Federalist, No. 84 in The Federalist 581 (Jacob E. Cooke, ed., 1961).

3. As Madison wrote to Jefferson during the ratification debates, "Experience proves the inefficacy of a bill of rights on those occasions when its control is most needed. Repeated violations of these parchment barriers has been committed in every State." Quoted in Jack N. Rakove, Original Meanings: Politics and Ideas in the Making of the Constitution 332 (1996).

4. For example, one delegate to the Pennsylvania ratifying convention pointed out that "it might be argued at a future day by the persons then in power — you undertook to enumerate the rights which you mean to reserve, the pretension which you make is not compromised in that enumeration, and, consequently, our jurisdiction is not circumscribed." Quoted in id., at 329.

5. *See* Alexander M. Bickel, The Least Dangerous Branch: The Supreme Court at the Bar of Politics (2d ed. 1986) *quoting* The Federalist No. 78 (Alexander Hamilton).

6. For an excellent account, see Jack N. Rakove, Original Meanings: Politics and Ideas in the Making of the Constitution 330–36 (1996).

7. 410 U.S. 113 (1973).

8. *See, e.g.,* John Hart Ely, The Wages of Crying Wolf: A Comment on Roe v. Wade, 82 Yale L. J. 920 (1973).

9. 394 U.S. 557 (1969).

10. 381 U.S. 479 (1965).

11. 410 U.S. 113 (1973).

12. *Compare, e.g.,* United States v. Knotts, 460 U.S. 276 (1983) (no invasion of reasonable expectation of privacy when beeper used to track movement of car in public view) *with* United States v. Karo, 468 U.S. 705 (1984) (invasion of reasonable expectation of privacy when beeper used to track chemical inside of house).

13. 376 U.S. 254 (1964).

14. 274 U.S. 357, 372 (1927).

15. 515 U.S. 557 (1995).

16. 478 U.S. 186 (1986).

17. As the Court explained: "If there were no reason for a group of people to march from here to there except to reach a destination, they could make the trip without expressing any message beyond the fact of the march itself. Some people might call such a procession a parade, but it would not be much of one. Real '[p]arades are public dramas of social relations, and in them performers define who can be a social actor and what subjects and ideas are available for communication and consideration.' S. Davis, Parades and Power: Street Theatre in Nineteenth-Century Philadelphia 6 (1986). Hence, we use the word *parade* to indicate marchers who are making some sort of collective point not just to each other but to bystanders along the way. Indeed, a parade's dependence on watchers is so extreme that nowadays, as with Bishop Berkeley's celebrated tree, 'if a parade or demonstration receives no media coverage, it may as well not have happened.' " Id., at 171. 515 U.S. 557, at 568.

18. 483 U.S. 378 (1987).

19. Id., at 380.

20. Id., at 387 (quoting New York Times Co. v. Sullivan, 376 U.S. 254, 270 [1964]).

21. Id., at 393.

22. 468 U.S. 609 (1984).

23. Id., at 618–20.

24. Id., at 626–27.

25. 250 U.S. 616 (1919).

26. Id., at 630.

27. Id., at 629.

28. Id., at 628.

29. For some similar rhetoric, see Justice Douglas' dissent from the Court's decision in Dennis v. United States, 341 U.S. 494, 588 (1951) upholding criminal convictions of leading Communists for violating the Smith Act: "If we are to take judicial notice of the threat of Communists within the nation, it should not be difficult to conclude that as a political party they are of little consequence. Communists in this country have never made a respectable or serious showing in any election. I would doubt that there is a village, let alone a city or county or state, which the Communists could carry. . . . The country is not in despair; the people know Soviet Communism; the doctrine of Soviet revolution is exposed in all of its ugliness and the American people want none of it. How it can be said that there is a clear and present danger that this advocacy will succeed is, therefore, a mystery. Some nations less resilient than the United States, where illiteracy is high and where democratic traditions are only budding, might have to take drastic steps and jail these men for merely speaking their creed. But in America they are miserable merchants of unwanted ideas; their wares remain unsold."

30. Debs v. United States, 249 U.S. 211, 214–15 (1919).

31. 381 U.S. 479 (1965).

32. *See* Bernard Schwartz, The Unpublished Opinions of the Warren Court 235 (1985).

33. Id., at 237.

34. Id., at 237–38.

35. 381 U.S. 479, at 486.

36. For a similar but not identical grouping, see Jerry Kang, *Information Privacy in Cyberspace Transactions,* 50 Stan. L. Rev. 1193, 1202–05 (1998).

37. 505 U.S. 833, 852 (1992).

38. *See, e.g.* Leonard Krieger, The German Idea of Freedom: History of a Political Tradition 90 (1957).

39. *See, e.g.,* Michael J. Sandel, Liberalism and the Limits of Justice 64 (1982); Michael J. Sandel, Democracy's Discontent 202 (1996); *and* Frank I. Michelman, *The Supreme Court, 1985 Term — Foreword: Traces of Self-Government,* 100 Harv. L. Rev. 4, 74–75 (1986).

40. *Cf.* Jed Rubenfeld, The Right of Privacy, 102 Harv. L. Rev. 737, 784 (1989) (conceptualizing privacy as "freedom not to have one's life too totally determined by a progressively normalizing state").

41. *See, e.g.,* Katz v. United States, 389 U.S. 347, 351 (1967).

42. *See, e.g.,* Richard A. Posner, *The Right of Privacy,* 12 Ga. L. Rev. 393, 399 (1978); *and* Richard A. Posner, Overcoming Law 531–51 (1995).

43. *Cf.* Jerry Kang, *Information Privacy in Cyberspace Transactions,* 50 Stan. L. Rev. 1193, 1203–04 (1998).

44. 476 U.S. 747 (1986).

45. Id., at 766.

46. U.S. Const. art. I, sec. 9, cl. 7.

47. This is a version of an argument made many years ago by Charles Fried. *See* Charles Fried, *Privacy,* 77 Yale L. J. 475, 482–83 (1968) (arguing that control of information is necessary to maintain intimate relationships). *See also* Ferdinand Schoeman, *Privacy and Intimate Information,* in Philosophical Dimensions of Privacy: An Anthology 403, 408–09 (Ferdinand Schoeman, ed., 1984).

48. *See* Jon Elster, Ulysses and the Sirens: Studies in Rationality and Irrationality (1979).

49. The discussion that follows is drawn from id., at 47–57.

50. Id., at 48.

51. *See* Guido Calabresi and Philip Bobbitt, Tragic Choices 57–72 (1978).

52. *See, e.g.,* Federal Judicial Center, Pattern Criminal Jury Instruction, Instruction 5 (1991) (warning jurors not to discuss case "with . . . people involved in the trial" until trial is completed); *and* id., at Instruction 58 (warning jurors not to reveal to judge "how you stand as to your verdict").

53. *See, e.g.,* United States v. Thomas, 116 F.3d 606, 617 (2d Cir. 1997) (holding that trial judges have "both the responsibility and the authority to dismiss a juror whose refusal or unwillingness to follow the applicable law becomes known to the judge during the course of trial"). *See generally* Nancy J. King, *Silencing Nullification Advocacy inside the Jury Room and outside the Courtroom,* 65 U.Chi. L. Rev. 433 (1998).

54. *See* Vincent Blasi, *The Checking Value in First Amendment Theory,* 1977 Am. B. Found. Res. J. 521.

55. *See* New York v. United States, 505 U.S. 144, 167–69 (1992).

56. *See, e.g.,* Industrial Union v. American Petroleum Institute, 448 U.S. 607, 687 (1980) (Rehnquist, J., concurring).

57. *See* Adarand Constructors, Inc., v. Pena, 515 U.S. 200 (1995); *and* City of Richmond v. J. A. Croson Co., 488 U.S. 469 (1989).

58. *See* United States v. Morrison, 528 U.S. 598 (2000); United States v. Lopez, 514 U.S. 549 (1995); *and* New York v. United States, 505 U.S. 144 (1992).

59. *See* Metropolitan Washington Airports Authority v. Citizens for the Abatement of Aircraft Noise, 501 U.S. 252 (1991); Bowsher v. Synar, 478 U.S. 714 (1986); *and* INS v. Chadha, 462 U.S. 919 (1983).

60. *See* 44 Liquormart, Inc., v. Rhode Island, 517 U.S. 484 (1996); Denver Area Educational Telecommunications Consortium, Inc., v. Federal Communications Comm'n, 518 U.S. 727 (1996); *and* Colorado Republican Federal Campaign Comm'n v. Federal Election Comm'n, 518 U.S. 604 (1996).

61. *See* Stenberg v. Carhart, 120 S. Ct. 2597 (2000); *and* Planned Parenthood of Southeastern Pennsylvania v. Casey, 505 U.S. 833 (1992).

62. *See* United States v. Virginia, 518 U.S. 515 (1996).

63. *See* Lucas v. South Carolina Coastal Council, 505 U.S. 1003 (1992); *and* Nollan v. California Coastal Commn., 483 U.S. 825 (1987).

64. *See* Miller v. Johnson, 515 U.S. 900 (1995); *and* Shaw v. Reno, 509 U.S. 630 (1993).

65. 478 U.S. 186 (1986).

66. 517 U.S. 620 (1996).

67. *See* The Federalist No. 10, at 56 (James Madison) (Jacob E. Cooke, ed., 1961).

68. See Cass R. Sunstein, *Naked Preferences and the Constitution,* 84 Colum. L. Rev. 1689 (1984).

69. *See, e.g.,* Bernard H. Siegan, Economic Liberties and the Constitution 260–303 (1980).

70. *See* Akhil Reed Amar, *The Bill of Rights as a Constitution,* 100 Yale L. J. 1131, 1132 (1991) (arguing that "[t]he main thrust of the Bill [of Rights] was . . . not to impede popular majorities, but to empower them").

71. *See* Cass R. Sunstein, *Naked Preferences and the Constitution,* 84 Colum. L. Rev. 1689, 1704–27 (1984).

72. 5 U.S.C. sec. 552.

73. Lochner v. New York, 198 U.S. 45, 75–76 (1905) (Holmes, J., dissenting).

74. 334 U.S. 1 (1948).

75. For a widely cited account of the two-tier approach, see Gerald Gunther, *Foreword: In Search of Evolving Doctrine on a Changing Court: A Model for a Newer Equal Protection,* 86 Harv. L. Rev. 1 (1972).

76. The fundamental-rights strand of the strict scrutiny doctrine was inaugurated in Skinner v. Oklahoma, 316 U.S. 535 (1942). For an early articulation of the suspect classification strand, *see* Korematsu v. United States, 323 U.S. 214 (1944).

77. *See, e.g.* Williamson v. Lee Optical, 348 U.S. 483 (1955); *and* New York City Transit Authority v. Beazer, 440 U.S. 568 (1979).

78. 394 U.S. 618 (1963).

79. Id., at 638.

80. 163 U.S. 537 (1896).

81. Id., at 559.

82. 347 U.S. 483 (1954).

83. For an example of this sort of reasoning in the abortion context, see Harris v. McRae, 448 U.S. 297, 298 (1980): ("[T]he Hyde Amendment [prohibiting government funding of abortions] leaves an indigent woman with at least the same range of choice in deciding whether to obtain a medically necessary abortion as she would have had if Congress had chosen to subsidize no health care costs at all").

84. 347 U.S. 483, at 494.

85. For example, in Green v. County School Board, 391 U.S. 430 (1968), the Court invalidated a facially race-neutral "freedom of choice" plan because it did not have the effect of desegregating the schools. Similarly, in Swann v. Charlotte-Mecklenburg Board of Education, 402 U.S. 1 (1971), the Court upheld a lower court order mandating busing in order to overcome the effects of residential segregation.

86. *See, e.g.,* Milliken v. Bradley, 418 U.S. 717 (1974) (holding that courts had only limited power to impose interdistrict remedies for school segregation); *and* Pasadena Board of Education v. Spangler, 427 U.S. 424 (1976) (holding that courts lacked the power to prevent resegregation after an initial desegregation plan had been implemented).

87. In recent years, the Court has undertaken to provide road maps for lower courts disengaging from the desegregation process. *See* Board of Education v. Dowell, 498 U.S. 237 (1991); *and* Freeman v. Pitts, 503 U.S. 467 (1992).

88. *See, e.g.,* City of Richmond v. J. A. Croson Co., 488 U.S. 469 (1989); *and* Adarand Constructors, Inc., v. Pena, 515 U.S. 200 (1995).

89. McAuliffe v. City of New Bedford, 155 Mass. 216, 220, 29 N.E. 517, 517 (1892).

90. Similarly, in Commonwealth v. Davis, 162 Mass. 510, 39 N.E. 113 (1895), Holmes wrote to affirm the conviction of a preacher who challenged the constitutionality of a statute prohibiting him from speaking on the Boston Common. According to Holmes, for "the Legislature absolutely or conditionally to forbid public speaking in a highway or public park is no more an infringement of the rights of a member of the public than for the owner of a private house to forbid it in his house." Id., at 511, 39 N.E., at 113.

91. Hague v. CIO, 307 U.S. 496, 515 (1939).

92. *See, e.g.,* Schneider v. State, 308 U.S. 147 (1939); Martin v. Struthers, 319 U.S. 141 (1943); *and* Cox v. Louisiana, 379 U.S. 536 (1965).

93. 376 U.S. 254 (1964).

94. 395 U.S. 367 (1969).

95. Id., at 389.

96. 411 U.S. 1 (1973).

97. 410 U.S. 113 (1973).

98. *See* 411 U.S. 1, at 33.

99. *See* id., at 112–13 (Marshall, J., dissenting).

100. *See* id., at 37.

101. *See* Maher v. Roe, 432 U.S. 464 (1977); *and* Harris v. McRae, 448 U.S. 297 (1980).

102. 426 U.S. 229 (1976).

103. *See* City of Richmond v. J. A. Croson Co., 488 U.S. 469 (1989); *and* Adarand Constructors, Inc., v. Pena, 515 U.S. 200 (1995).

104. For limitations on the public-forum doctrine, *see, e.g.,* Heffron v. International Society of Krishna Consciousness, 452 U.S. 640 (1981); Greer v. Spock, 424 U.S. 828 (1976); *and* Members of the City Council of Los Angeles v. Taxpayers of Vincent, 466 U.S. 789 (1984). For limitations on *New York Times* and *Red Lion,* see Gertz v. Robert Welch, Inc., 418 U.S. 323 (1974); *and* Turner Broadcasting System, Inc., v. FCC, 512 U.S. 497 (1994).

105. *See, e.g.,* Adarand Constructors, Inc., v. Pena, 515 U.S. 200, 236 (1995) (strict scrutiny of affirmative-action programs not always "fatal in fact").

106. *See* Bush v. Vera, 517 U.S. 952, 977 (1996) ("If the State has a 'strong basis in evidence' . . . for concluding that creation of a minority-majority district is reasonably necessary to comply with [the Voting Rights Act] and the districting that is based on race 'substantially addresses the . . . violation,' . . . it satisfies strict scrutiny").

107. *See* 517 U.S. 620, at 628.

108. Id., at 631.

109. 526 U.S. 489 (1999).

110. *See, e.g.,* Rosenberger v. Rector and Visitors of the University of Virginia, 515 U.S. 819 (1995); *and* Lamb's Chapel v. Center Moriches Union Free School Dist., 508 U.S. 384 (1993).

111. 518 U.S. 515, 558 (1996).

112. The Court "assumed for purposes of this decision that most women would not choose VMI's adversative method" but held that the question was "whether the State can constitutionally deny to women who have the will and capacity, the training . . . that VMI uniquely affords." 518 U.S. 515, at 541.

113. Id., at 565 (Rehnquist, J., concurring).

114. Id.

115. Id.

116. Holden v. Hardy, 169 U.S. 366 (1898).

117. *See* Lochner v. New York, 198 U.S. 45, 69 (Harlan, J., dissenting).

118. For the *Lochner* majority's acknowledgment of the legitimacy of these powers, see id., at 52.

119. Id., at 58–59.

120. 431 U.S. 494 (1977).

121. Id., at 498.

122. 416 U.S. 1 (1974).

123. 517 U.S. 620, at 635.

124. Id.

125. Id.

126. Id., at 648 (Scalia, J., dissenting).

127. Id., at 652 (Scalia, J., dissenting).

128. 515 U.S. 819 (1995).

129. Id., at 863 (Souter, J., joined by Stevens, Ginsburg, and Breyer, J.J., dissenting).

130. I borrow this matrix from Ira C. Lupu, *The Trouble with Accommodation,* 60 Geo. Wash. L. Rev. 743, 779–781 (1992).

131. *See, e.g.,* Michael W. McConnell, *Accommodation of Religion,* 1985 Sup. Ct. Rev. 1 (arguing for expansive right of accommodation of religion under free-exercise

clause); *and* Michael W. McConnell, *Coercion: The Lost Element of Establishment*, 27 Wm. & Mary L. Rev. 933 (1986) (arguing against "rigorous separationist" view of establishment clause).

132. *See, e.g.,* Santa Fe Independent School Dist. v. Doe, 120 S. Ct. 1266 (2000) (Stevens, J.) (holding that student-led prayer at high school football game violated establishment clause); *and* Goldman v. Weinberger, 475 U.S. 503, 510 (1986) (arguing against free-exercise religious accommodation for a Jewish military officer who wished to wear a yarmulke).

133. *See, e.g.,* Employee Division, Dept. of Human Resources v. Smith, 494 U.S. 872 (1990) (Scalia, J.) (sharply restricting scope of constitutionally mandated free-exercise accommodations); *and* Lee v. Weisman, 505 U.S. 577, 631 (1992) (Scalia, J., dissenting) (rejecting establishment-clause challenge to prayer at high school graduation ceremony).

134. *See, e.g.,* Goldman v. Weinberger, 475 U.S. 503, 513 (1986) (Brennan, J., dissenting) (arguing in favor of constitutionally mandated free-exercise accommodation for military officer wishing to wear yarmulke); *and* School Dist. of Abington Township v. Schempp, 374 U.S. 203, 230 (1963) (Brennan, J., concurring) (arguing that prayer in public schools violates establishment clause).

135. Among contemporary First Amendment scholars, perhaps Ira Lupu comes closest to defending this position. *See* Ira Lupu, *The Trouble with Accommodation,* 60 Geo. Wash. L. Rev. 743, 772 (1992) (arguing for mandatory, but against permissive, accommodation).

136. For a good example of how Justice Brennan wrestled with the contradiction between establishment and free-exercise clause values, *see* Corporation of the Presiding Bishop of the Church of Jesus Christ of the Latter-Day Saints v. Amos, 483 U.S. 327, 339 (1987) (Brennan, J., concurring).

137. *See* United States v. Miller, 307 U.S. 174 (1939) (upholding national ban on possession of unregistered sawed-off shotgun against Second Amendment attack).

138. *See, e.g.,* Stephen P. Halbrook, That Every Man Be Armed: The Evolution of a Constitutional Right (1984). *Cf.* Printz v. United States, 521 U.S. 898 n. 1 (1997) (Thomas, J., concurring) (citing "impressive array of historical evidence" supporting personal right).

139. *See, e.g.,* 1 Laurence Tribe, American Constitutional Law 898–900 (2000); *and* David C. Williams, *Civic Republicanism and the Citizen Militia: The Terrifying Second Amendment,* 101 Yale L. J. 551 (1991).

140. For good examples, see Akhil Reed Amar, The Bill of Rights 52 (1998); *and* Don B. Kates, Jr., *Handgun Prohibition and the Original Meaning of the Second Amendment,* 82 Mich. L. Rev. 204 (1983).

Conclusion

1. For some unsatisfactory musings that go on at greater length, see Louis Michael Seidman, *This Essay Is Brilliant/This Essay Is Stupid: Positive and Negative Self-Reference in Constitutional Practice and Theory,* 46 UCLA L. Rev. 501 (1998).

2. *See* Alvin W. Gouldner, The Future of Intellectuals and the Rise of the New Class (1979).

3. Freud himself attacked his critics by claiming that their theories were generated by neurosis. *See* Peter Gay, Freud: A Life for Our Time 223 (1988) (characterizing Freud's attack on Adler as "denunciation as diagnosis").

4. For an economic analysis of the incentives to include economics in the law school curriculum, see Warren F. Schwartz, *The Future of Economics in Legal Education,* 33 J. Leg. Educ. 314, 330–36 (1983).

5. For a discussion, see J. M. Balkin, *Deconstructive Practice and Legal Theory,* 96 Yale L. J. 743, 764–67 (1987).

6. *See* John Rawls, Political Liberalism 11–13 (1996).

7. *See, e.g.,* Ronald Dworkin, Life's Dominion: An Argument about Abortion, Euthanasia, and Individual Freedom (1993); *and* Richard Epstein, Takings: Private Property and the Power of Eminent Domain (1985).

8. *See* John Rawls, Political Liberalism 133–68 (1996).

9. *See* id., at 150–52.

Index